ISBN 978-1-332-24705-9
PIBN 10303829

1 MONTH OF
FREE
READING

at
www.ForgottenBooks.com

By purchasing this book you are eligible for one month membership to ForgottenBooks.com, giving you unlimited access to our entire collection of over 1,000,000 titles via our web site and mobile apps.

To claim your free month visit:
www.forgottenbooks.com/free303829

REPORT

OF THE

METROPOLITAN COMMISSIONERS IN LUNACY,

TO THE

LORD CHANCELLOR.

PRESENTED TO BOTH HOUSES OF PARLIAMENT BY COMMAND
OF HER MAJESTY.

LONDON:
BRADBURY AND EVANS, PRINTERS, WHITEFRIARS.

1844.

LONDON:

BRADBURY AND EVANS, PRINTERS, WHITEFRIARS.

COMMISSIONERS.—1843 & 1844.

LORD SEYMOUR.

LORD ASHLEY.

RIGHT HON. R. VERNON SMITH.

ROBERT GORDON, Esq.

COLONEL WILLIAM HENRY SYKES.

JAMES MILNES GASKELL, Esq.

JOHN BARNEBY, Esq.

FRANCIS BARLOW, Esq.

JAMES ROBERT GOWEN, Esq.

DOCTOR THOMAS TURNER.

DOCTOR JOHN BRIGHT.

DOCTOR HENRY HERBERT SOUTHEY.

DOCTOR JOHN ROBERT HUME.

DOCTOR THOMAS WATERFIELD.

DOCTOR FRANCIS BISSET HAWKINS.

DOCTOR JAMES COWLES PRICHARD.

JAMES WILLIAM MYLNE, Esq.

BRYAN WALLER PROCTER, Esq.

JOHN HANCOCK HALL, Esq.

R. W. SKEFFINGTON LUTWIDGE, Esq.

EDWARD DU BOIS, Clerk and Treasurer.

Office, 12, *Abingdon Street,*
Westminster.

TABLE OF CONTENTS.

TO THE

LORD HIGH CHANCELLOR,

OF ENGLAND.

WE, the Metropolitan Commissioners in Lunacy, beg
to submit to your Lordship the following Report,
relating to the several matters entrusted to our care.

As our duties have been materially increased, by
the provisions of the Act 5 & 6 Vic. c. 87, which have
enabled us to inspect the condition of the various public
and private Asylums throughout England and Wales,
beyond as well as within the limits of the Metropolitan
district, we think it right to report to your Lordship the
result of our experience, in a more minute and specific
way than we have heretofore been accustomed to do.

Your Lordship is aware that the legislative provisions now in force relative to Lunatic Asylums in
England, are for the most part comprised in the public
Acts of 9 Geo. IV. c. 40; 2 & 3 Will. IV. c. 107;
and 5 & 6 Vic. c. 87.

The Act 9 Geo. IV. c. 40, relates mainly to the formation and management of County Asylums; and several
other Statutes have been subsequently passed, by means
of which various Lunatic Establishments, not originally

*Legislative pro-
visions now in
force.*

*9 Geo. IV. c.
40.*

B

erected for County purposes, have been brought within the regulations of that Act. There are, however, several other Asylums of a mixed character, supported wholly or partially by charitable contributions, to which the Act last referred to does not apply.

2 & 3 Will. IV. c. 107.

The Act 2 & 3 Will. IV. c. 107, (enlarged and continued by later Acts) relates to all licensed Lunatic Asylums throughout England and Wales ; and directs certain of the Metropolitan Commissioners (amongst other things,) to visit the several licensed Houses within the limits of the County of Middlesex, and of certain specified portions of Surrey and Kent, (which limits are now known as the Metropolitan district,) four times in each year, and to report to your Lordship as to their condition. This Act also directs, that three Justices, together with a Medical Attendant, shall be appointed at the General Quarter Sessions to visit all Houses Licensed for Lunatics, in the various counties of England, three times in every year.

5 & 6 Vic. c. 87.

The Act 5 & 6 Vic. c. 87, relates to all Lunatic Asylums in England and Wales, whether private or public, except to the Hospital of Bethlem; and by this Act certain of the Metropolitan Commissioners are directed, twice a year, to visit and report on the Licensed Asylums in the provinces, and once a year to visit and report on the County and other Asylums regulated under the Act of 9 Geo. IV. c. 40; and your Lordship is also empowered to direct us to visit the Royal Military and Naval Hospitals, and all other public Asylums for the reception of insane persons in England and Wales, except the Hospital of Bethlem. This power your Lordship has thought proper to exercise, in order that we might have a more complete opportunity of ascertaining the present state of Lunacy in this Country, and of judging of the sufficiency of the existing laws relating thereto.

We have thought it right to mention the general purport of these Acts, as it will be necessary to advert to some of them in subsequent parts of this Report.

The total number of Lunatic Asylums, public and private, which we have thus been authorized to visit, amounts to 166; viz.:— *Number of Asylums.*

17 County Asylums or Asylums brought within the scope of 9 Geo. IV. c. 40., viz.:

    12 County Asylums.

    5 County and Subscription Asylums.

11 Asylums of a mixed character, maintained partly by subscription and partly by income arising from charitable foundations.

2 Military and Naval Hospitals.

99 Houses licensed by the Justices in Session; viz.:

    59 which receive private patients only.

    40 which receive paupers as well as private patients; of which, 4 are parts of Workhouses.

37 Houses licensed by the Metropolitan Commissioners; viz.:

    33 which receive private patients only.

    4 which receive paupers as well as private patients.

A list of Asylums, with the weekly charges for pauper patients, and the number of patients in each Asylum on the 1st January, 1844, will be found in Appendix (A). *Appendix (A.)*

In addition to the Asylums above enumerated, 4 Houses have been licensed by the Justices in Session, and 3 by the Metropolitan Commissioners, since the 1st January, 1844. *Additional Houses license since Jan. 1, 1844.*

The Asylums above mentioned, with the addition of the Hospital of Bethlem, comprehend all the Asylums for Lunatics in England and Wales, which are at present expressly recognised by law.

Division into
districts for
visitation.

Before entering into a more minute examination of
the subject, which it is our duty to bring before your
Lordship, we beg to state that in pursuance of the
7th section of the Act 5 & 6 Vict. c. 87, a Board
of the Metropolitan Commissioners was assembled,
at which the whole of England and Wales was
divided into four districts; regard being had. to the
number of public and private Asylums necessary to
be visited, and also to the numbers of patients confined
therein; and that each of these districts was again subdivided into two parts, for the purpose of more
conveniently distributing the visitations amongst the
Legal and Medical Commissioners.

Inquiries made
by Commis-
sioners.

Throughout the course of the visitations, made in
pursuance of this arrangement, we have endeavoured to
carry into full effect the spirit as well as the letter of the
Acts of Parliament: and with this view, we have extended our inquiries to many subjects beyond those
which are specifically mentioned in those Acts.   Our
experience within the Metropolitan district has suggested
some of these inquiries; and we have also obtained information from intelligent persons acquainted with the
provincial Asylums, as to their general character and
management.   It has been our endeavour to ascertain
the treatment to which the lunatic (particularly the pauper lunatic) has been subjected from the commencement
of his disease, previously to his reception in an Asylum,
to his final discharge.   For this purpose, we have
visited various Workhouses and other places; have
observed the condition of the inmates; have learned
how and upon what principle the insane poor have
been removed thence to Lunatic Asylums; to what
extent their comfort has been afterwards secured;
how often and with what care they have been visited;
what benefit they have derived from medical treatment;
and what may be the impediments to, or facilities for
their liberation when they are restored to health.   The

excellencies or defects in certain points which we have found existing in some institutions, have instructed us to direct our attention to the same points in others.

We have examined, minutely, into the management of various Asylums, their resources, their security, superintendence, and general arrangements, including their domestic economy, and also their external government and supervision: it being quite obvious that many abuses and defects might exist undiscovered in these establishments, if the mere condition and appearance of each place, at the period of our visit, were admitted as a sufficient criterion of its condition, at all other times and seasons. We have deemed it right to inspect the clothing, bedding, and food, of the patients, and to inquire into every circumstance connected with their subsistence, comfort, and general management; more especially in all establishments for paupers. We have perused the Magistrates' reports, and have inquired into the frequency of their visits, the nature and extent of the inquiries instituted by them, and the general result of their investigations. We have examined all the registers, with a view to ascertain, as much as possible, the amount of intelligence and care exercised in reference to Lunatic Patients, by the visiting Medical Officers; and we have also (as directed by the Acts) given our attention to the questions of religious exercises, classification, and restraint.

In addition to the foregoing subjects, we have, in some instances, thought it advisable to make inquiries as to the origin of the Asylum, and the funds out of which it is supported; as to the experience of the Medical Attendant, his duties, and the remuneration given to him; as to the particular duties of the Matron, and various attendants, and their wages; as to the opportunities afforded of learning the previous history of Patients, the mode of ascertaining their convalescence, and of obtaining their discharge; as to the remedies employed, especially in the cases of dirty and helpless patients; as to the number of cures, deaths, relapses, and other statistical matters, which will be hereinafter specially referred to; as to the Dietary, and the means of adapting it to the exigencies of the disease; and as to various other points, involving the general comforts of Lunatic Patients.

General statement of condition of Asylums.

The Asylums thus brought before our view, exhibit instances of almost every degree of merit and defect. Some are constructed on an extensive scale, and combine most of the advantages and comforts of a wealthy establishment. Others are mean, poor, confined within narrow bounds, and almost wholly without comforts or resources of any kind. Some are situate in open and healthy places, in the midst of large airing grounds, and cheerful prospects. Others are in the centre of towns or populous suburbs, without good air, and without space sufficient for daily exercise. In some places, books and amusements are furnished abundantly for the benefit of Patients, and various means of occupation, adapted to their capacities and previous habits, are provided. In others, the Lunatic is left to pass his time listless and unoccupied, or occupied only with the delusions that disturb him, and which thus, being diverted by no amusement or employment, in the course of time become strengthened, and not to be removed.

Asylums for lunatic poor,

The Asylums in which the lunatic poor are received, have however been the subject of our most especial enquiries. These places (even such of them as are upon the most extended scale) are, we regret to say,

filled with incurable patients.

filled with incurable patients, and are thus rendered incapable of receiving those whose malady might still admit of cure. It has been the practice, in numerous instances, to detain the insane pauper at the workhouse or elsewhere, until he becomes dangerous or unmanageable; and then, when his disease is beyond all medical relief, to send him to a Lunatic Asylum where he may remain during the rest of his life, a pensioner on the public. This practice, which has been carried on for the sake of saving, in the first instance, to each parish some small expense, has confirmed the malady of many poor persons, has destroyed the comfort of families, has ultimately imposed a heavy burthen upon parishes and counties, and has, in a great measure, nullified the utility of public Lunatic Asylums, by converting them into a permanent refuge for the insane, instead of hospitals for their relief or cure. For years past, we have endeavoured, within the Metropolitan District, to diminish this evil practice; but it still prevails; and we doubt whether it will be altogether suppressed, unless some plan be adopted and enforced, for removing, from time to time, each Lunatic as he becomes incurable from the Asylum to which he has been sent, and supplying his place by another whose case, from the recent nature of the attack, may still admit of cure; and unless, also, there be a strict and frequent supervision, not only of Asylums, but of all Workhouses, and other places in which the lunatic poor are detained. We beg to refer your Lordship to the subsequent pages of this Report, for more detailed information on this important point.

The number of insane persons ascertained to exist in England and Wales, exceeds 20,000; and there is every reason to believe that this is considerably below the actual amount. They belong to every station in society; but by far the largest proportion of them (exceeding in fact two-thirds of the whole), are objects of charity, and are maintained entirely at the public expense. These unhappy persons are, for the most part, necessarily removed from their homes, and consigned to the protection of a Lunatic Asylum, by their relations and friends. We have, therefore, entered upon the discharge of our duty, with a strong sense of the claims of the Insane upon our vigilance and care. We are desirous, at the same time, to do justice to those to whose charge the

Number of insane persons in England and Wales.

Two thirds maintained at the public expense.

Insane are committed; and, with this view, we beg leave to bring before your Lordship's notice one class of persons, who, in the course of our labours, have rendered us the most cordial and valuable assistance,—we refer to the resident Medical Officers and Superintendents of the great public Institutions and well-conducted private Asylums throughout the kingdom. We entertain a high opinion of the ability and zeal with which these gentlemen devote themselves to the performance of their arduous duties; and we feel bound to state, that, although on many occasions we have been compelled to impose upon them much trouble, they have afforded us their assistance with the utmost readiness.

Assistance rendered by Medical Officers and Superintendents of Asylums to Commissioners.

After these preliminary observations, we proceed to call your Lordship's attention to the present condition of Lunacy in England; and for the greater convenience of shewing the result of our investigations, we shall divide the subject into the following heads, viz.:

Subject divided into heads.

    I. The different Classes of Lunatic Asylums, their Construction, Condition, Management, and Visitation.

    II. Condition of Paupers, on Admission.

    III. Forms of Disease, Medical Treatment, Diet, and Classification.

    IV. Occupations and Amusements.

    V. Restraint.

    VI. Religious Services.

    VII. The Admission and Liberation of Patients.

    VIII. Statistics of Insanity.

    IX. Criminal Lunatics.

    X. Wales.

THE DIFFERENT CLASSES OF LUNATIC ASYLUMS, THEIR CONSTRUCTION, CONDITION, MANAGEMENT, AND VISITATION.

The distinctions which exist between the various Lunatic Asylums in England, and the nature and extent of their accommodations, will be better understood, if the Asylums are divided into classes, and a brief enumeration is given of the principal points in which they differ from each other. They may be divided into five classes :— *Asylums divided into five classes.*

First.—County Asylums, which have been established under the the Acts of 48 Geo. III. c. 96, and 9 Geo. IV. c. 40, and have been erected by Counties, and paid for wholly out of County rates, for the reception of Paupers; but in some of which private Patients have nevertheless been received. In this class, are included the Asylums for the Counties of Bedford, Chester, Dorset, Kent, Lancaster, Middlesex, Norfolk, Suffolk, Surrey, and for the West Riding of the County of York : in this class, also, may be included the Asylum at Haverfordwest, St. Peter's Hospital, Bristol, and the Workhouse at Hull, which have been declared County Asylums under special Acts of Parliament. *County Asylums.*

Secondly.—County Asylums united with Subscription Asylums, which have been established under the last-mentioned Acts, and have been erected by Counties and subscribers, and paid for partly out of County rates, and partly by private subscription. In this class are included the Asylums for the Counties of Cornwall, Gloucester, Leicester, Nottingham, and Stafford. *County Asylums united with Subscription Asylums.*

Thirdly.—The Lunatic wards of the Royal Military and Naval Hospitals, supported by, and under the control of the Government.

Military and Naval Hospitals.

Public Hospitals, &c. supported wholly or in part by voluntary contributions.

Fourthly.—Public Hospitals, and parts of Hospitals or other Charitable Institutions, supported wholly or partly by voluntary contributions. Of this class are the Lunatic Asylums at Exeter, Lincoln, and Northampton; the Warneford, (formerly called the Radcliffe,) at Oxford, the Retreat at York, the York Asylum, St. Luke's Hospital, the Bethel Hospital at Norwich, the Lunatic ward of Guy's Hospital, the Hospital at Manchester, and the Liverpool Asylum.

Licensed Houses;

Lastly.—Licensed Houses, which receive Private Patients only, Private and Pauper Patients jointly, or Pauper Patients only. This class includes the licensed parts of the following Workhouses, viz., the House of Industry for the Isle of Wight at Carisbrooke, the Workhouse at Devonport, the Houses of Industry at Kingsland near Shrewsbury, and at Morda near Oswestry.

including parts of certain Workhouses.

Bethlem Hospital not included above.

The Royal Hospital of Bethlem is not included in the above enumeration.

Workhouses not licensed, containing Lunatic wards.

Besides the several Asylums already described, there are numerous Workhouses belonging to Parishes and Unions, which are not licensed for the reception of the Insane, but which, nevertheless, contain wards exclusively appropriated to Lunatics, and receive large numbers of Insane persons, dangerous as well as harmless; such as the Workhouses at Birmingham, Manchester, Sheffield, Bath, Leicester, Redruth, in Cornwall, the Infirmary Bethel at Norwich, and others.

1. County Asylums.

County Asylums erected under 48 Geo. III. c. 96, and 9 Geo. IV. c. 40.

The existing County Asylums have been erected under the provisions of the Acts of 48 Geo. III. c. 96, and 9 Geo. IV. c. 40. The former of these Acts directs

the Visiting Justices to fix upon an airy and healthy
situation, with a good supply of water, affording
a probability of the vicinity of medical assistance,
and to provide separate wards, day rooms, and airing
grounds for males and females, and for the convales-
cents and incurables, and dry and airy cells. The Act
of 48 Geo. III., is repealed by the Act of 9 Geo. IV.
c. 40, except as to matters done before the passing of
the latter Act. This latter Act omits the directions as
to the site, and plans of Asylums; but gives special
directions as to the contracts for the purchase of land,
and for the erection of County Asylums.

We made inquiries at the County Lunatic Asylums
as to the mode in which contracts for the purchase of
land for the erection of buildings have been entered
into, and carried into execution: but these contracts,
and all orders relating thereto, being directed to be kept
amongst the records of the different counties, we found
that scarcely any information upon the subject could
be obtained at the asylums. We have, however, procured the most accurate statements we could obtain of
the cost of the land, and the buildings of many of the
Asylums, and these, together with other particulars,
will be found in Appendix(B). Your Lordship will perceive from the perusal of these statements, that the
County Asylums which have hitherto been erected
have caused a heavy expense to the rate-payers, an
expense which we fear has prevented the increase of
these most useful establishments*. Although we have

Contracts for purchase of land for buildings.

Appendix (B).

* The Magistrates of the North Riding of Yorkshire are about to
erect a County Lunatic Asylum for their Paupers. There are several
Corporate and Borough towns in the North Riding which are believed
to be desirous of uniting with the County Magistrates in the erecting
of their Asylum, but it has been considered that the Acts of 9 Geo.
IV. c. 40, and 5 & 6 Will. IV. c. 76, do not authorize such unions.
Our attention has been drawn to this subject by the Chairman of the
Quarter Sessions for the North Riding of Yorkshire; and we think
that it is desirable that the Act of 9 Geo. IV. c. 40, should be
amended in this respect.

no wish to advocate the erection of unsightly buildings we think that no unnecessary cost should be incurred for architectural decoration; especially as these Asylums are erected for persons who, when in health, are accustomed to dwell in cottages.

Comparative cost of Union Workhouses and Asylums.

The best Union Workhouses have in general cost not more than 40*l*., whilst Pauper Lunatic Asylums, have, in some cases, cost upwards of 200*l* per head, for the persons whom they will accommodate. It is true that Lunatics cannot be properly taken care of in the manner in which paupers are provided for; and there are many expensive arrangements essential to a Lunatic Asylum, which are not required in a Workhouse. We have been informed that nearly half the expense of

Increase of expense by making building fire-proof.

an Asylum is caused by the number of separate cells, and by making the building fire-proof; whereas if ordinary dormitories, sufficiently large to contain a moderate number of patients, were principally used, and that part of the house most exposed to danger only were made fire-proof, a large proportion of the cost might be saved.

Use of single cells.

In reference to the question, whether many single cells are necessary or not, we observe that the larger proportion of patients in almost every County Asylum have separate cells, whilst in almost all private Houses licensed for paupers, single cells are rarely used, except for a few of the more violent and dangerous inmates; the general body of the patients sleeping in dormitories containing several beds, varying in number according to the size

Dormitories.

of each room. In 1842, some of the corridors at Stafford, owing to the crowded state of the Asylum, were converted into dormitories, and divided by folding partitions, which allowed perfect ventilation when closed at night. At Lincoln a large proportion of the patients' beds are placed in galleries, an arrangement that is considered to be advantageous, and in all the large County Asylums there are some sleeping-rooms containing numbers of beds. We have seldom seen any sleeping rooms for paupers more comfortable, and more cleanly or better ventilated, than some of the dormitories in the Licensed Houses at Bethnal Green, Fairford, Devizes, and Market Lavington, each of which contains seven or eight beds, or more.

The dormitories in these and in some other licensed Houses appear to us to possess every comfort which the paupers either wish for or require. They, moreover, better accord with the pauper's previous habits than sleeping alone in a solitary cell with a single window; and the companionship of others in the same room does not seem to interfere with their nightly rest. We rarely visit a licensed House containing paupers without asking some of the patients how they sleep at night, and we are generally answered that they sleep well. These persons almost invariably occupy sleeping-rooms containing several beds. In many good Licensed Houses, also, private patients, of a superior class, frequently sleep, to the number of four or five, or even more, in separate beds in the same room. Upon the whole, we are of opinion that dormitories containing several beds are much preferable, as a general arrangement, to cells or single-bedded rooms; although a limited number of the latter is doubtless necessary in every large Asylum, for the use of violent, noisy, and mischievous patients, and for such as are labouring under a paroxysm of insanity. The introduction, however, of any great number of single cells in an Asylum is objectionable, by reason of the space which they occupy, and of the expense incident to their erection; to which may be added the circumstance of their small guarded windows giving a gloomy character to the building. For, when so much is in operation to afford cheerfulness and remove restraint within, it may not be without advantage to abolish the prison-like aspect which marks the exterior of some of the old Asylums.

The question whether Lunatic Asylums for Paupers

Comfort and advantage of Dormitories.

Great number of single cells objectionable.

should be made fire-proof, has been brought under our consideration, and is specially connected with the subject of the cost of these buildings. The Public Hospitals for the Sick in London and in the country, and the large Public Hospitals for the Insane, at Northampton, York, Exeter, and elsewhere, are not built fire-proof; and of all the private licensed Houses for the Insane, we know of only two which have been so built.* The importance of rendering the building fire-proof is obviously increased if a large proportion of the patients sleep in separate cells; for, in the event of a fire, the difficulty of unlocking a great many doors would much impede the removal of the patients to a place of safety.

Having called your Lordship's attention to the question of the cost of County Asylums, we now proceed to remark on the site for such buildings, and on what is necessary in their construction, in order to render them fit for the reception of Lunatics.

An Asylum should be placed upon elevated ground, and should command cheerful prospects: the soil should be dry, and there should be a plentiful supply of water, and means of proper drainage. The want of water, in places where large numbers are collected, of whom many are invalids, and many extremely dirty, is obviously a serious calamity. The buildings should be surrounded with land sufficient to afford out-door employment for the male, and exercise for all the patients, and to protect them from being over-looked, or disturbed by strangers. In the best asylums (such as

---

* It is singular that in one of these houses two, and in the other one person, have lost their lives by fire in their separate rooms. There was a fire at the York Asylum, in the year 1813, in which four persons lost their lives. There has also been a slight fire at the Gloucester Asylum, in the main building, and in a gas house at Hanwell, but no accident happened, and little excitement took place among the patients on the happening of either of these events.

After the Surrey Asylum was made fire-proof in the part occupied by the patients, the chapel was required to be made fire-proof, and this was effected at a very considerable additional cost.

15

those for the counties of Surrey, Kent, and the West Riding of Yorkshire) these and other important matters* have been attended to; but in others they have been partially or wholly neglected.

St. Peter's Hospital, Bristol, is situate in the centre of the most crowded part of the city, and has for the purposes of exercise, only half of a small paved court for the males, and for the females an equally small court, used, also, as a road, and which is, in every respect, quite unfit for the purpose to which it is appropriated. The Asylum for the county of Pembroke, at Haverfordwest, was once a town Gaol, and, in its present state, is an ill-constructed Prison. For its total unfitness for the care of pauper lunatics, we must refer to the description of it, in a subsequent part of this Report. The site of the Asylum at Nottingham is partly surrounded, and commanded by adjoining buildings. It contains 177 patients, but has not more than three acres of land, besides what is occupied by the buildings, garden and yards, and we understand that there is no opportunity of purchasing any more adjoining ground. The present medical superintendent himself took a farm, for some time, with the view of finding employment for the male paupers, but his other duties prevented his continuing to occupy it. Inconvenience has been experienced at the Asylum for Dorset, and at Lancaster, from the yards and wards being too close to the boundary wall. At Hanwell, the ward for the worst class of females, and the large exercising ground for the women, are both liable to the same annoyance, being only separated from the land of other proprietors by a wooden paling. At Leicester,

St. Peter's Hospital, Bristol.

Asylum at Haverfordwest;

Nottingham;

Dorset;
Lancaster;
Hanwell;

Leicester;

* The Galleries and Day Rooms at the Leicester and Dorset County Asylums, are very good. The Yards of Gloucester, and the Grounds at Hanwell, are spacious and very well adapted for exercise. Many of the arrangements at Stafford have been much approved; and amongst other important advantages, the Kent and Lancaster Asylums have detached Infirmaries for each sex.

containing 131 patients, there are only four or five acres of land, besides the site of the buildings.

The Norfolk Asylum, with 220 patients, has only five acres of land, of which not more than one acre and a half, used as a kitchen garden, can be applied to

the employment of the patients. At Lancaster, where there are 611 patients, they had originally only five acres, subsequently increased to fifteen; and last year the magistrates of the county were obliged to apply to Parliament for, and obtained an Act to enable them

to purchase the additional land, which was essential for the proper care of their patients. At the Asylum at Bedford, with 139 patients, there are only six acres, besides what is covered by the buildings and yards, part of which is used as a burial ground. The great value of out-door occupation as a means of restoring the insane poor, (even those whose employments have been previously sedentary,) to health of mind, and of promoting tranquillity, renders the want of a sufficient quantity of land a very serious defect in the above-mentioned Asylums ; and this, in some instances, cannot be remedied without removing the Asylum altogether.

The Asylum of Bodmin is frequently short of water, and had been so during a whole week at the time of our visit to it in 1843, when the discomfort and evils resulting from this deficiency were very perceptible. There has also been considerable difficulty about the

supply of water at the Lancaster Asylum. At Hanwell, one well has failed, and this large establishment was mainly dependent on the Grand Junction Canal for its supply, which was obtained at a cost, during several years, of 140l. a year; but the Company having refused to continue the supply, the Visiting Justices have been compelled to sink an Artesian well, which has cost 1,483l.

The importance of warmth, ventilation, and dryness, in Lunatic Asylums, will be understood by the fact that at Stafford, as was stated to us, in 1842, that " an improved system of warming and ventilation had been recently introduced with success, since which no cases of dysentery, formerly prevalent, had occurred ;" and at the Dorsetshire Asylum, in 1843, we were informed, that, "from the floors having been damp, the patients were formerly subject to dysentery, but they had been taken up and relaid, and not one of the patients admitted since the alteration had suffered from dysentery." Many Lunatics are not only sickly, but are so filthy in their habits, that they nearly frustrate all attempts to keep them clean, and can only be allowed to sleep upon straw or other bedding which may be thrown away, or washed every day. In cases of this sort, a free circulation of air is very important. The ventilation at the Asylums for the counties of Kent, Surrey, and some others, is very good; whilst at Hanwell, and at Bodmin, it is in some parts extremely defective.

It is indispensable to the comfort and health of the inmates of Lunatic Asylums, that proper provision should be made for warming and ventilating the Galleries and Dormitories, so that the Patients may breathe a pure atmosphere, of a moderate and even temperature. It is also essential to their enjoyment, that the interior of the building should be light and cheerful. A large proportion of the Patients, more particularly the Females, spend a great part of the day in the Wards; and it is very desirable that the Galleries should be so constructed and lighted as to form convenient places of exercise and recreation in rainy weather, and in the winter season. It is especially important that these considerations should be kept in view, in the erection of Asylums. If they are neglected in the first instance, much additional expense must be incurred in remedying the original defects : whilst the evils arising from tainted air, and an unequal temperature, can, in many cases, be only partially abated by subsequent alterations.

Arrangements for warming and ventilation in Asylums visited.

We have endeavoured to ascertain, as regards Warming and Ventilation, what arrangements are made in the several Asylums which we have visited, and what plans have been found, most successful.

Steam Apparatus, &c.

The mode of warming frequently adopted is by means of a circulating steam or hot-water apparatus, which, in the older Asylums, has, in most instances, been substituted for the open fires, or stoves, formerly in use.

In adopting this arrangement, consideration has been had to economy of fuel, to the saving of trouble to the Attendants, and to lessening the risk of danger to the

Advantage of open fires.

inmates; but open fires have the advantage of cheerfulness, and chimneys materially promote ventilation at those seasons of the year when artificial heat is not

Mode of warming Chester Asylum;

required. In the Chester Asylum, on the occasion of our first visit, in August, 1842, we found open fires still in use on the Female side, principally, as we were informed, with a view to the enjoyment of the Inmates, who much preferred them to a heating apparatus, as being more cheerful. The Male Division was warmed by means of hot-water pipes, passing through the upper Galleries; the furnace to the boiler answering the purpose of a Stove for the Basement Story, in which the Patients of uncleanly habits were placed.

Nottingham Asylum;

At the Nottingham Asylum, steam pipes have been substituted for a hot-air apparatus, the latter having been found ineffectual for its purpose. The steam is generated by the boiler of an Engine, by means of which water is pumped up into a Reservoir above the level of the upper Galleries. Over this Boiler is an excellent Drying Room.

Leicester Asylum;

The interior of the Leicester Asylum is "warmed by atmospheric air conducted in brick drains, and passed over iron plates and pipes made hot with boiling water;

and the air, when heated, is conveyed by brick tubes to the several Dormitories and Galleries, and the vitiated air is allowed to escape through Conductors into the roof, from whence it is discharged by turn-caps, or cowls, regulated by vanes."

At the Kent Asylum, the warming and ventilating arrangements were designed and carried into execution at the time the Buildings were erected, and consist (as described by the Architect) of " a large volume of pure atmospheric air, passing from the yard, through channels under ground, into a Chamber where it is warmed in winter, by passing over a large surface of hot-water pipes, and from thence enters the Galleries in a large volume near the ceiling, and into the Sleeping Rooms.—It is from thence drawn off through apertures near the floor, and into air drains which communicate with fires in the Cellar; thus ensuring a constant change of the air, as the fires are supplied entirely by the vitiated air from the Galleries and Sleeping Rooms." The apparatus has been in use several years, and has been found to answer perfectly. The Superintendent, to whom we are indebted for the foregoing particulars, adds that hot water is the medium used for warming the air in the new Building ; but that in the old Building, the air is warmed by a cockle and tubes, the principle in other respects being the same. Hot-water tubes or pipes are consiered by him preferable to the latter, " as the air cannot be heated above the temperature of boiling water, and consequently is never burnt."

In reply to our inquiries at the Gloucester Asylum, we have received from the Superintendent the following statement :—" In the Refractory Wards, the Sleeping Rooms are both warmed and ventilated by air passing through chambers, inclosing pipes of warm water. The same principle is here adopted as at the Pentonville Prison ; and was one of Mr. Haden's first attempts to effect the circulation of warm air from above down-

Kent Asylum ;

Gloucester Asylum ;

c 2

wards. It is very good, and answers extremely well."—
Upon two several occasions, however, when this Asylum was visited by the Commissioners, the ventilation
of the Basement Story, especially in the cells appropriated to the dirty class of Patients, appeared to be
extremely indifferent.

Surrey Asylum; . In respect to the Surrey Asylum, (the last County
Asylum which has been erected,) the House and Galleries
generally are warmed by the circulation of Steam, and
the introduction of Hot Air through apertures in the
floor. The temperature is regulated by stop-cocks,
and kept between 56° and 58°. There are open fires,
with proper guards, in the several Day Rooms on the
Female side; and it is proposed to adopt them also in
the Male division. We drew the attention of the Superintendent to the defective ventilation of some of the
Pauper Dormitories on the third floor, which we were
informed by him had also been noticed by the Visiting
Justices.

We have elsewhere adverted to the want of proper
ventilation in some of the Wards or Sleeping Rooms
Hanwell Asy- in the Hanwell Asylum, more especially in the Base-
lum defective; ment Story on the Female side. And we have, when
visiting other Asylums, pointed out similar defects to
the Superintendents and Medical Officers.

St. Luke's Hos- . The Galleries in St. Luke's Hospital, which are spa-
pital; cious and airy, are not artificially warmed; and complaints were made to us of their being cold in winter. The
only fires in the Wards are those in the Day Rooms and
Nurses' Apartments. We were informed, however, that
plans were under consideration for the introduction of a
hot-water apparatus, with grated openings in the lower
part of the doors of the Sleeping Rooms. The ventilation of these rooms, when we visited the Hospital, appeared to be imperfect.

Lincoln Asy- At the Lincoln Asylum; the Day Rooms, of which
lum. there are eight in each division of the Asylum, are

warmed by open fires. The Galleries, which appeared to us as likely to be very cold in winter, are not artificially warmed, the stoves and flues formerly in use having been discontinued in the year 1836. Upon this subject, the Board of visitors, in January, 1843, amongst other Regulations for the Medical Treatment of the Patients, passed the following Resolution : " That no system of warming this house, by means of which the Patients may breathe a heated atmosphere, be introduced."

We proceed to offer a few observations upon the size and arrangement of the Dormitories and single Sleeping Cells. In respect to the latter, it appears desirable, on every account, that they should be on only one side of the Gallery, and that they should not be ranged back to back, as is the case at Lancaster and Gloucester. Galleries, with Sleeping Rooms on both sides, are generally gloomy, and the ventilation is necessarily imperfect. Where the original construction of the Asylum, or the number of Patients to be accommodated, renders such an arrangement unavoidable, it is desirable that recesses extending to, and lighted by windows in the outer wall could be left at intervals between the sleeping rooms, so as to form part of the galleries, the ventilation and general cheerfulness of which will be thereby materially promoted. Light should also, in all cases where it is practicable, be admitted at the extremities of the Galleries. The Galleries in the Surrey Asylum, in which there are Sleeping Rooms on both sides, are wide and airy; those on the upper floor being well lighted by cupolas. This plan, in some degree, diminishes the force of the objections that we have stated.

Upon the subject of single Rooms as connected with ventilation, we would observe that, unless they are perfectly ventilated, Dormitories, with a limited number of beds, are preferable. Such Dormitories present the advantage of a more free circulation of air, and more even temperature. Single Rooms, where adopted, should be of good size.

Observations on dormitories and single cells.

Galleries in Surrey Asylum.

Dormitories preferable to single rooms.

Those in the new Wings at the Bedford Asylum, which are constructed only on one side of the Galleries, are of inadequate dimensions, being only six feet six inches in length, by six feet in width, and about eight feet high. We found them, however, clean and free from any offensive odour. The usual size of the single Cells in County and Public Asylums is from nine to ten feet in length, and seven feet in width; and the average solid measure of each is about 700 cubic feet.

Use of base-
ment stories for
Patients to be
avoided.

The use of basement stories below the level of the adjoining ground should be avoided as much as possible for occupation by Patients. They are used in the Suffolk Asylum and at Nottingham and Hanwell. Some of the cells on the basement floor at Nottingham can scarcely be considered as fit for invalids; and many of the sleeping-rooms on the basement story at Hanwell, are dark, cold, and ill ventilated. Much has been done at the Surrey Asylum to render the basement story cheerful and airy, by making the windows open upon green grass slopes, instead of into areas; and the same plan has, also, been partially adopted at Hanwell.

An Asylum
should have
cheerful and
spacious day
rooms.

An Asylum should have cheerful and spacious day rooms, easily accessible from the yards. An opinion was expressed by the Resident Physician of Hanwell, before a Committee of the House of Lords, that it was desirable to have the day rooms formed in the galleries: but the other Medical Officers and Engineer of that Asylum did not, on our mentioning the subject, concur in this opinion. One of the galleries for females, in Hanwell, is in the form of three arms of a cross, and has one arm entirely occupied by a table and benches. At Bodmin, the day rooms generally form parts of the galleries, and partitions have been erected to keep the patients away from their bed rooms in the day time, and to prevent the smell and inconveniences resulting from their using the galleries as dining rooms.

Use of galleries
as day rooms;

at Hanwell;

Bodmin;

Kent Asylum.

In the Kent Asylum, the galleries constitute the

23

only day rooms for the patients, an arrangement which
we think of very doubtful advantage in this otherwise
excellent establishment. Galleries are intended as places
for exercise for invalids, and for all the patients in bad
weather, and the necessity of placing chairs and tables
in them, and the preparations and removals before and
after meals, greatly interfere with this object.

The yards of Asylums should be constructed so as to Construction of yards.
have as much light, sun, and prospect as possible. With
this view, there were raised, in the yards of the Asylum
at Wakefield, (erected in 1815,) mounds affording a view
of the country over the walls. Similar but more perfect arrangements have been made since at the Surrey,
Lancaster, and other Asylums. The yards, however, at
Bodmin, Nottingham, and Leicester, are for the most
part dull and gloomy, from being surrounded by high
walls. Many of the yards at Hanwell are enclosed by
walls and buildings, and some are placed between the
main building, the farm-yard and piggeries. The
yards in the Asylum for the county of Norfolk,
are extremely defective; and those in the Asylums for
the counties of Dorset and Kent, are not cheerful or well
laid out. Every yard ought to contain a shed for shelter
from the sun.

Another point connected with the construction of Limitation of size of County Asylums;
county Lunatic Asylums, and which requires much
attention, is the size to which each should be limited.
Out of fifteen county Lunatic Asylums already erected,
ten have accommodation for not more than 200
patients, whilst the remaining five have room for larger
numbers. The Asylum for Kent will contain 300; for
Surrey, 360; for the West Riding of York, 420; for
Lancaster, 600 patients; and the Asylum for Middlesex
has beds for 1,000 patients. From the best opinions
that we have been able to collect, and from the result of
our own observations and experience, we think it is
desirable that no asylum for curable lunatics should should not contain more than 250 patients.
contain more than 250 patients, and that 200 is perhaps

. 24

as large a number as can be managed with the most benefit, to themselves and the public, in one establishment.*

It has been generally considered to be an advantage
in England, that our public hospitals are less in size
than they are in France and on other parts of the Con-
tinent, and that the patients are on this account better
attended to in our hospitals. We have, in other parts of
our Report, alluded to some evils and inconveniences
which have been experienced at Hanwell, owing to its

Magnitude of Hanwell inconvenient. extreme magnitude. The two resident Medical Officers
have, between them, nearly 1,000 patients to attend,
and are required by the rules to see every patient
twice a day. Each of these Officers has an average
of 30 persons on the sick list, and about 50 on the
extra-diet list. Besides these duties, they have to mix
the medicines, and to keep the registers and diaries.
Some attention is also required to be paid to chronic
cases, in which the general health and state of mind are
often varying. This Asylum contains 100 officers
and servants, residing in the buildings besides employing
between 50 and 60 out-door labourers and mechanics.

Consequences of disuse of restraint. The diminution and disuse of restraint in Asylums
have been accompanied by an increase in the number
of attendants, and by confiding to them a greater
power of control over the patients. The delegation of
so much authority, as, in large asylums, is now necessarily placed in the hands of attendants, demands a
proportionate increase of vigilance in the Superintendents. At Hanwell, much importance is attached to
having a superior class of attendants, to be employed
in carrying into effect the system of management which
exists there; but we found that a large proportion of the
female attendants had been in the Asylum only a short
period, and had not previously been employed in any

* The Legislature has recognised the expediency of limiting the size
of Asylums by enacting (1 and 2, Geo. IV., c. 33), that the District
Asylums in Ireland, " shall be sufficient to contain not more than
150" Patients.

similar establishment. There is, however, sometimes
great difficulty in finding good attendants for Asylums,
and where more than eighty are employed, it is probable that there must necessarily be frequent changes.
We think that the assembling, under one roof, of so
many patients and servants, as are now in Hanwell
Asylum, is calculated to render it difficult to main-
tain that order, regularity, and subordination, which are
essential to the good management of a receptacle for
the insane. These considerations are especially important at a time when, as we are informed, there exists an
intention to increase the Asylums (already so large) for
the Counties of Middlesex and Lancaster. We trust
that the Magistrates of those districts will deliberate
seriously before they resolve upon a measure of such
doubtful expediency.

By the Act 9 Geo. IV. c. 40, sect. 8., it is enacted
that, in the case of every County Asylum " it shall be
" lawful for the major part of the Justices of the Peace,
" at the Michaelmas General Quarter Sessions in each
" year, to elect a Committee of Visiting Justices, for the
" Management of such County Lunatic Asylum, and to
" fill up any vacancy in the number of such Committee as
" may have occurred by death, or resignation ;" and by
the 30th sect. of the same Act, the Visitors are required
" from time to time, to make regulations for the man-
" agement and conduct of the Asylum ; in which regu-
" lations shall be set forth the number and description
" of Officers and Servants to be kept, and their respec-
" tive duties and salaries ;" such Officers and Servants
to be appointed and dismissed by the Visitors. The
first of these provisions appears to be in general complied
with, but the regulations are frequently neglected to be
made.

In the Asylum for the County of Bedford, however,
there seems to be no Committee elected ; the whole body
of Magistrates being appointed Visitors, and almost the
entire control of the County Asylum being delegated to

Difficulty in finding good attendants; and of maintaining order. Election of Committee of visiting justices for County Asylums, under 9 Geo. IV. c. 40, s. 58. Regulations frequently neglected.

the Medical and General Superintendent, who appoints and dismisses servants, and occasionally discharges patients of his own authority. There is also no set of rules, for the direction of the officers and servants of this

Appointment and dismissal of servants.

Asylum. We consider that the appointment and dismissal of servants is a trust of great importance, which is vested in the Visiting Justices for the purpose of checking any undue power or influence being used by the superintendent over the servants of an Asylum.

In the County of Chester, at our first visit, no Committee of Visiting Justices had been elected, but all the Magistrates acted as Visiting Justices. They seldom visited the Asylum, the superintendence and management of which was confided, until lately, almost exclusively, to the Visiting Physician, upon whom a very serious responsibility was thus thrown. In some other Asylums, the hiring and dismissal of servants appear to be entrusted to the Medical Superintendent and Matron.

Rules for management of County Asylums left by law entirely to Magistrates.

The law has left the formation of rules for the management of County Lunatic Asylums entirely to the Magistrates. Whilst these institutions were comparatively new, this might be unobjectionable; but now that they have become numerous and of great importance, and are maintained at a large public cost, we think that some

General rules desirable.

general rules should be laid down for their management, and some uniform but concise tables framed for their use, in order to their making periodically certain statistical

Publication of annual accounts important.

returns. It is important that an account should be published of the annual expenditure of every County Asylum, (as is already done in many cases,) as well as of the original cost, and all the current expenditure, in proper detail. Some opinion might then be formed as to the comparative good management and efficiency

Rules for relief of certain pauper lunatics when discharged important.

of each of these Asylums. We think it of importance that some rules should be laid down for the relief of certain Pauper Lunatics when discharged. Pauper Lunatics who are sent from a Parish, or a Workhouse, have, on being discharged, either their own home

or the Workhouse to return to, until they can find
employment and the means of subsistence. Paupers,
however, whose Parishes are unknown and who are sent
as County, or Vagrant Paupers, and are maintained at
the charge of Counties, have, frequently, on being discharged, no home or Workhouse to which they can
resort until they can obtain work. Our attention has
been called to this subject, on more than one occasion.

At the Bethnal Green Asylum, whenever any County
Pauper has been discharged as cured, it has been the
custom, if the Patient has conducted himself well, to
give him permission to return to sleep and have some
meals, until he can find employment. This has been
charitably allowed from a conviction that such persons,
if suddenly turned adrift without a home, or the means
of procuring food, would, in most cases, be soon sent
back under a relapse brought on by destitution. When
it is stated that in 1842 there were, in the County Asylum of Lancaster, 118, and in 1843, in the County
Asylum for Middlesex, 126 County Paupers, or
Vagrants, who, upon their discharge would have no
Workhouse, and probably no home to repair to—it
will probably be thought worth while to make some
provision for Patients of that class in the event of their
liberation.

Practice at Bethnal Green Asylum on discharge of Pauper Lunatics.

Some provision for such Patients necessary.

The destitute condition of many Pauper Lunatics on
leaving Asylums, has induced benevolent individuals to
raise funds for their assistance. A gentleman of the
name of Harrison left a sum of 1000l. to the Asylum
at Wakefield for this purpose. The Adelaide fund
having the same object, was set on foot by the charitable exertions of the Visiting Magistrates at Hanwell,
and in 1842, amounted to 5000l. At the Gloucester
Asylum, where there is a similar fund, amounting to
about 800l., small sums of money and occasionally
also tools, are lent to Patients on their liberation.
There is a similar fund, instituted by Lady Middleton,
at Nottingham; and upon the same principle, assistance

Charitable funds for relief of discharged Pauper Luna-tics.

is given to poor Patients on their discharge at St. Luke's.
It may deserve consideration whether, some arrangement should not be adopted generally with a view to
provide assistance for poor Patients on their discharge.
Relapses are frequently attributed to the want of some
such relief.

Rule adopted
by Middlesex
Magistrates as
to Pauper
Lunatics' settle-
ments.

At the suggestion of the Visiting Justices of Hanwell,
the Magistrates of the County of Middlesex have agreed
not to adjudicate Paupers as County Patients, without
previous notice to the County Solicitors, and a minute
investigation of each case. The result of this judicious
arrangement has been, that the Settlements of many
Paupers, previously charged upon the County, have been
discovered, and a considerable saving to the County has
been thus effected.

Recommenda-
tion as to ap-
pointment of
resident Medi-
cal Officer in
Public Asy-
lums;

By the Act 2 & 3 Will. IV. c. 107, every licensed
Asylum containing 100 patients (or more), is required to
have a resident Medical Officer, and it is important that
a similar regulation should be made in reference to
Public Asylums. It is to be observed that all the County
Asylums possess resident Medical Officers, except those
of the counties of Bedford, Norfolk, and Pembroke,
(Haverfordwest). We think it, also, in many cases,

and Visiting
Physician in
County Asy-
lums.

desirable that County Asylums should have a Visiting
Physician, in addition to the resident Medical Officer.

In the case of the Asylum at Hanwell, the Visiting
Justices have lately appointed a gentleman (formerly an
Officer in the Army), who has had no previous experience in the management of the Insane, as the Governor.
The appointment appears to have become necessary in
order to preserve good order in this large Establishment;
and for that purpose, the Governor has the power of suspending, not only the servants, but even the Medical
Officers and Matron of the Asylum. He has also the
entire control over the classification, employment, amusements, instruction, and general management of the
patients both male and female, subject only to the
general control of the Visiting Justices.

It is apparent, from the foregoing remarks, that although a few of the existing County Asylums are well adapted to their purpose, and a very large proportion of them are extremely well conducted; yet some are quite unfit for the reception of the insane, some are placed in ineligible sites, some are deficient in the necessary means of providing out-door employment for their paupers, some are ill-contrived and defective in their internal construction and accommodations, some are cheerless and confined in their yards and airing-grounds, and some are larger than seems consistent with the good management of their establishments and the proper care and health of their patients. When in addition to these defects in the Institutions themselves, the very large cost at which they have been erected is taken into account, it appears to be deserving the consideration of the legislature, whether the erection of Public Asylums for the insane poor of the country may not be advantageously regulated by some independent authority. Although county magistrates have properly the control of the expenditure of funds to be raised in their own districts, it can scarcely be expected that they should devote so much attention as is really necessary to make them conversant with the various points which involve the convenience, comfort, and security necessary to be provided for in large Asylums for the insane, and they are therefore liable to be misled as to their proper cost and construction.*

General remarks on County Asylums.

* Surveyors and architects should be especially directed to visit the best constructed Lunatic Asylums, previously to the preparation of plans for new Establishments. The plan of the Asylum for the County of Devon, not yet opened, has been much objected to: it is somewhat similar to that of the Lunatic Asylum for the County of Cornwall, which has been found ill suited to the purposes for which it was erected. Whilst visiting the Asylum at Hanwell, we met several parties examining the buildings, with a view of preparing plans for a Pauper Lunatic Asylum for the County of Derby; and from perusing the printed minutes of a Committee of Magistrates of that County, we fear that they have been led to adopt some of the defects of the Hanwell Asylum.

Pauper Lunatics have unfortunately become so numerous, throughout the whole kingdom, that the proper construction and cost of Asylums for their use, has ceased to be a subject which affects a few counties only, and has become a matter of national interest and importance.

2.—County Asylums, partly supported by Contributions.

Asylums erected under 48 Geo. III. c. 96, and 9 Geo. IV. c. 40.

In respect to the Asylums for the counties of Cornwall, Gloucester, Leicester, Nottingham, and Stafford, which have been established at the joint expense of counties and subscribers, it is to be observed that they were erected under the provisions of the Acts 48 Geo. III. c. 96, and 9 Geo. IV. c. 40. From the recitals in the former of those Acts, the intention of the Legislature appears to have been to encourage Asylums of this description; first, on the ground of the payments of the richer being applied towards the maintenance of the poorer classes of Patients; and secondly, on account of the advantages which they were likely to afford to Pauper Lunatics.

We have not been able to ascertain, with accuracy, what has been the extent of the relief contributed in these Asylums to the poorer private Patients, from the excess of the payments of the richer private Patients, and we are therefore unable to say, how far the charitable objects of the Legislature have been realised in this respect. But, as regards the advantages which have been conferred by these Institutions upon Pauper Lunatics, it appears to us that they scarcely equal those of County Asylums erected exclusively for Paupers; whilst the maintenance of Paupers in them is fully as expensive as in Asylums established solely for paupers.

Weekly payments for paupers in certain County Asylums.

In the Asylum for the county of Cornwall, the payments of the higher classes of private patients are applied in diminution of the expenses of the paupers, for whom the weekly payment is 5s. 6d. The weekly payment for paupers at Leicester, is 8s. 6d.; and at Stafford, 7s., in each case, exclusive of clothing; and at Gloucester, 9s. and at Nottingham, 8s., including clothes. In some of these Asylums, the better part of the buildings and airing grounds are given up to the private patients, to the exclusion, in a great measure, of the paupers.

It is right, however, to observe, that the defects of some of these Institutions may be attributed to their having been amongst the first Public Asylums that were erected, and that the contributors and subscribers to them were amongst the first promoters of a mild and humane system of treatment for the insane of all classes. Whether Institutions may be formed, in which private patients shall have all the comforts which their circumstances afford, and the poor may also be properly taken care of at a diminished expense to the country, is a question upon which we do not at present offer an opinion.

Contributors and subscribers first promoters of a mild system.

No opinion offered as to formation of improved mixed Asylums.

3. MILITARY AND NAVAL HOSPITALS.

The Military Hospital at Fort Clarence, near Chatham, is well situated. That part of the fort which is appropriated to the residences of the Officers is very gloomy, and ill suited for a receptacle for Insane persons. Some of the sleeping-rooms for the private soldiers are sufficiently good, but others are dull and cheerless. The exercising-ground for the Officers, and the yards for the soldiers, are cheerful, but are not sufficient in number or size. The buildings and grounds admit of great improvement; but we understand that the inmates of this Hospital are about to be removed to a new Asylum.

Military Hospital at Fort Clarence, described.

New Asylum about to be opened.

That part of the Naval Hospital at Haslar which is set apart for Officers of the Navy and seamen afflicted with Insanity, is admirably adapted to its purpose. The

Naval Hospital at Haslar.

rooms are lofty, spacious, and airy; and they command a view of the entrance to Portsmouth harbour. There are excellent exercising-grounds between the Hospital and the shore, and the Patients are frequently taken out in boats.

4. PUBLIC HOSPITALS, SUPPORTED WHOLLY OR PARTLY BY VOLUNTARY CONTRIBUTIONS.

General remarks on Public Hospitals.

Having obtained authority from your Lordship to visit the different Lunatic Hospitals in the kingdom coming under this class, it will be expected that we shall make some remarks upon their condition. These Hospitals differ materially from other Hospitals for the Sick in this respect, that although most of them derive some portion of their income from a charitable foundation, the patients admitted into them invariably pay the greater part, and sometimes the whole, of the expense of their own maintenance and medical attendance. The Lunatic Ward

Guy's Hospital, and Bethel at Norwich.

of Guy's Hospital, and, to a certain extent, the Bethel Hospital at Norwich, are exceptions to this rule. The sum received from private patients, and for board and

Comparative receipts from private patients.

lodging, in the year 1842, at the Retreat, York, was 4139l. 2s. 11d.; at St. Luke's, 1526l. 8s.; at Lincoln, (1843), 3559l. 19s. 11d.; at Exeter, 1735l.; at the Warneford, near Oxford, 1098l. 10s. 6d.: and at Northampton, 5141l. 18s. 5d. Private patients who have been

Advantages enjoyed by them.

in better circumstances, derive much benefit from the comforts and advantages which these Institutions supply, at a moderate rate of payment.

Payments at Lincoln and Northampton for paupers.

There were eighty-three pauper patients, in 1843, at the Lincoln Asylum, for whom the payment made by their parishes was 10s. per week for each person, and at Northampton there were 192 paupers, for whom the payment was 9s. per week for each person, not including clothes in either case. These sums are higher than are usually charged for paupers in licensed houses.

The founders, however, of these Institutions did not intend them for the benefit of rate-payers.

The internal accommodations and grounds of the Retreat, near York, are admirably adapted to promote the benevolent objects for which that Asylum was established. The Lincoln Asylum is extremely well situated, and the buildings are commodious and well suited to their purpose, but at the time of our visit, there was no land for employment. Some of the rooms at Exeter are cheerful, and command good views, but the yards are surrounded by unusually high walls. The Warneford Asylum, near Oxford, is well situated, and the grounds are well laid out. Saint Luke's Hospital is ill placed, and is extremely deficient in airing-grounds. The galleries, however, are very spacious. From the curative wards of this Hospital, cases of epilepsy, paralysis, and idiocy, and also cases of more than a year's standing are excluded; but there is a ward appropriated to incurables, limited to 100 patients. The Asylum at Northampton is well situated: the buildings are well arranged; it has several walled yards, and also extensive grounds, in which the patients who can be trusted, take exercise, and which, from the circumstance of their being bounded by banks and hedges, instead of high walls (as is usual in other Asylums) possess a character of great cheerfulness. The Bethel Hospital at Norwich, and the Asylum at Manchester, from their sites and accommodations, are very ill adapted for receptacles for the Insane.

In some of these Public Hospitals, the Governing Bodies claim, on behalf of their Institutions, an entire exemption from Visitation. We cannot, however, but think, that all places receiving and detaining in custody any class of Her Majesty's subjects, should be open to inspection by proper authority; and we do not perceive anything in the constitution of Hospitals of this nature that distinguishes them from other Public Asylums, or

Comparative accommodations.

Exemption from visitation claimed in some cases.

D

provides any sufficient security against the chances of abuse.

5. Licensed Houses.

Licensed
Houses consist
of three classes.

The Houses which are licensed for the reception of Insane persons consist, first, of those which admit only Private Patients; secondly, of those which admit both Private and Pauper Patients; and lastly, of the licensed parts of Workhouses, which receive Paupers only.

Our object, in this Report, is to bring before your Lordship's especial notice, such instances of existing evils in Lunatic Establishments in general as are of magnitude, and require immediate correction ; leaving such as are of less importance, and appear to be in a state of progressive amendment, to the effect which a strict investigation cannot fail, in the course of time, to produce. With this view, we think it expedient, on the present occasion, to advert more especially to the character of the Licensed Houses which receive Paupers, and which are necessarily resorted to on account of the Public Asylums being wholly insufficient for that class of Patients. It is in these Houses that the principal defects have been found. In regard to Licensed Houses which receive Private Patients only, although many of them are susceptible of improvement, their prosperity is more essentially dependent on their good conduct, and they therefore present less occasion for animadversion.

Some of the Establishments, which receive Private Patients only, possess every accommodation and convenience which comfort, or even luxury, can require; and in them the Patients are generally treated kindly and judiciously. We abstain from pointing out specially the Houses of this class which we consider to be the best, in order that we may not indirectly affect the character of others, which, although inferior in accommodation and arrangement, are nevertheless well conducted. These remarks, it should be observed, apply not only to Houses, receiving Private Patients only, which are situated in the Metropolitan district, but to some in the Provinces. The former have for many years been under our exclusive jurisdiction, and their condition has been frequently the subject of former Reports to your Lordship; and although very great improvements have been made in many of them, and no important defects in their management demand particular notice from us at present, we are nevertheless convinced that some of these very houses, of which we now speak in terms of commendation, would soon become the scenes of great abuses, were it not for the checks interposed by the constant and watchful visitation to which they are subjected.

It is due to the Proprietors of Licensed Houses in the provincial districts, to state that alterations to a considerable extent have been already made by several of them, upon our suggestions; that others are in progress; and that, upon the whole, a decided improvement has already taken place in some parts of these Establishments, though much still remains to be done. There are some of these Houses, however, which require to be greatly altered before they can be considered as fit receptacles for the Insane; but the Proprietors having expressed a willingness to make improvements, we shall not call particular attention to them on the present occasion. Should our expectations of amendment not be realised, we shall think it our duty to bring before your Lordship's notice such defects as may continue to exist, in our next Report. It will be necessary, however, even in our present Report, to advert to certain irregularities and partial defects in some of these Houses, which ought not to be passed over. *Alterations and Improvements.*

At the Licensed House of the Rev. Dr. Chevallier, at Aspall Hall, in the county of Suffolk, who is a practising Physician, as well as an officiating Clergyman and acting Magistrate of the county, there were at our first visit, in 1842, three certified Patients, and eight other ladies and gentlemen, who were reported to us as not Insane, residing *Irregularities at Dr. Chevallier's, Aspall Hall, Suffolk;*

there as boarders. One of these gentlemen was stated to be the Curate of a neighbouring church, and he was therefore not examined: it was, however, afterwards ascertained that he had been previously confined as Insane. The other boarders were examined. One of them was a Clergyman who had been previously confined under certificates, and was still low-spirited; another was an imbecile young man, not fit to be trusted in society; a third was a lady who was manifestly Insane; a fourth was a gentleman who fancied that he was becoming Insane; and a fifth was his companion. The remaining two boarders were ladies of weak minds and nervous habits.

The Visiting Justices subsequently examined five of these boarders, and came to the conclusion that three of them were of sound mind, that one was Insane, and that the mental condition of the fifth was doubtful. At our second visit, we were satisfied that one of the male boarders, whose case was considered as doubtful by the Justices, was decidedly of unsound mind; and he afterwards became so manifestly Insane, that he was removed in a hopeless state to another licensed house, as a certified Lunatic. This gentleman had been permitted to execute some deed or instrument during his residence in Dr. Chevallier's House, with his privity and approbation, by which some cottages were said to have been leased or disposed of.

At Dr. Allen's, High Beach, Essex; At our first visit to the House of Dr. Allen, at High Beach, in the county of Essex, in September, 1842, we found a gentleman, residing as a boarder without certificates, whom we had known as a certified Patient in one of the Houses in the Metropolitan district: this person was evidently unfit to be at large. Dr. Allen stated that he had been in the habit of sometimes receiving low-spirited or desponding persons as boarders. He also said that he had, on several occasions, permitted patients in his Establishment to execute deeds affecting property, but that

before doing so he always satisfied himself that the act
was proper.   There are three different houses belonging
to Dr. Allen at High Beach, which are licensed, and also
a cottage which is not licensed, but to which patients are
nevertheless sometimes removed.*   These houses, at the
times of our visiting them, were not in a good state of
repair.

At our second visit, in 1843, to the house of Mr. At Mr. Ogil-
Ogilvie, at Calne, in the County of Wilts, we found that Wilts.
he was in the habit of receiving from time to time, a gentleman without certificates, who had been previously confined
in his House as a Patient. This practice was objected to by
us in the Visitor's book, and the Visiting Magistrates, on
two subsequent occasions, expressed their entire concur-
rence in our views upon this subject.   At our fourth visit
to this House, in April, 1844, there were three persons,
who it was said were not Insane, residing in the house as
boarders. One of these persons was the gentleman who had
been previously confined under certificates at Mr. Ogilvie's,
and another was a person who had been a certified Patient
in two other Houses, and who, if not positively Insane, was
in a very doubtful state of mind. He had quarrelled with
his own relations, who are highly respectable, and he expressed a desire to be reconciled to them.   The person
and property of this individual both seemed to be under
the control of a solicitor, and we regretted that he was
not under the care of the members of his own family.
Mr. Ogilvie advertises, that he receives Nervous as well
as Insane Persons in his establishment.

Houses which are Licensed for the reception of Insane Nervous persons
Persons, ought to be kept exclusively for that purpose ; received in
and the reception of nervous, imbecile, and dejected per- Houses licensed
sons, amongst those who are Insane, and often dangerous, for the Insane.
is for obvious reasons open to serious objection.   The
admission of such persons without orders and certificates,

* This cottage has since been included in the license granted in
October, 1843.

appears, however, to be contrary to law, and is assuredly liable to great abuse. The practice is, or may be, made a subterfuge for receiving, as nervous, those who are manifestly of unsound mind. In the Houses above noticed, some of the boarders had been previously in confinement as certified Patients; one of them subsequently became maniacal, and was removed to another Licensed House; and others were manifestly Insane at the periods of our visits. The great object of the Laws for the regulation of Licensed Houses is, to insure to every person confined in them the advantage of being regularly visited, and thus to provide a security against improper acts, affecting either the person or the property of the Insane. Every individual confined under certificates is examined by official visitors, whose duty it is to satisfy themselves not only that he is properly treated, but that he is also a fit person to be detained; and such investigation is some protection against persons of unsound mind being induced to make dispositions of their property. It is questionable, whether a proprietor of a Licensed House who receives boarders of this class, or who permits deeds to be executed by persons who are under confinement as Patients, ought to be entrusted with a License.

Reasons for bringing the subject forward in a special manner.

We have brought this subject before your Lordship's notice, in a special manner, because Boarders, represented to be of sound mind, have been removed from several Licensed Houses upon our suggestions, whilst at the Houses of Aspall Hall and at Calne, the practice of receiving them has been persisted in, notwithstanding our repeated remonstrances. Your Lordship is aware that we formerly prosecuted a person for improperly receiving insane persons as Boarders, and procured his conviction and imprisonment, and that we have lately applied to you for authority to visit Houses in which Boarders have been illegally taken, with a view to the prosecution of the Proprietors.

Dr. Finch at Laverstock, in the County of Wilts, occupies a private residence near to his Licensed House, but entirely separated from it. In this House, although it is not licensed, he has been in the habit of keeping Patients. This practice has been objected to by us as irregular, and Dr. Finch stated at our last visit, that the Clerk of the Peace thought the objection would be done away with by merely inserting in the next License the word "Houses" instead of "House." By the 22nd section of 2 & 3 Will. IV. c. 107, such a License would be invalid. Dr. Finch has also another House in Salisbury which is not Licensed, but in which he has admitted that he sometimes had more than one Patient. These practices are irregular and very objectionable.

Irregularities at Dr. Finch's, Laverstock, Wilts;

The Asylum at Cranbourne, in the County of Dorset, has been visited three times. At the third visit, on the 11th of Oct., 1843, the Proprietor was absent thirty miles from Cranbourne, having left home on the Tuesday, and not being expected to return until Friday. There was no Superintendent, Keeper, or Nurse, to take charge of the Patients, and there was only one female servant, and a boy, sixteen years old, in the House. We were told that there was a farming man who might be sent for, in case any of the Patients should be violent. A female who resides in an adjoining House comes to the Asylum daily, and presides at meals, and assists in the Establishment. There was also a Female who had been a Patient, and was still a Boarder in the House, who assisted in the management of it. The Proprietor of this House has not been at home at any one of the visits of the Commissioners. If the engagements of the Proprietor of an Asylum take him so frequently, and for long periods, from home, some responsible and competent person ought, we think, to be left in charge of the Patients.

Asylum at Cranbourne, Dorset;

At Ringmer, near Lewes, in the County of Sussex, a female is permitted to be almost entirely without

Ringmer, near Lewes, Sussex;

clothing; and although the Patients seem to be kindly treated, the House requires great improvement. At Halstock, in the County of Dorset, the Proprietor seems kindly disposed towards his Patients; but the rooms occupied by two of them have been reported upon at our different visits as defective in every respect. At the last visit, they were described as low, dirty, and without any furniture except a wooden bedstead.

Halstock,
Dorset;

Belle Grove
House, near
Newcastle;

At Belle Grove House, near Newcastle, more restraint has been found in practice than is met with in well conducted Houses, and the Establishment is not in a good condition, nor under proper management. The beneficial interest in this House appears to have been transferred to the gentleman who now has the License, either as a Creditor, or as a Trustee for the Creditors of the former Proprietor.

Loddon,
Norfolk.

The state of the Licensed House at Loddon (in Norfolk) has been reported anything but satisfactory or creditable. The apartments in general are small, low, and ill-ventilated, and the whole House dilapidated and cheerless. One place, which is used by two Male Patients as a sitting-room, is very objectionable. In this House, little provision appears to be made for the comfort or cure of its unfortunate inmates. Although the Magistrates who visit it generally make favourable Reports upon its condition, it has been found on our visits in the condition above described.*

Medical Journal
often neglected.

In many Licensed Houses receiving Private Patients only, and in some also receiving Paupers, the Weekly Medical Journal, required to be kept by 2 & 3 Wm. IV. c. 107, sect. 33, has been altogether neglected. In some cases, the Proprietors, being Medical men, have contended that they are not required to keep such a journal.

---

* Very recently, and since this Report was prepared, the House has been again visited by two of the Metropolitan Commissioners, who state it to be now somewhat improved.

There is, in our opinion, no ground for this construction; a journal being required to be regularly kept in every house, without exception, which is licensed for the reception of Insane persons.

We now proceed to notice those Houses which, although they admit private Patients, are more particularly devoted to the reception of Paupers.

Amongst the provincial Houses which are licensed to receive Paupers, the best-conducted are those at Fairford, Market Lavington, Devizes, Newcastle (Drs. Smith and Mackintosh), Bensham and Dunston Lodge, near Newcastle, at Hull (the Refuge), and at Droitwich. The Proprietors of the Houses at Fairford, Market Lavington, Dunston, and Devizes, occupy farms and land, which afford employment for their Paupers: but it may be doubted if the Houses at Bensham and Newcastle, and the Refuge at Hull have sufficient ground for the employment of the Patients. The yards belonging to these last-mentioned Establishments, with few exceptions, are confined. In some of these Houses improvements have been made, and in others, alterations are in progress, which are quite necessary. The alterations at Bensham are very extensive. We have been desirous, on the ground of expense, not to press alterations too hardly upon the Proprietors. The Establishments at Newcastle and Hull belong to Medical Men. The Proprietors of the Houses at Fairford, Market Lavington, and Devizes are not Medical Men, but have Resident Physicians or Apothecaries. The Diet in all these Houses is good, and in some of them very liberal. *(Provincial Houses licensed to receive paupers.)*

We have observed that Houses which have been formerly private Mansions frequently require extensive alterations, to make them fit for Asylums: that the Mansion is sometimes engrossed by the Proprietor, his family, and a few Private Patients; and that the Paupers are consigned to buildings which were formerly used as offices, and out-houses. Of this description are the *(Asylums formerly private houses.)*

Houses at Lainston, and Nursling, in the County of Hants, Bailbrooke, near Bath, Plympton, in the County of Devon, Derby, and Duddeston, near Birmingham. The House at Duddeston has only one dull Yard for the Male, and one, for the Female Paupers; and at Bailbrooke, there was, until very lately, and even after we had remonstrated on the subject, only one Yard for the alternate use of the Male and Female Paupers; the Males had no day-room, except the confined space in a narrow sleeping-gallery, and some of the Paupers still sleep in a cellar-like place on the basement story, which we consider unfit for such a purpose. These Establishments possess the means of affording their inmates exercise in their Gardens and Grounds, but we have not satisfied ourselves that they are allowed a sufficient use of them. Although we consider the Houses at Bailbrooke and Duddeston, in their present state, to be ill-adapted for the care of Pauper Lunatics, we think that the Proprietors treat their Patients with kindness.

System adopted at Duddeston and Hilsea in connection with Workhouses.

Two Licensed Houses, namely, those at Duddeston and Hilsea, deserve particular notice on account of the manner in which they have been established and carried on in connection with Workhouses, which send to them only their unmanageable Patients, and afterwards remove them when they become tolerably tranquil, without reference to the propriety of their remaining at the Asylum, for the purpose of cure.

Asylum at Hook Norton, Oxfordshire;

The Asylum at Hook Norton, in the County of Oxford, has lately been taken by a Medical Gentleman, who appears disposed to make improvements; but at present some of the Yards are small and dull.

Fisherton House, Salisbury;

The accommodations for the Paupers at Fisherton House, near Salisbury, require great alteration and improvement. The Proprietor has lately purchased some land adjoining the House, and states his intention to make additions to his premises, which are quite essential.— Some of the apartments at the Licensed House at Gates-

head Fell, near Newcastle, were very defective; but considerable improvements have been lately made in them, at
our suggestion.—The House at Gate Helmsley, near
York, is, in its interior, commodious, and well adapted
for an Asylum, having been built expressly for the purpose. The Yards, however, are extremely gloomy and
confined. The Proprietor is desirous to improve them,
but there are local difficulties.—The House at Dunnington, near York, is of an inferior description: until
very lately there was only one Airing Court for the
Males and Females, and the Males were consequently
locked up during a great part of the day. Some of the
sleeping-rooms in this house are very bad.

The parts of the Workhouses at Morda, near Oswestry, in the County of Salop, and at Stoke Damerel,
near Plymouth, which are Licensed for the reception of
Insane persons, are extremely ill-suited for the purpose.
The Patients at Stoke Damerel are, however, under
excellent management.—At the Licensed part of the
House of Industry at Kingsland, near Shrewsbury,
containing from eighty to ninety Insane persons, they
were nearly all fastened to their beds at night by chains
to the wrists. In consequence of our remonstrances,
this restraint has been in a great measure discontinued.
—The Licensed Workhouse at Carisbrooke is much
improved, and has very good accommodation for the
Patients, and good grounds and Yards for exercise. It has
never been the practice to detain any curable persons
at this Workhouse.

There are four Houses in the Metropolitan District
receiving Paupers and private Patients; namely, the
Asylums at Hoxton and Peckham, and the Red and White
Houses at Bethnal Green, which adjoin each other. The
one is appropriated to Males and the other to Females.
The premises comprise about nine acres of land, and
are in a populous neighbourhood: not more than two

Marginal notes:

Gateshead Fell, near Newcastle;

Gate Helmsley, near York;

Dunnington, near York;

Workhouses at Morda, Salop, and Stoke Damerel, Devonport;

Kingsland, near Shrewsbury;

Carisbrooke.

Asylums in Metropolitan District:

Bethnal Green;

44

of these nine acres are used for the out-door employment
of the Male Paupers. The Houses were, until lately,
old and inconvenient, and the yards not well arranged.
Almost the whole of the Buildings, however, are in the
course of being taken down and rebuilt, and the Establishment is undergoing extensive improvements. We
have visited few, if any, receptacles for the Insane, in
which the Patients are more kindly or more judiciously
treated than in these two Houses. The abuses which
existed in this and some other Asylums, previously to
the year 1828, led to the introduction of the system of
Visitation by Commissioners in the Metropolitan district.
The Houses at Bethnal Green which were amongst the
worst, now rank with the best receptacles for the Insane.

Hoxton House; The Asylum at Hoxton is situate in a densely-
crowded neighbourhood: the Yards are dull and confined,
and the internal accommodations are inconvenient and
defective, and it has no land whatever for employing its
Peckham Paupers.—The Peckham Asylum has great advantages
House; over those at Bethnal Green and Hoxton, in its site and
grounds, and the internal accommodations are in general
good. This house, however, has always been a source of
trouble to us, upon the subject of its diet. It has, on
several occasions, been specially visited on this account,
and frequent remonstrances have been made. Application has been lately made for licensing the House for
the reception of a larger number of Patients. The grant
of the License, however, has been delayed, until we shall
be satisfied as to the diet of the Pauper Patients.—It
may be asked, perhaps, if we have not been too lenient
in renewing, from time to time, the Licenses for the
Peckham and Hoxton Asylums. Your Lordship, however, must be aware, that in consequence of the deficient
accommodation in Public Asylums, if Licenses were
withdrawn from Houses containing large numbers of
Paupers, there would be no alternative, but to send the

Patients to Workhouses, or to board with other Paupers, where they would not have the care which they now receive under regular visitation and supervision.

Many of the Licensed Houses are the freehold of the Proprietors, and others are held upon lease, and some only by tenancy from year to year. We notice this circumstance, as it of course influences the adoption or rejection of any improvements that may be suggested by us, which involve much expense. _{Influence of tenure of Licensed Houses on improvements involving expense.}

It is only fair, to state that very important and extensive improvements have been already made in several of the Licensed Houses since the commencement of our visits. Additions to the yards, grounds, and buildings have been made at the Houses at Gateshead Fell, Bensham Asylum and Dunston Lodge, near Newcastle, at Bailbrook House, near Bath, at Laverstock, near Salisbury, at Carisbrooke, in the Isle of Wight, at Belle Vue House, Devizes, and at Fairford; but other improvements are still requisite in some of these Establishments. In many of the other Houses which we have noticed, and in some others which we have not remarked upon, some alterations are essential. We have found, in a few Houses and Asylums, a practice of permitting two men to sleep in the same bed, and in many Houses and Asylums of allowing only two men to sleep in one room. This practice has been discontinued at the York Asylum, and at Newcastle (Smith and Mackintosh's), at Hanwell, and in many other instances, upon our suggestion. At Dunston Lodge, the practice is still continued, notwithstanding our remonstrances; and it still continues also at the Chester Asylum; although alterations have been lately made there, we believe, in some of the rooms (which are capable of holding two beds only) at our suggestion.

6. Abuses and Defects.

Having thus called your Lordship's attention to the Asylums of all classes which have partial defects, it is now our duty to bring under your consideration the condition of the Asylums and Licensed Houses which deserve almost unqualified censure.

Haverfordwest; Commissioners' Report in 1842, recited.—Asylum formerly a gaol.

The Asylum at Haverfordwest was first visited by the Commissioners on the 13th of September, 1842. Their Report states that this Asylum was formerly a small gaol, for the criminals of the town, but was (in 1822), by virtue of an Act of Parliament, appropriated to the reception of Lunatics. It did not appear that any addition or alteration whatever had been made, so as to adapt it to the accommodation of patients. On the contrary, all the cells and rooms were apparently in their original condition, not even windows having been added, except in the part which faces the public street.

Number of patients in 1842.

The Asylum, at that time, (1842,) contained eighteen Patients, nine being Males and nine Females; and the Corporation of Haverfordwest contracted with a person to supply the Patients with food and other necessaries.

Extreme deficiency of comfort and convenience.

The Commissioners felt it their duty to report that the Asylum was deficient in every comfort, and almost in every convenience; the rooms being small and ill ventilated, some of the lower rooms (originally cells for Prisoners), being almost dark, and the interior of the Asylum altogether out of repair. The two day rooms, in which the less violent Patients were confined, (one having seven Males and the other five Females), each measured about twelve feet by nine feet: the floors were of soft stone, but parts of it (in the Female ward considerable parts), had been torn up and destroyed. There was no seat, or table, or any article of furniture in the Women's Room, and nothing, except a table, in the Men's Room. The Men were standing; the

Women standing or sitting on the floor. On the circumstance being noticed by the Commissioners, a long board or seat was brought into the Men's Room from the airing-ground, and fixed against the wall. It was not sufficient for the seven Male Patients who were in the room to sit on. Four of the Men, however, sat down on it; the others remained standing. In the airing-ground belonging to the Women, there was a bench, which apparently belonged to their Room. There were large holes in some of the walls and ceilings. The airing-courts were very small and cheerless, particularly that belonging to the Men, and they were both strewn with large stones, which had fallen or been forced from the Building. There were two mischievous Patients, unrestrained, amongst the Men, (in whose hands these stones might be formidable weapons,) and another fastened in a chair, in a separate room or cell.

The dress of the Patients was, in almost every instance, dirty, ragged, and insufficient. One of the Female Patients pulled off her shoes and stockings, which were nothing more than rags, such as are occasionally seen on heaps of rubbish. The Commissioners were informed that there was not a single change of linen (either for the beds or for the person), throughout the Asylum. This fact was complained of by the Matron. Indeed, the Commissioners could not discover any linen whatever, except upon the persons of some of the Patients, and the dirty cases of the straw beds, throughout the House. There were only sixteen single beds for the eighteen Patients confined in the Asylum. One Patient (a Boy of nineteen) slept on loose straw, on the stone floor, in a small dark cell; and one other Patient (a Girl), who was convalescent, slept in the same room with the Keeper and his Wife, on a bed belonging to them. She must otherwise have slept upon the floor, and apparently without bedding.

Bad state of clothing.

48

Want of bedding.

The Commissioners caused many of the beds to be uncovered, and found that there were no sheets or blankets, and little more than a single rug to cover the Patients.. In more than one instance, the scrap of blanket (allowed in addition to the rug) was insufficient to cover half the person. The beds were of straw, and almost all of them were inclosed in coarse linen cases; but although there were several dirty Patients, there was not more than one case for each bed. Some of the cases were soiled, and all of them appeared dark, as if from long use. The Matron stated that she had applied repeatedly for more bed-clothes and for linen, but without effect; the Contractor would not send them. She complained to the Commissioners, that the state of the Asylum (in reference to its want of repair, comfort, and accommodation, and the destitute condition of the Patients) was dreadful; and she expressed her earnest hope that some person would speedily interfere on behalf of " the poor creatures confined there."

Restraint.

In regard to restraint, the Commissioners found that no belts, hand-locks, or strait-jackets were allowed, but the refractory Patients were confined in strong chairs, their arms being also fastened to the chair. Two were thus confined, separately, in small rooms, into which scarcely any light entered through the gratings. One was the Boy before mentioned, who slept at night on the floor of the same room; the other was a Woman who was entirely naked, on both the days on which the Commissioners visited the Asylum, and without doubt during the whole of the intermediate night. Both these were dirty Patients. In the Woman's room, the stench was so offensive, that it was scarcely possible to remain there.

Want of exercise and employment.

During wet weather, there was no place whatever for exercise; and at other times there was not sufficient space for the purpose. No attempt was made to employ any of the Patients, and no books or other amusements were provided. Prayers were never read, and no Clergyman ever visited the Asylum, although one of 'the Female Patients, who was occasionally depressed, and imagined that she had not done her duty to a child who had died, appeared especially to require such consolation as a Clergyman might afford.

The Keeper and his Wife (the Matron) appeared well-disposed towards the Patients, but they were themselves scarcely above the rank of Paupers. They were allowed the same rations as the Pauper Patients, and a salary of 20*l.* a year, between them. They had no assistant or servant, for the purpose of keeping the Asylum or the Patients clean, for cooking the food, for baking the bread, or for any other purpose connected with the Establishment. At our first visit, the Keeper was absent. The Commissioners were informed that he was at work for some person in the neighbourhood.

The Patients were allowed water only for their drink; culm and clay for firing; straw (chopped and whole) for the beds—of the clean as well as of the dirty. The bread was dark and heavy, and was made of barley-meal and wheaten flour. The Matron said that the yeast allowed was insufficient, and that the oven was out of repair, and that consequently she could not make the bread good or wholesome. She had repeatedly complained of these things without effect.

As evidence of the spirit in which this establishment was upheld, the Commissioners were informed that a few years ago a person was directed by Government to examine the buildings constituting the Asylum, and that, some notice being had of his expected arrival, workmen were employed during the whole of the preceding night upon the repairs, so that when the Governmen Agent visited the building in the morning, he found it undergoing repair. These repairs, however, were discontinued immediately after the Agent left the Asylum, and

Allowance to keeper and his wife.

Insufficient provisions.

Bad spirit evinced in the management.

E

have never since been proceeded with. These facts were stated to the Commissioners by the Matron.

As the Commissioners had no opportunity of seeing any of the County Magistrates, they thought it advisable to make the following entry in the book kept at the Asylum, in order that their opinion might be known :—

" The undersigned Metropolitan Commissioners in Lunacy have this day visited this Asylum, which, they regret to observe, is deficient in almost every comfort and accommodation which a Lunatic Asylum should possess. The place imperatively requires repair and enlargement. There is a deficiency of bedsteads, of seats, of wearing apparel, and a great and most culpable deficiency of linen and bedding.

" They think it their duty to call the attention of the Magistrates of this district to the miserable condition of the poor persons confined in this Asylum, and to urge their immediate interference in their behalf.

" They suggest that some employment should be provided for the Patients; that prayers (which are now never read) should be read regularly; that means should be afforded of dividing the violent from the tranquil Patients; and that larger rooms and more extensive airing-grounds should be provided. They beg further to suggest that a liberal contract for the supply of food and clothes, &c. to the Patients, should be entered into and *enforced* upon the contractor, who at present appears to be irregular in his supplies, and to be disgracefully inattentive to the applications which the Commissioners understand have been made to him, for the supply of clothes, linen, and beds to the Patients.

" The Medical Superintendent is requested to communicate these observations to the Magistrates of the district, and to entreat their attention to them."

On the 3rd of November, 1842, being the first quarterly meeting of the Metropolitan Commissioners that took place after the Asylum of Haverfordwest had been visited, the case was brought before the Metropolitan Board, and they resolved that the opinion of the Law Officers of the Crown should be taken as to "the parties amenable for the great and cruel abuses existing in this Asylum." They also ordered a copy of the Visiting Commissioners' Report to be sent to the Lord Chancellor, and to the office of the Secretary of State for the Home Department, accompanied by a letter, intimating that the importance of the case had induced the Metropolitan Commissioners to take the opinion of the Law Officers of the Crown. The copies of the Report were accordingly sent, and on the 28th of January, 1843, Sir J. Graham acknowledged the receipt of the letter sent to his office from the Metropolitan Board, and enclosed a letter from Mr. Leach, Chairman of the Quarter Sessions for the County of Pembroke, relative to the care and custody of the Lunatics in the Haverfordwest Asylum. On the 7th of February, 1843, Sir J. Graham wrote to the Metropolitan Board, requesting to have the opinion of the Law Officers of the Crown as to this Asylum, when it should be obtained. In the meantime, a case, stating the facts, accompanied by a Report of the Visiting Commissioners, had been laid before the Attorney and Solicitor-General. After some time the opinion of the Attorney-General was obtained; but upon perusing it, it was found necessary to call his especial attention to some points arising out of the case, and a conference subsequently took place between him and the Solicitor-General; and on the 30th of May, 1843, they gave their joint opinion that the "cause of the state of the Asylum appeared to be the neglect and want of attention on the part of the Justices of the Town" (of Haverfordwest): but that it was difficult to say that there had been any breach of the provisions of any of the Acts of Parliament, which could be the subject of legal proceedings. And they concluded by recommending "that a strong remonstrance and representation should be made to both the Justices of the Town and of the County of Pembroke ;" and by saying, that if the Justices of the Town had not made a Code of Regulations for the Asylum, they might be compelled to do so, by mandamus.

Second Report of Commissioners, in 1843. Asylum wholly unfit for treatment and care of Insane.

At the second visit made to this Asylum, in August, 1843, the Commissioners reported that some improvement had been made, but that the great want of accommodation in the Asylum, and the very narrow dimensions of the yards, almost precluded the possibility of providing the Patients with suitable occupations or amusements. Occasionally, one or two of the Patients, it appeared, were taken out for a walk into the town ; and within the precincts of the Asylum, a few of the women sometimes assisted a little in the household work. A Surgeon, practising in the town, visited the House once, and occasionally twice, a week; but the Commissioners could not find, from any of the documents, that he made any Reports or Entries relative to the Patients or the Asylum. It appeared that the House had then lately been visited weekly, by the Mayor or one of the Magistrates of the Borough, and sometimes by both, accompanied by a Police-Constable. The arrangements regarding the diet appeared to the Commissioners to be on a scale of extreme parsimony ; and they considered that although symptoms of some improvement were manifest the place was wholly unfit for the treatment and care of the Insane.

State of St. Peter's Hospital, Bristol.

The part of the Bristol Workhouse called St. Peter's Hospital, set apart for the Pauper Lunatics of the city, is without any day-room, eating-room, or kitchen, for the Females, distinct from their sleeping apartments ; and the only place in which they (40 in number) can take exercise is a small passage or paved yard at one end of the Hospital. It is part of the road for carts to the Workhouse, and measures about thirty-seven feet by eighteen, and is, from its pavement and extent utterly unfit for an airing-ground. The accommodations for the men are somewhat better, but they have only part of a paved yard, very little larger than that appropriated to the Females. The Workhouse itself is in the centre of the City of Bristol, and is totally unfit for an Asylum for the Insane. There are no means of classification, of exercise, or employment. Praise, however, is due to the Medical and other Officers of the house, for the attention paid by them to the Patients, considering the means at their disposal. There were small wooden closets, or Pens, for confining the violent and refractory Patients. Those for the men were seven feet long by three feet three inches broad, and about nine feet high, and were warmed by pipes, and had a hole in the door, and also a hole in the ceiling for ventilation. The Pens for the Women were smaller and were not warmed, and were ill-ventilated. The walls of each were of wood, but not padded. Formerly, Patients were occasionally kept in those Pens during both day and night, but the Pens are now very rarely used. The entire body of Lunatics ought to be removed to more spacious premises, and to a more airy and healthy situation. In addition to the jacket and leg-locks, a sort of open mask of leather passing round the face, and also round the forehead to the back of the head, and fastened by leather straps, was at one time placed over the heads of such Patients as were in the habit of biting; but this mask (as the Commissioners understand) has been for some time disused.

At the Asylum at West Auckland, first visited on the 5th of December, 1842, there were 13 Males, and 16 Females. Each sex had only one sitting-room, with windows that did not admit of any prospect from them, and the violent and quiet, and the dirty and clean were shut up together. There was only one small walled yard, and when the one sex was in it, the other was locked up. One of the Male Patients said that they were made so tender by their confinement that their health

State of Asylum at West Auckland.

was destroyed. There were two small grass closes belonging to the House, but they appeared to be little used for the employment of the Males. In the small, cheerless day-room of the Males, with only one unglazed window, five men were restrained, by leg-locks, called hobbles, and two were wearing, in addition, iron hand-cuffs and fetters from the wrist to the ankle: they were all tranquil. The reason assigned for this coercion was, that without it they would escape. One powerful young man, who had broken his fetters, was heavily ironed, and another was leg-locked and hand-cuffed, who was under medical treatment, and in a weak state. One woman was leg-locked by day and chained to her bed at night. Chains were fastened to the floors in many places, and to many of the bedsteads. The Males throughout the House

In Commissioners' opinion unfit for Insane Persons.

slept two in one bed. The Commissioners who first visited the Asylum, stated their opinion to be, that it was entirely unfit for the reception of Insane Persons. It was also visited on the same day by two Magistrates, who entered the following Minute in the Visitor's Book:—

5th December, 1842.

Report of Visiting Magistrates on day of Commissioners' first visit.

"We this day visited the Asylum, and found that the Commissioners had just left it. We found every thing in good order."

Three Magistrates, with one Medical Attendant, on the 24th January, 1843, entered the following Minute in the Visitor's Book :—

24th January, 1843.

" Visited this House and found everything in proper order, and the House in a clean state."

Second visit of Commissioners to West Auckland.

On the 16th of May 1843, two other Metropolitan Commissioners visited this house and found the Patients all locked up in their day-rooms, with the exception of two or three who were employed about the House ; the restraint had been removed from all the Patients but one, without accident or inconvenience of any kind, but the House was in the same state in which it was at the previous visit. The Patiénts were listless, without amusement, occupation, or exercise. The Medical Attendant considered that ."bleedings, blisters, and setons" were the principal resources of Medicine for relieving Maniacal Excitement. The Asylum was visited a third time by different Commissioners, on the 27th day of August, 1843; and lastly, on the 19th of April, 1844 ; and the several Commissioners, on both occasions, reported that, notwithstanding. some alterations and slight improvements made in consequence of their suggestions, they concurred entirely in the opinions repeatedly expressed by the other Metropolitan Commissioners, as to the total unfitness of these premises for a Lunatic Asylum. *Commissioners' third and fourth visits.*

At the Wreckenton Asylum near Gateshead, first visited on the 2nd of December, 1842, the day rooms, of which there are three on the Male side, and the same number on the Female, were confined and gloomy. Chains were attached to the floor in several places, and it was the-practice to chain Patiénts by the leg, upon their first admission, in order, as it was said, to see what they would do. In a small dirty room or cell, on the Male side, in which a Patient was placed at night, was observed a heavy chain attached to the wall, by which it was admitted that a Man had been confined within the last twelve months. The bedding was in a filthy state, and the cell very offensive, as were also most of the sleeping-rooms and beds throughout the house. The whole place was in bad order; and the Male Patients especially presented a ragged and uncleanly appearance and were listless and unemployed. The Females were in a better state, in regard to clothing, and some of them were employed in needle-work. An old Woman, who had attempted to commit suicide, was, at the time of our visit, on that account chained by the leg to the fireguard, and she was stated to be usually fastened in a *State of Wreckenton Asylum, near Gateshead.*

similar manner to her bed at night. This place was visited again the next day, when the benefit of our enquiries was manifest; the whole house having apparently been cleaned in the meantime, and fresh linen placed upon the beds. The Commissioners considered the premises in their then state unfit for an Asylum. The

Commissioners' second visit.

second visit to this Asylum was made on the 17th of May, 1843, by two other Commissioners, and although some improvements had been effected, and others were in progress, they considered that the place was still not a proper Receptacle for Lunatics. At the third visit, in August, 1843, the place was clean, and the Patients tolerably comfortable : at the last visit, in 1844, the Commissioners considered that, although considerably enlarged and improved, it was, in many respects, still unfit for an Asylum.

State of Licensed House at Derby.

At the Licensed House at Derby, first visited on the 21st of October, 1842, the straw in the Paupers' beds. was found filthy, and some of the bedding was in a disgusting condition from running sores, and was of the worst materials, and insufficient. Two Cells, in which three sick epileptic Paupers slept, were damp, unhealthy, and unfit for habitation. The beds of some of the Private

Nearly all the provisions of the law violated.

Patients were in an equally bad state. Nearly all the provisions of the Law for the regulation of Licensed Asylums were violated. A lady was found confined in

Case of a Patient represented to be a visitor.

this House, who was represented to be a Visitor, and not a Patient, but who, upon investigation, was proved to have been brought to this House from another Lunatic Asylum, where she was a certified Patient. Her name was entered, in the Private Account Book of the Proprietor, as a Patient, and he had given a Certificate that she was confined in his Asylum, for the purpose of authorising her Trustee to pay over to her husband dividends to which she was entitled, only a few days previously to the visit of the Commissioners. The Magistrates of the Borough, who are its Visiting Justices, had not

visited the House for the space of a year, minus eight
days. This lady had been, during the whole of her residence in this place, from the month of May until October, anxious to see some Magistrate, with a view to
demand her liberty. She was afterwards liberated upon
our remonstrances. This Asylum was found in a better
state at the second visit, but when visited for a third
time, on the 18th of October, 1843, it was again in a
very bad state. The Paupers were still occupying what
had been the coach-house and stables. The Cells, which
had been objected to, were not used, but the male Paupers (fifteen in number) were sleeping in the upper floor
or loft. One room, measuring seventeen feet long by
nine in width, had four beds, two rooms had two beds
each, and there were four single rooms, only six feet six
inches by six feet. Three beds were placed in the common passage. The rooms were low, comfortless, and ill
ventilated. An Epileptic was in bed in a dying state,
and the windows and door of his room being closed, and
there being no opening or other means of producing a
free circulation of air, the apartment was most offensive.
Some sawdust had been thrown upon the floor to absorb
the urine, but nothing had been done to purify the air.
—This Asylum has lately been transferred to another
Proprietor.

Commissioners' second visit.

The Asylum at Lainston, in the County of Hants,
was first visited on the 14th of October, 1842. The
Buildings appropriated to the Paupers consisted of
stabling and out-houses converted to that purpose, and
were quite unfit to be used as an Asylum. At the
second visit, these evils were so manifest, that the
Visiting Commissioners expressed a hope that means
would be found to put an end to them, either by refus-
ing the license, or otherwise. At the third visit, on
the 22nd of August, 1843, the house was found altogether in a bad state. The rooms on the ground-floor,
both for the Males and Females, were in an extremely

State of Asylum at Lainston, Hants.

Commissioners' second visit.

Commissioners' third visit.

58

filthy condition. Seven Female Paupers were restrained with iron hand-locks and chains, and strait-waistcoats; and the same seven Women, and three others, were chained to their beds at night. We expressed our strong disapprobation at the use of hand-locks and chains, but the Proprietor said that he employed them because they were essential to safety. Previously to the third visit, this house had been several times visited by the Magistrates. They had entered in the Visitor's Book, at one visit, a remark, that the sleeping-rooms for the dirty Male Patients, and for the Females on the ground-floor, were "unwholesome and damp;" and that the clothing of one of the Patients was scanty and insufficient; at another visit, that the yards of the Females were wet and filthy; and, at a third visit, that there was no classification, and that their previous recommendations upon this head were unattended to. The Paupers in this House are tolerably well-fed, but have been always found dirty and ill clothed. It was visited again in April, 1844, and was still in so indifferent a state, that the Commissioners again repeated their opinion as to the urgent necessity of erecting a Public Asylum for the county.

With regard to the house at Nursling, in the same County, the Commissioners, who first visited it on the 12th of October, 1842, reported that the Buildings appropriated to the Paupers had been offices, and were in a dilapidated state. Their construction was bad, and they could not, in the Commissioners opinion, be made comfortable. The rooms were small and close, and the airing-courts extremely limited in point of space. The Commissioners who next visited this Asylum, on the 25th day of June, 1843, made a similar Report, and objected that the main part of the house, as at Lainston, was reserved for the Private Patients and the family of the Proprietor, and that the out-buildings were set apart for the purpose of receiving Insane Paupers, without

Use of hand-locks and chains.

Magistrates' remarks in Visitor's book.

Commissioners' fourth visit.

State of House at Nursling, Hants.

Commissioners' second visit.

much consideration as to their general comfort or eventual cure. At the third visit, on the 24th August, 1843, a similar Report was made, and the bed-rooms for the dirty classes, both of the Male and Female Paupers, were offensive and confined, and had unglazed windows, and only wooden shutters, as a protection against the outer air. Commissioners' third visit.

Kingsdown House, at Box, near Bath, was first visited in September, 1842. Amongst its great defects, is the want of airing-grounds. The space allowed for exercise, considering the number of Patients, is wholly insufficient. One of the wards, in which were fifty Female Paupers, had only a very small yard attached to it, and this, being on an abrupt descent and uneven throughout, was not only unfit for exercise, but was insufficient for half the number of Patients; and they were consequently congregated in a small room at one extremity of the yard. Every seat there was occupied, and the room itself being ill-ventilated, there existed an offensive odour that must have been detrimental to the bodily health of the Patients. The airing courts for the Females is surrounded by very high walls, and is dull and cheerless, and the only yard for the Male Paupers is but little better. At the second visit, on the 18th of April, 1843, the straw-rooms for both sexes on the ground floor, were pointed out by the Commissioners as unfit for use. There being only one day-room and one airing court for each sex, the noisy, violent, refractory, dirty, and dangerous Patients, were crowded together in the same small space with those who were clean, convalescent and quiet, and the noise and confusion were extreme. There were seven Females under restraint; two had strait-waistcoats, two had their arms fixed in iron frames, not allowing the freedom of hand-locks, and three had iron leg-locks; one Female was chained by her legs to a wooden seat in a paved passage, to prevent her, as it was stated, hurting herself in her fits. Eight or ten of the Females were State of Kingsdown House, Box, near Bath. Commissioners' second visit.

fastened by straps and chains to their beds at night. One Male was chained by his leg to a seat in the yard, and another Male was chained to his bed at night. At our last visit, on the 24th of April, 1844, a trifling enlargement had been made in the yards, one of which was covered with macadamized stones, but the House was in the same unsatisfactory state, and the same harsh and cruel system of restraint was in practice.

Commissioners' third visit.

The Asylum at Plympton, in Devonshire, was first visited in October, 1842, when ten persons were found under restraint. One of them had been restrained for two months, merely for breaking windows. From the Reports of the Visiting Justices, it appeared that complaints had been repeatedly made of the state of the Buildings, but apparently without any beneficial results, as they were then in a very objectionable condition. One room, in which seventeen Patients lived during the day, measured only sixteen feet six inches by twelve feet. There was no table in it, and there was sitting-room for no more than ten Patients. Several of the bed-rooms were cheerless and wet, from the damp or rain, and the walls were besmeared with filth. Close to some small crib-rooms, in which some Girls (violent patients) slept, there was a bed-room for a Male Patient, who, it appeared, had access to the room in which the Girls slept. At the second visit, on the 14th of July 1843, the condition of the Pauper Patients continued wretched in the extreme. Some of the buildings, to which attention had been directed by the previous Report, were in the same objectionable state as then described; the day-room being most offensive, and the airing-court comfortless, and rendered dangerous by a quantity of loose stones scattered about. In a day-room, in a state of furious mania, was a young woman, who had been delivered of a child five or six weeks previously, confined by a strait-waistcoat, and chained by the arm and leg to a bench. Another Woman in this ward, in a strait-

State of Asylum at Plympton, Devon.

Complaints of Visiting Justices unattended to;

Commissioners' second visit.

waistcoat, was lying in a hole in the middle of the airing court, without covering to her head, or anything to shelter her from the broiling sun. Ten Curable Patients and two Idiots were under the charge of a Lunatic, who was himself confined by a chain from the wrist to the ankle, at the arrival of the Commissioners, principally to prevent him escaping: this chain was soon afterwards taken off at his own request, in order that he might not be:seen, by the Commissioners, so restrained. The day-room of this ward was extremely small, with an unglazed window and no table. A series of sleeping cells for dirty Patients, connected with this yard, were dark, damp, and offensive : they were occupied at night by four Males, two in one; cell, and two in single cells. The dirty Male Paupers slept in a room, formerly the dairy, in which were six beds; it was damp, ill ventilated, and offensive. There was only one small window unglazed, which was closed with a shutter at night. There were chains and wrist-locks attached to nine of the beds on the Male side, which were constantly used at night, partly to prevent violence, and partly to guard against escape. Four of the Female Paupers, represented to be subject to violent paroxysms after epilepsy, were ordinarily confined to their beds by chains and wrist-locks.

At the third visit to this House, on Oct. 2, 1843, three Women were found chained by their legs to the benches. One of them, mentioned in the previous Report, had, besides the chain to her leg, another chain passing round her waist, to which were fixed, by an iron ring, two hand-locks in which both her hands were confined. Besides this restraint, there were twenty-one Patients who were chained to their beds at night: two of these were Private Patients, and the others were Male and Female Paupers. The three sleeping-rooms in the Women's cottage, could not, in the judgment of the Commissioners, have been cleaned for some days : the wooden cribs were filthy, the floor was in holes, and soaked with

Commissioners third visit;

urine, and in parts covered with straw, and excrement. We can give no other general description of it, than that it was most disgusting and offensive. In a crib, in one of these wretched places, a Female Private Patient who was cleanly, had been compelled to sleep : she implored us only to remove her to a better part of the House. The remainder of the third Report of this House by the Commissioners, is a detail of numerous other abuses.

Extract from Commissioners' third report on Asylum at Plympton.

The following is an extract from it :—" In one of the " cells in the upper Court for the Women, the dimen- " sions of which were eight feet by four, and in which " there was no table, and only two wooden seats, fast- " ened to the wall, we found three Females confined. " There was no glazing to the window, and the floor of " this place was perfectly wet with urine. The two dark " cells, which adjoin the cell used for a day-room, are " the sleeping-places for these three unfortunate beings. " Two of them sleep in two cribs in one cell. The floor " in the cell with the two cribs, was actually reeking " wet with urine, and covered with straw and filth, and " one crib had a piece of old carpet by way of bedding, " besides the straw, but the other appeared to have had " nothing but straw without any other bedding. In " the other cell, the Patient who slept in it had broken " her crib to pieces, and a part of it was remaining in the " cell, but the straw was heaped up in one corner, and " as far as we could rely upon what was said, she had " slept upon the straw, upon the ground, at least one " night. The straw itself was most filthy, the floor was " perfectly wet with urine, and part of the straw had " been stuck to the wall in patches with excrement. It " must be added that these two cells, and one other " adjoining to it, have no window, and no place for " light, or air, except a grate over the doors, which " open into a passage. The persons of these three " unfortunate Women were extremely dirty, and the " condition in which we found them and their cells

" was truly sickening and shocking. Adjoining to the
" two sleeping-cells of these Women, and opening into
" the same passage, was a third cell which was occupied
" as a sleeping-place by a Male criminal of very dan-
" gerous habits, and an Idiotic Boy. This cell was
" dirty and offensive, and the floor of it wet with urine,
" but it was not in so filthy a state as the other two.
" The criminal was fastened at night to his bed with a
" chain. We strongly objected to these Men being con-
" fined in a cell closely adjoining to the females. The
" whole of these cells were as damp and dark as an
" underground cellar, and were in such a foul and dis-
" gusting state, that it was scarcely possible to endure
" the offensive smell. We sent for a candle and lan-
" tern to enable us to examine them."

So far from any good having resulted from the pre- Comments on
the disgraceful
condition of the
house.
vious remonstrances of the Commissioners, the House
was found, at this third visit, even in a worse condition
than at the previous visits. The visiting Commissioners stated, that in their opinion, it was highly disgraceful to the Proprietor to keep his Paupers in the
wretched condition in which they found them, and that
his conduct in this respect loudly called for some prompt
and effective interposition. This Proprietor received
10s. 6d. per week for each Pauper, besides a guinea
upon admission. The Magistrates, who appear to
have formerly attempted to improve this House, had
not at our third visit inspected it since the last preceding visit of the Commissioners, and on the 2nd of
October, 1843, it seemed to have been visited only once
by the Magistrates since the 14th of October, 1842;
namely, on the 14th of June, 1843. We are decidedly
of opinion, that a person who keeps his Patients in the
disgraceful condition in which the Paupers were found
in this Asylum, ought not to be entrusted with the care
of Insane Persons.

The Asylum at Nunkeeling, near Beverley, in the State of Asy-

64

county of York, first visited on the 10th of September, 1842, was found in an indifferent condition, but the Proprietor promised to remedy the defects objected to. At the second visit in 1843, no alterations had been made. The sitting-room and chambers in which the Pauper Patients were lodged, and the yards, the only places out of doors to which they had access, were extremely small and cheerless. Seven Females were confined in a room about twelve feet square, where there was no furniture of any kind, except one seat not large enough to accommodate more than four persons, so that the rest were obliged to stand or to sit on the brick floor. Some of the bed-rooms, which had been before objected to, were dark, small, and offensive. In one bed-room for females, the windows had been all broken for three weeks, and in a sleeping-room on the ground-floor was a woman, a dirty Patient, curled up in her bed, which was wet and filthy, and consisted of chaff and some rags, and she herself was in a wretched condition. This House requires very great improvement, to render it fit for the reception of Insane Persons.

On the third visit of the Commissioners to the Asylum at West Malling, in Kent, on the 2nd of September, 1843, they were much astonished at discovering six sleeping-places for Males in an outhouse, at the upper end of the Male Paupers' yard. These places had not been laid down in the plan of the House, and they had never been shown either to the Visiting Justices, or to the Metropolitan Commissioners, who had previously visited the Asylum. They were wooden closets, six feet long, six feet high, and three feet two inches wide; three being on each side of a passage, which was between two and three feet wide. These places had a raised floor, upon which the bedding was placed. They were all extremely close, but the two centre ones had no means of ventilation. They had been regularly

(margin notes)
lum at Nunkeeling, near Beverley, Yorkshire.

Commissioners' second visit.

Discovery of six concealed sleeping places on third visit to West Malling, Kent.

used, and were occupied by five Males on the night before they were discovered, and were made up for use when first seen. They were, of course, quite unfit for sleeping-places.*

—Having thus detailed the particulars of some of the more flagrant abuses which have come under our observation, we think it right to state to your Lordship that we have made various endeavours to procure their correction and removal. We have before stated what steps were taken with respect to the Asylum at Haverfordwest. As regards the Hospital of St. Peter's, at Bristol, we received a communication, through Secretary Sir James Graham from the Visiting Justices, immediately after our first visit to it. In consequence of that communication, we made a second visit to the Hospital, and upon a proposal being made by the Magistrates of Bristol to enlarge the present premises for the purpose of an Asylum, we reported that, in our judgment, such a measure was highly inexpedient.

Although a new County Lunatic Asylum was in progress for the County of Devon, we felt that the condition of the Paupers at Plympton called for some prompt interposition, and we therefore addressed a letter to the Chairman of the Quarter Sessions for the County of Devon, on the 10th of August, 1843, after our second visit, calling his attention to the state of the House. No answer had been received to this letter at the period of our third visit, on the 2nd of October, 1843, when the House was found in even a worse state than at the second visit. Subsequently to our third visit, a letter upon the subject was addressed by Lord Ashley, as Chairman of this Board, to the Earl of Devon, who thereupon took immediate steps with a view to remedy the abuses complained of.

Marginalia: Endeavours of Commissioners to remove abuses; at Haverfordwest and Bristol; at Plympton;

* These closets have since been pulled down and the building shut up.

F

at Derby; The Paupers who were confined in the Licensed House at Derby having been nearly all sent thither by the Magistrates of the County, we addressed a letter to the Chairman of the Quarter Sessions at Derby, on the 10th of November, 1842, bringing the state of the Paupers in that House under his notice. We received an acknowledgment of the receipt of our letter on the 1st of March, 1843, but no further communication. We wrote at the same time to the Magistrates of the Borough, and received an immediate answer. The Paupers, however, on our third visit to this House, were found in the condition which we have above described.

at West Auckland and Wreckenton; A letter was written to the Chairman of the Quarter Sessions of the County of Durham, on the 15th of February, 1843, accompanied with extracts from our Reports, and we submitted to the Magistrates whether it would be expedient to renew the Licenses of the Houses at West Auckland and Wreckenton, without requiring effectual alterations to be made in them, and security for their better management in future. No answer has been received to this letter. The House at Wreckenton is considerably improved; but that at West Auckland remained nearly in the state which we have above described, when visited, on the 19th of April, 1844.

The Commissioners who first visited the Licensed Houses at Lainston, Nursling, and Hilsea, in the County of Hants, in October, 1842, called the attention of the Visiting Justices to the urgent want of a Public Lunatic Asylum for the Paupers of the County. The Justices at Lainston; who have visited the House at Lainston since our first visit, have, in the Visitor's Book, condemned in unqualified terms the management of that large Asylum. Nevertheless, the Commissioners who visited this place in April, 1844, found no material improvement, and could only earnestly repeat their call upon the Magistrates of the County of Hants to provide a proper receptacle for their neglected Paupers.

In reference to the Licensed House at Box, near at Box; Bath, in the County of Wilts, we have repeatedly pointed out to the Visiting Justices the very reprehensible state of its yards, and the harsh and cruel system of restraint which is there practised. The Visiting Justices concurred in our views, but the same defects as before were in existence in April, 1844. We have called attention to the unfitness of the Licensed House at Bailbrook, near Bath, in the County of Somerset, in at Bailbrook; its present state, for the care of Pauper Lunatics; and we have made similar remarks as to the Licensed House at Duddeston, in the County of Warwick. We have also, at Duddeston; in various other instances, made such remarks, in the Visitor's Books at the different Licensed Houses, as at other houses. seemed to us calculated to excite the attention of the Magistrates, to the condition of Houses requiring alterations and improvements.

—By the Act 2 & 3 Will. IV. c. 107, it is directed that Visitation of Asylums in Borough towns. three Justices, together with a medical attendant, shall be appointed, at the General Quarter Sessions, to visit all licensed Lunatic Asylums throughout England and Wales, (except those in the Metropolitan district), three times in every year. This power, or duty, so far as respects the visitation of certain Asylums situate within the limits of borough-towns, is now, by virtue of the Municipal Corporations Act, exercised by the Magistrates of those boroughs.

The country is much indebted to the County and Services rendered by County and Borough Magistrates. Borough Magistrates for their services, under these acts, in all cases where their visitations have been carefully and regularly made; and we are desirous of bearing testimony to the solicitude which they have, in many instances, evinced to perform a very painful duty.

It is not our intention to enter into any minute

Irregularity in
visits by Magis-
trates.

examination of these visits, with a view of testing their
efficiency, in particular districts ; but we feel bound to
state certain facts which have come under our notice,
and to offer a few remarks, in order to bring the subject
of these provincial visits fairly under your Lordship's
consideration ; the value of which must depend upon
their frequency, upon their being made without notice,
and at uncertain intervals ; upon the minuteness of the
investigations that take place ; and, above all, upon the
firmness with which the visitors enforce the provisions
of the Acts of Parliament.

Oulton, near
Stone, Stafford.

The Licensed House at Oulton, near Stone, in
Staffordshire, had not (in October 1843), been visited
by any magistrate for the space of two years and a
half. It is right to state, however, that the Medical
officer appointed to attend the magistrates had himself
visited this Asylum frequently during that period. The

Shillingthorpe,
Lincoln.

Asylum of Shillingthorpe, in the county of Lincoln,
(which, however, is in excellent order, and so far
excuses the neglect of its visitors), is inspected by the
Magistrates once a year only, instead of three times a

Great Wigston,
Leicestershire.

year.—After our visit to Great Wigston Asylum, near
Leicester, (in October 1843) we found that the magistrates had visited it only once during the preceding

Visits to
Heigham Hall,
Norfolk, com-
paratively use-
less.

twelve months. On visiting Heigham Hall Asylum, in
the county of Norfolk, (in August, 1843,) we found
that the Magistrates visited the place regularly, but that
their inspection was rendered comparatively useless,
by their always sending beforehand for the visitors'
book, which gave the proprietors notice of their intended
visits. The visitations of Magistrates to the Asylum at
West Auckland have been already adverted to.

Magistrates'
visits, in many
instances, regu-
lar, and made
with care.

Having felt it our duty thus plainly to express our
opinion of the neglect, in some few instances, of the Visiting Magistrates, we have the satisfaction of stating that,
in many instances, the visits of the Magistrates have
been regular, and that their inspection of the Asylums,

and their investigation as to the comforts and general treatment of the lunatics, have been made with much care; with evident solicitude to perform the duties imposed upon them ; and with that benefit to the patients which must necessarily arise from gentlemen of station and local influence giving up their time and attention to this subject.

It has however rarely happened that all the points to which we have thought it our duty to direct our inquiries, have entered into the consideration of the county Magistrates. They appear, generally, to have limited their attention to the number, cleanliness, and bodily condition of the patients confined, and to the ventilation and general fitness of the wards appropriated to their use. And these, without doubt, are subjects of great importance to the comforts, and in some degree to the recovery, of persons afflicted with insanity. Nevertheless, there are other subjects equally deserving of inquiry, to which we do not, generally speaking, observe that the attention of the visiting justices has extended. The first and most material of these is the state of mind of the lunatic, in reference to his fitness for liberation. Secondly, the nature and effect of the employments provided for the patients, with a view of diverting their disease. Thirdly, the character of the medical reports, as indicative of the care and intelligence bestowed upon the mental condition of the patients, by the medical officer; and, fourthly, the food (both as to quality and quantity) afforded to the pauper patients, the rates of payment made for them, and the attention bestowed on them by their parish officers.

Magistrates rarely attend to all the points to which Commissioners direct their inquiries.

Points usually neglected.

In the more careful reports of the Magistrates, some of these subjects are occasionally adverted to, but in others both these and other points remain unnoticed. In a great proportion of cases, the reports are couched in general terms, expressive of the satisfaction of the Visitors at the condition of the Asylum, without indicating any particu-

Remarks on Magistrates' reports.

lar matter as deserving of notice. This species of report, although it may be less objectionable in cases where Asylums are appropriated exclusively to the reception of private patients of the wealthier classes; yet in establishments which receive paupers and persons but little above the rank of paupers, we have ourselves almost always remarked some defect, or have suggested some obvious improvement, in reference to the condition of the place or of the patients; and upon these occasions, we have thought it right to make a special statement to that effect, in our entry, in the visitor's book, with a view to future amendment; and we have the satisfaction of adding that these suggestions have, in many instances, met with attention from the Visiting Magistrates. Notwithstanding the influence, however, of these gentlemen, and notwithstanding such improvements as those to which we have alluded and many others, it must, we think, be apparent from the state of the Asylums and Licensed Houses at Haverfordwest, St. Peter's, West Auckland, Wreckenton, Plympton, Derby, Lainston, Nursling, Loddon, Aspall Hall, High Beach, Calne, Box, Bailbrook, and others, that the visits of Magistrates have not had the effect of correcting the irregularities and the abuses existing in many of these Establishments, or in putting an end, in some few instances, to cruelties of a very flagrant character. Much, indeed, remains to be done, in order to render many of the existing Asylums proper and sufficient receptacles for the Insane.

Additional caution necessary in granting Licenses.

Amongst other means of insuring good conduct in the management of Asylums, it has occurred to us that some additional caution might be observed in the grant of Licenses. Your Lordship is aware that Licenses in the Metropolitan district are granted by us, and we are careful that the Reports of the different Houses should be brought under the consideration of the Board, before each renewal. We cannot, therefore, finish our remarks upon the performance of the duties assigned by law to the county Magistrates, without recommending that they

Commissioners' practice in granting Licenses recom-

should follow the same course in renewing the Licenses
of the provincial Houses. We are of opinion that the
proprietor of a Lunatic Asylum should always attend at
the Quarter Sessions when an original or renewed License
is applied for, with a view of answering such questions
as may be put to him ; and that the reports of the Visiting Magistrates, and of the members of this Board, relative to the state of his House, should be then read. We
could further suggest, that in the advertisements usually
inserted in the county papers, announcing the business proposed to be done at each sessions, special notice should be
entered of the intention of parties to apply for Licenses.
This is already done in Hertfordshire, and we believe in
a few other counties.* It is also essential, previously to

* On our first visit to the Retreat near York, we were accompanied
by Mr. Tuke, a gentleman well acquainted with the management of
most of the principal Lunatic Asylums, and who has for many years
made the treatment of Lunacy the subject of his especial observation,
and he called our attention to the necessity of a more frequent and
vigorous supervision of all Asylums. As he has already expressed his
sentiments on this subject, in a publication relating to Hospitals for
the Insane, we have thought it right to lay them before your Lordship.
"The appointment of visitors at the Quarter Sessions, to these
places, may afford a little check against abuse, and some facility for the
investigation of complaints; but I do not hesitate to say, that it is a
most imperfect and unsatisfactory system of visitation, and so I know
it is felt and acknowledged to be by some who act under the appointment. A physician is appointed at the Sessions in conjunction with
three magistrates, to visit the private houses four [three] times in the
year. The magistrates will, of course, be much influenced in their
judgment by their medical companion, and thus he is often called upon
to judge the conduct of his professional neighbours, who may be either
his rivals or his particular friends. It is no imputation on the honour
of any man to say, that it is not for the public good that he should be
placed in such a position."—"We shall not, I apprehend, secure
efficient visitation, until we have an appointment of a number of competent persons to visit, under the authority of Government, all the
places of whatever description, private or public, chartered or unchartered, in which the insane are confined ; to compare the degrees of
human misery in these abodes,—to ascertain how it may be most
effectually provided for and alleviated,—to collect information under
uniform heads from all these institutions,—and to report annually to
the public the results of their observations and inquiries."—Introduction to "Jacobi's Treatise on Hospitals for the Insane."

granting a License, to ascertain the fitness and security of the premises.

Escapes from Licensed Houses.

We have made inquiries upon the subject of escapes from Licensed Houses, returns of which are required to be made to our Board, and have not found in general much cause of complaint upon this head. Some cases, however, have occurred which call for animadversion, and some matters relating to the safe custody of certain classes of Insane Persons, demand notice at our hands.

Penalty imposed by 9 Geo. IV. c. 40' on officers, &c. of County Asylums permitting escapes, but not on officers, &c. of Licensed Houses.

The Act 9 Geo. IV. c. 40, has imposed a penalty upon Officers and Servants of County Asylums who permit escapes through neglect or connivance. There is no similar provision with respect to the Servants of Licensed Houses, although it would seem that the safety of the Insane, and of the Public, and also of the Proprietors of Licensed Houses, equally calls for legislative protection. In the course of last summer, a Servant at a Licensed House assisted a Lady, who was a Patient,

Danger of permitting escapes.

to escape. Escapes are not only to be guarded against on account of the hazard to others of permitting dangerous Lunatics to be at large, but also for the excitement which they are apt to cause to the Insane themselves.

Case of Epileptic Lunatic at Gateshead Fell.

An Epileptic Lunatic who escaped from Mr. Kent's Asylum, at Gateshead Fell, near Newcastle, in December, 1842, was, at the time of his escape, employed with a number of other Patients upon the Proprietor's farm. He was immediately pursued, but was not retaken. Application was made by the Proprietor to the police, but the wife of the Lunatic interceded, and he was not sent back to the Asylum. He escaped on the Saturday afternoon, and on the Monday night after his escape he murdered his wife and daughter, in a violent paroxysm of epileptic mania, in a most savage and horrid manner.

This wretched man is now a furious criminal maniac in the Licensed House from which he escaped, although he was so far recovered as to be on the point of being

discharged. When he had escaped, he became so apprehensive of being retaken, that he did not dare to go
to his own house, and it was only upon the intercession
of his wife with the authorities that he was permitted
to remain at large.

At a private Asylum at Dunnington, near York, Escapes at Dunnington, near York ;
there were when we visited it three dangerous Patients,
one of whom had threatened the life of a brother,
another the life of his wife, and a third the lives
of his wife and child. All these three individuals
had escaped at different times from the Asylum.
Another Patient, an old woman, had also escaped and
had not been since heard of. It was surmised that she
might have met with some accident. In this Asylum,
there was only one insufficient yard both for the Males
and Females, and the House was unfit for the safe custody of the Patients without locking them up in their
day rooms.

At Sandfield, near Lichfield, a Patient had escaped, at Sandfield, near Lichfield, and at Plymp-ton ;
and at Plympton, a criminal Patient had escaped, for the
third time, and neither of them had since been heard of.

At Nunkeeling, in Yorkshire, a most dangerous at Nunkeeling, in Yorkshire.
Patient had escaped three times. We found him in confinement after his third escape. His legs were confined
by leg-locks; one arm was chained to his legs, and
both his arms were fastened behind him. He had twice
nearly succeeded in killing his keepers, and once in setting
fire to the Asylum. Both the restraint employed, and
the extremely small yard in which this man was confined
were calculated to injure his health. At a Licensed
House in Yorkshire, we found two Male Patients confined
in strait-jackets. We thought the restraint improper, and after some remonstrance with the keeper,
they were removed. The restraint used for one of these
Patients was, it was said, to prevent his escaping. He
promised us not to attempt to escape for a limited time.
He kept his word; but after the lapse of the period which

was fixed, he made his escape. This Patient had an

Improper restraint. attendant entirely for himself. The improper restraint which we have met with in the Houses at Lainston, Plympton, and elsewhere, has been defended on the ground of the apprehension of escape. The use, however, of restraint is not a proper remedy against escape, except, perhaps, in cases of very violent or dangerous Patients.

Escapes at Hanwell. We were informed that the escapes from Hanwell had been numerous, and we have since been furnished with an account of them. From the years 1831 to 1843, both inclusive, it appears that the escapes have been in all 245. These do not include those cases in which a Patient has been almost immediately retaken by the servants of the Asylum. The total cost of retaking these persons has been 73*l.* 14*s.* 9*d.* The greatest number of escapes that took place in any one year from 1831 to 1837, was seventeen; and from 1837 to 1843, both inclusive, the highest number in any year was thirty-eight. We are not aware, however, that any serious mischief arose from these escapes.

Consequences of escapes. The above remarks are not made with the view of offering any suggestions, but merely of calling attention to the fact that very calamitous consequences may result from escapes, and that therefore it is important to take every possible precaution to prevent them; not by the use of restraint, but by vigilance and care. It is desirable, also, to ascertain, before a License is granted to the Proprietor of a House, that there are proper means to keep the inmates in safe custody, without resorting to such improper restraint, and confinement in gloomy places, as we found practised at West Auckland, Nunkeeling, and elsewhere, and which are calculated to destroy the bodily health of the patients.

Visitation of Paupers by Parish Officers. In regard to the visits of the officers of parishes and unions, to their paupers, we observe that the Medical officer in each case generally visits them regularly, and at no very distant intervals; excepting only when the paupers are sent from distant counties, when there appears, for the most part, neglect in this respect. We are of opinion that no pauper should be sent to any Asylum which is at a great distance from the parish or union to which he belongs; in order that there may be no excuse for not visiting him regularly, and no motive (such as the saving of expense) to prevent or delay his removal home, when reported convalescent.

Paupers should not be sent to distant Asylums.

We find, upon inquiry at various provincial Asylums, that the friends of pauper patients are allowed to visit them on certain days in the week, or on all days of the week, excepting Sundays. It is worth consideration, whether the Asylums should not be open, during certain hours, on Sundays also, to the visits of the friends of poor lunatics, whenever they are in such a state of health as to render such visits not injurious. Those friends, for the most part, belong to the labouring classes of the community, and if they are to be precluded from visiting the patients on the only day on which they themselves are unoccupied, the probability is that the pauper lunatic, whilst he remains in an Asylum, may be altogether denied the comfort of a visit from his friends. In all cases where it may be advisable to refuse the admission of the friends, the reasons for such refusal should be stated in writing by the Medical officer.

Visits of friends of Pauper Lunatics.

In regard to the visits made to private patients, these appear, in general, to be made with sufficient frequency, so long as any probability of cure exists. When the patients become incurable, these visits, in many cases, become more rare.

Visits to Private Patients.

It is customary, in all respectable Licensed Houses, to allow any near relation of the patient to visit him, at proper times, unless the state of his health should render such visits unadvisable. There are, however, occasions when the proprietor of the Asylum considers himself bound to submit, in this respect, to the directions of the person under whose authority the patient is first confined. In one instance, the trustee of an insane lady, confined in the Asylum at Laverstock near Salisbury, was for a long time refused admittance to the patient, by the directions of the person who had authorised her confinement; and the Proprietor of the Asylum, in answer to our question on that head, said that he considered himself bound to obey those directions, whether the visit of the Trustee to his Patient would be likely to benefit her health or not. In another case, where a male patient was confined at the Asylum at Southall, in Middlesex, on the authority of his son, his daughter was, by the son's order, arbitrarily prevented from visiting him. There did not appear to be any reason for the exclusion. The power thus vested in any person to prevent the access of a child, or near relation, is obviously liable to great abuse.

Position of Lunatics with respect to their property.

Our attention has been drawn to the position in which Lunatics, who have not been the subjects of Commission, are placed with respect to their property, whilst they are confined in Asylums.

Liberality usual towards Lunatics.

Many persons are most liberal to their unfortunate friends whom it has become necessary to put under the restraint of an Asylum, and we have seen many instances of great liberality on the part of the Proprietors of Licensed Houses, in maintaining their inmates, for many years, as Private Patients, at considerable expense, with little, and in some cases

Cases of Peculation.

no prospect of reimbursement. Some cases, however, have been stated to us where the party is believed to be entitled to a considerable income, and a small portion of it only is applied to his maintenance; others, where the whole property has been applied by Trustees, or others, to their own purposes, and the Lunatic has thus been left entirely destitute. Other cases again have occurred, in which the patient has been allowed, whilst in the Asylum, or during a temporary visit to his friends, to execute instruments materially affecting his property. We have not had the means of testing the accuracy of these statements.

Our attention has been called, in the course of our visitations, to the following, among other cases, upon the correctness of which we have every reason to rely.

W——, an Imbecile, was for many years confined at Dr. Warburton's House, at Bethnal Green. Upon his father's death, he was allowed to go out of the Asylum for some hours : he went to his sister's house, and, whilst there, signed some deeds, the nature of which he did not understand, but was told that he was to share in his father's property, whose heir he was. He is now a Pauper, in the Asylum for the County of Surrey. Case in Dr. Warburton's House ;

A Gentleman, now in Dr. Finch's House at Laverstock, had formerly a large property. For many years Dr. Finch has received nothing, and there is a very large sum owing to him for his maintenance, and he is still furnished gratuitously with the comforts and accommodations of a private Patient. in Dr. Finch's House ;

Mr. H., an Idiot in Mr. Jackson's House at Turnham Green, had £400 a year in the funds, left to him by his father. The executors paid the dividend, for some years, but ultimately absconded, having misappropriated the funds, and the poor Idiot is now destitute. Miss B., who was under confinement for several years at Dr. Tukes' House, had £2000 left to her by her father. The executor employed this sum in his business, and the whole was lost. in Mr. Jackson's House ;

There are two brothers, Paupers in Dr. Warburton's House, the elder of whom, we are informed, is supposed to have become entitled to property worth £20,000. One of them is generally employed as a tailor, but he is so lost that he does not know where he comes from, and the other brother is in a worse state. in Dr. Warburton's House;

We would also recall your Lordship's recollection to a case, which not long since came before your Lordship in consequence of a commission of lunacy, namely, that before the Lord Chancellor.

of R. P. H., who was very properly placed by his bro_ther in an Asylum, and which brother immediately took possession of all his property, producing an income of upwards of 400*l.* a year, and remained in possession of it until his death in 1840, applying only a very trifling part of such income to the Lunatic's support and then died insolvent.*

Provision for protection of Lunatics' property where no Commission issued recommended.

· We beg to submit for your Lordship's consideration, whether some provision might not be made for the protection of the property of Lunatics, who shall have been in confinement for more than a fixed period, and where no Commission has been applied for. It has been suggested that where a Lunatic has been confined for six or twelve months, a verified statement might be required to be made by the persons upon whose order he is detained, as to the amount and nature of his property ; and some security might be required for its due adminis-. tration, or an official Trustee be appointed for that purpose.

It has also been suggested, that in cases where the

* The particulars of this case are as follows :—In July, 1805 R. P. H. was placed by his brother in the Asylum of Dr. Burman at Henley in Arden. He was at the time entitled to freehold property in Northamptonshire, and Somersetshire, and Gloucestershire, now producing an income of more than 460*l.* a year ; and was also the owner of the advowson of a living worth 300*l.* a year and upwards. He also held a commission in the army. The brother sold the commission, and cut timber, and received the proceeds of each, and the rents of the freehold property from 1805 to October, 1840, when he died. He was also in 1807, being a clergyman, instituted to the living, under a paper to which he procured the signature of his brother, when in the Asylum.

The brother died in 1840, perfectly insolvent, and having only applied about 120*l.* a year for the maintenance of the Lunatic, and even that sum was often much in arrear, and for some period before his death was not paid at all. The brother had also received money in respect of a fee-farm rent of the Lunatic, which he professed to sell, and also in respect of a further mortgage, which he professed to make on the Lunatic's property. On the death of the brother a commission was taken out in 1841 by Messrs. Burman, and the jury found R. P. H. to have been of unsound mind from the 2nd of July, 1805, and the property has since been protected.

malady is likely to be of short duration, or the property
of the Patient is small, a competent portion of the
income might, during a limited period only, be applied
for his maintenance, under the sanction of one of the
Commissioners in Lunacy,* acting with the consent of
the nearest relatives, and of the former having the control of the fund : and that the written instructions of
the Commissioners to that effect, issued under such
circumstances, should be a sufficient warrant for such
application.

We are aware that these are matters of considerable
delicacy ; and that they do not, at least directly, fall
within our proper province. At the same time, as they
have not unfrequently come under our observation in-
cidentally, and appear in themselves to deserve serious
consideration, we hope to be excused for having thus
ventured to call your Lordship's attention to the subject.

II.

CONDITION OF PAUPERS ON ADMISSION.

No subject to which our attention has been given,
is of deeper interest and importance than the inquiry
directed to be made (5 & 6 Vic. c. 87, s. 11) "into
the condition as well mental as bodily of the pauper
patients when first received into Asylums, and whether
this has been such as to prevent or impede the ultimate
recovery either mental or bodily of such patients." And
this subject is of the greater moment, inasmuch as
the evils resulting from the delay in sending pauper
lunatics to Asylums is, we fear, to some extent, appli-

Evils resulting from delay in sending Pauper Lunatics to Asylums.

* Appointed under the 5 and 6 Vict., c. 84.

cable to the cases of private patients, in all classes of society.

Although it appears that pauper lunatics, in some few districts of England, are sent to Asylums soon after the first attack of mental disease, we have found that the practice of detaining them for long periods subsequently, (either in Workhouses, or as boarders with their friends, or elsewhere,) prevails to a very large extent throughout the kingdom. In order to bring this subject in a more distinct manner, before your lordship, and to show the evils which result from it, we beg to call your

lordship's attention to Appendix (C.) at the foot of this report. This appendix contains the answers given to our inquiries, by the Medical Superintendents and Visiting Physicians of the different County Asylums and Public Hospitals for lunatics, and by the proprietors of a large number of licensed houses into which paupers are admitted.

In the Asylums of Lincoln, Leicester, Nottingham, and Northampton, the Superintendents and Visiting Physicians of those institutions have expressed their unanimous opinion, that pauper lunatics are sent there at so late a period of their disease, as to impede or prevent their ultimate recovery. Opinions, to nearly the same effect, have been given by the medical superintendents of every County Lunatic Asylum, with the exception of those of the Asylums for the counties of Bedford and Stafford. It is right to remark that, in some instances, there has been a reluctance to express any opinion as to the bad and hopeless condition in which pauper lunatics have been taken to Asylums, from a fear of offending either parish officers or other persons.

At the Retreat, York, at the Asylums of Lincoln and Northampton, and at the Asylum for the county of Suffolk, tables are published, exhibiting the large proportion of cures effected in cases where patients are admitted within three months of their attacks, the less proportion when admitted after three months, and the almost hopelessness of cure when persons are permitted to remain in Workhouses or elsewhere, and are not sent into proper Asylums until after the lapse of a year from the period when they have been first subject to insanity. The Asylums for the counties of Lancaster and Middlesex and for the West Riding of the county of York have published statements to the same effect. In the Dorset County Asylum, out of thirty-seven cases admitted in the year 1842, only six were received within three months after their first attack. Five of these six recovered, and were discharged within four months from the time of their admission, and the sixth, a female, aged seventy-five, was improving at the time of our visit.

In the year 1842, the cures in St. Luke's Hospital averaged seventy, and in the year 1843, sixty-five, per cent., a fact which, even taking into account the circumstance of their receiving only recent cases, and such as are supposed to be curable, is calculated to remove the reluctance commonly felt to send the insane to Asylums, and to exhibit the great importance of removing Lunatics as soon as possible after the first appearance of disease, to institutions where proper medical treatment can be obtained. *Average of cases at St. Luke's.*

The reasons principally assigned for the insane poor being sent so late to Lunatic Asylums, have been the ignorance of overseers and guardians of the poor as to the importance of early medical treatment in cases of insanity, and their reluctance to send paupers to Lunatic Asylums, on account of the great additional expenses incurred in those establishments beyond the ordinary cost of maintenance in Workhouses or in lodgings. There can be no doubt that both these causes have operated to a great extent, in improperly detaining paupers from Lunatic Asylums. There are, however, other circumstances, which, as we conceive, have still greater influence *Reasons assigned for poor being sent so late.*

in causing this serious evil. Even if there did exist on the part of guardians and overseers of the poor a full knowledge of the importance of early treatment, and the most earnest desire to avail themselves of its advantages, throughout almost the whole of England, and in the whole of Wales, there is so great a want of accommodation for the reception of the insane poor, that they could not carry their views into effect.

Want of accommodation for insane poor.

A mere summary of the total number of insane poor, and of the total amount of accommodation provided for them in the different public and private Asylums throughout the kingdom, would not, by showing the general insufficiency of Asylums for their reception, expose all the inconveniences and evils which result from the present system of managing pauper lunatics. We shall submit, however, as accurately as is in our power, the details of the numbers of insane poor, and the extent of accommodation provided for them in different counties; for the purpose of explaining the grounds upon which we have formed our opinion, as to the causes which combine, with the reluctance and mistaken economy of parish authorities, to produce this serious evil.

Appendix (D).

We have annexed, in Appendix (D), a detailed account of the numbers of pauper lunatics, and of the accommodation for them :—First, in those counties which have Lunatic Asylums erected exclusively for paupers, and also in those counties which have Lunatic Asylums for paupers erected in union with subscription Asylums;—Secondly, a statement of the numbers of pauper lunatics in every county, and the entire accommodation whether public or private for them;—And thirdly, a list of those counties and districts which have no Lunatic Asylums of any description, either public or private, and the numbers of pauper lunatics contained in them.

From the statements in Appendix (D), it is apparent,

first, that in those counties in which Lunatic Asylums have been erected exclusively for paupers, and also in those in which Lunatic Asylums for paupers have been erected in union with subscription Asylums, there are large numbers of insane poor for whom there is no room, owing to nearly all the Asylums being full of patients. Even in those counties, therefore, where there are public Asylums, there frequently exists difficulty in obtaining admission for recent cases. Secondly, it will be seen that in those counties where there are public and private, and in some instances, only private Asylums receiving paupers, there is a striking deficiency of accommodation. Thirdly, it is apparent that in eleven counties in England and in all the counties in Wales, with two exceptions, there are no public or private Asylums of any kind, and consequently the insane poor must be sent to distances from their own homes, at a greater expense than if there were Asylums near at hand. This circumstance is of itself calculated to increase the unwillingness of overseers and parish officers to send patients, in proper time, to these Establishments.

Difficulty of obtaining admission for Pauper Lunatics in recent cases.

As regards the state of pauper Lunatics in counties having County Asylums, we must remark that the Asylums for the counties of Chester, Cornwall, Dorset, Lancaster, Middlesex, Stafford, Suffolk, and for the West Riding of York, have all been reported to our board as having been found in a very crowded state. In the Workhouse at St. Austle in Cornwall, the Visiting Commissioners found a woman in a state of raving mania. The master of the Workhouse had applied to the County Asylum at Bodmin, for the admission of this person, but it was so crowded, that her admission had been refused, and it was only upon urgent application that she was subsequently received. In this County, there were 153 lunatics in Workhouses and other places out of the County Asylum. At the Asylum, at Forston, for the County of Dorset, where the Superintendent has

State of Pauper Lunatics where there are County Asylums.

for a long time exerted himself to expose and remedy the evils resulting from cases being kept back from the Asylum, the Visiting Commissioners met with another instance during their visit, in which the admission of a patient was delayed for want of room. In this County, there were 114 pauper lunatics in Workhouses and other places out of the County Asylum.

Asylums have been necessarily enlarged.

In addition to the above facts, it must be observed, as a remarkable circumstance, with respect to Counties having public pauper Lunatic Asylums, that it has been found necessary to enlarge almost every Asylum of that sort that has hitherto been erected. The Asylums for the counties of Bedford, Cornwall, Gloucester, Kent, Lancaster, Leicester, Middlesex and Nottingham, and for the West Riding of York, have all been enlarged, and some of them several times. The Leicester Asylum was opened in 1837, and had additional accommodation made for fifty paupers in 1841. The Bedford Asylum has been twice enlarged. We were informed that the second additions were made with the view of receiving pauper lunatics from other counties, and thus diminishing the cost of maintaining the pauper lunatics of the county of Bedford. This circumstance may, in some degree, explain the reason, why in the county of Bedford, paupers have been sent in good time to the county Asylum. In the Hanwell Asylum, and also in the Surrey Asylum, (opened only in 1841,) and in some of the other Asylums, the basement stories have, contrary to the original intention, been brought into occupation for patients.

Increasing number of *incurable* cases.

We have mentioned these instances, as we are anxious to draw your Lordship's attention to the important fact that, however sufficient for the pauper lunatics of a county any Lunatic Asylum may have been at the period of its original erection, it has subsequently, and in many instances in a very short period, become insufficient, and is at the present time crowded with a large and increasing number of *incurable cases.* And that we do not assert this on slight grounds, the following Table, exhibiting the number of inmates in every county Asylum erected exclusively for paupers, and also in every county Asylum for paupers erected in combination with subscription Asylums, will make abundantly evident.

County Asylums.				County and Subscription Asylums.			
	Curable.	Incurable.	Total.		Curable.	Incurable.	Total.
Bedford . .	27	112	139	Cornwall .	13	120	133
Chester .	48	116	164	Glos'ter .	59	198	257
Dorset . .	14	139	153	Leicester .	63	68	131
Kent . . .	22	227	249	Nottingham	37	88	125
Lancaster .	65	546	601	Stafford . .	48	197	245
Middlesex	58	917	975				
Norfolk . .	108	56	164				
Suffolk . .	27	179	206				
Surrey . .	20	362	382				
York W. R.	48	384	432				

Your Lordship is aware that the Legislature has not only given to Justices of the Peace the management of County Asylums, but also, (as a necessary adjunct, to carry into effect the objects for which they are erected,) the disposal of all the Pauper Lunatics in their respective counties. By the act of 9 Geo. 4, c. 40, sec. 36, the Justices " acting for any county in England " are required to issue their warrants to Overseers to return lists of all insane persons chargeable to their respective parishes, specifying the " name, sex, and age of each insane person, and whether such insane person be dangerous, or otherwise, and for what length of time they have been disordered in their senses, and where confined, or how otherwise disposed of." These lists are to be verified on " oath, with a certificate as to the state and condition of every insane person, from a physician, surgeon, or apothecary," and are to be transmitted to the Clerk of the Peace, to be laid before the Justices at the next

Disposal of all Pauper Lunatics entrusted to Justices.

Return required from overseers by 9 Geo. IV. c. 40, s. 36.

General Quarter Sessions. By section 37, any Overseer*
neglecting to give information of any insane person
chargeable to his parish, is subjected to a penalty : and
by section 38, any Justice is empowered to require
any insane pauper to be brought before two Justices,
who may cause such pauper to be conveyed to the
County Asylum, or, if none, to some public Hospital or
Licensed House.

No system adopted by County Magistrates for early admission of Pauper Lunatics into Asylums.

The Visiting Justices of County Lunatic Asylums
have usually taken an interest in the internal management of their Asylums, and have framed rules for their
government. We have not, however, met with any
instance in which the County Magistrates have availed
themselves of the information afforded them by the
above-mentioned Acts, or have established any system
for securing the early admission of pauper lunatics into
the County Asylum. These lunatics are amongst the
persons for whose benefit the establishment has been
erected at a great expense to the county.

Provisions of the law have not been carried into effect.

Whether County Magistrates have not been aware of
the serious evil that was rapidly growing up throughout
the kingdom, or have been reluctant to rely upon their
own judgment, or unable to obtain satisfactory medical
advice for their guidance, it is manifest that the provisions of the law have not been carried into effect,
and that the public and the poor have been equally
deprived of the benefits of these salutary enactments.
The management of the pauper Lunatics of the county
of Middlesex, and their present condition, will illustrate
our remarks.

Establishment and subsequent increase of Asylum at Hanwell.

The County Asylum at Hanwell was originally erected
for 300 patients, and was opened in the year 1831. In
1837 additional wings were built for a further number
of 360. In 1832, the building, which had been erected

* The duties imposed by this Act on Overseers, are now transferred
to the Guardians, as to Parishes which are in Unions.

for 300, was made to accommodate 500 patients, and the Asylum, enlarged so as to contain 650 patients, has been made to hold 1000 beds. This has been effected by appropriating to the use of the patients, rooms intended for a kitchen, and also offices and places on the basement floor, under the level of the adjoining ground, not intended to be inhabited. Thus there has been introduced a number greater by 350 than the Asylum was constructed to hold; and at the time of our visit, in 1844, there were 984 patients in the house.

There were also in the county of Middlesex, as appears by the return made to the Quarter Sessions in 1843, 429 pauper Lunatics for whom there was no room in the County Asylum. In the Lunatic wards of the Marylebone Workhouse there were admitted in the years 1842 and 1843, 190 paupers considered as insane. Some few of these, however, were stated to be only under temporary excitement. The overseers of this parish could obtain admission into the Hanwell Asylum for only twenty-seven of these 190 cases, and they therefore ceased to apply for admissions, and left a notice at the Asylum, requesting to be informed when any vacancy might occur. They also requested the Committee of Visiting Justices to permit them to exchange some of their old incurable patients at the Asylum for recent curable cases from the Workhouse. This the Justices refused to do, on the ground that the diet was better at Hanwell than at the Workhouse, and that the patients enjoyed more comfort at the County Asylum.

Number of Paupers for whom there was no room in County Asylum in 1843.

Refusal of Justices to allow Incurable Patients to be exchanged for curable ones.

The Rule for the admission of patients in Hanwell is, that every parish is entitled to send one patient for every 7000*l.* of its rated rental, and every parish not rated so high is entitled to send one patient. The Magistrates take no steps to ascertain the nature of the cases previously to admission, with a view to the preference of recent cases. The Parish Officers frequently

Rule for admission of Patients at Hanwell.

88

merely mention the number, without even the names, of the patients requiring admission. This was the information given to us at the Asylum.

Attempts of Justices to compel overseers to send recent cases.

The first Committee of Visiting Justices gave notice, in 1831, that they intended to take measures for compelling the overseers to send to the County Asylum "those of their patients whose cases admitted there "should be the greatest probability of curing." In 1832, they called the attention of the County Magistrates to the fact of recent cases not having been sent to the Asylum, and they declared the delay to be illegal; and they have since repeatedly published Tables and Reports, showing the great advantages to be derived from cases of insanity being received at the Asylum in the earliest stages of the complaint, and the great evils

The House filled with old and incurable cases.

resulting from an opposite course. The resident Physician called the notice of the Magistrates, in 1834, to the "melancholy fact of the house being filled by old and incurable cases," which he attributed "almost entirely to the neglect of proper remedies in the early stages of the disease;" and in 1836 he also stated "that the additional room made for the patients "during the year had been almost entirely filled up by "old and incurable cases, only ten, said to be of recent "date, having been admitted." The resident Physician has, from time to time, called attention in his Reports to the incurable state in which paupers have been brought to the Asylum.

Visiting Magistrates have not taken steps to secure admission of recent cases.

From the foregoing statement it will appear that no steps have been taken by the Visiting Magistrates of Middlesex, pursuant to their notice in 1831, to secure the admission of recent cases, and that, in reference to the populous parish of Marylebone, they refused to exchange old incurable for recent and curable cases.

The cure of insanity the main object of a County Asylum.

But the professed and indeed the main object of a county Asylum is, or ought to be, the cure of insanity. The patient who has had the benefit of a trial in the

Asylum where he has become incurable, should, we submit, give way to the afflicted pauper who is in the Workhouse or at home, and is probably curable, and equally entitled to be received at the Asylum, where, by prompt and proper treatment, he may be restored to health and to his family, instead of being permitted to become an incurable lunatic, a source of expense to others, and of suffering to himself. A County Asylum is erected for the benefit of the whole county, and is to be considered not merely as a place of seclusion or safe custody, but as a public Hospital for cure. A large number of the patients now in Hanwell derive no substantial advantage from the means of exercise and employment furnished in that Asylum, and might be provided for in a separate Establishment; thus making room for patients who are susceptible of cure.

Many patients enjoy no benefit from the Asylum.

The result of the system, adopted by the Justices in Middlesex, is, that the County Asylum is nearly filled with incurable Lunatics, and almost all the recent cases are, practically, excluded from it. When we visited it in March last, there were 984 patients, of whom only 30 were reported curable; and there were 429 patients belonging to the County out of the Asylum, and 40 applications for admission had been refused within less than three months from the commencement of the present year.

Result of the system.

In 1831, there were 300 patients, for whom there was no County Asylum whatever; and in 1844, although there *is* an Asylum holding 984 patients, there are 429 pauper Lunatics unprovided for, and who, if they wait for the rota before they are admitted, will probably have become incurable, and will be lunatic annuitants upon the county or their parishes.

There is some difficulty in ascertaining the exact cost of the Asylum at Hanwell; but we believe that at least 160,000*l.* has been expended upon the land and buildings. The maintenance of paupers in this Asylum in the year

Cost of Establishment at Hanwell.

90

1843, cost their parishes 24,049*l.* 12*s.* 6*d.*, which does not include a sum of about 4000*l.* a year paid by the county for the yearly cost of furniture, and the wages of mechanics and labourers employed about the ordinary repairs and work of the establishment. Notwithstanding this annual expenditure of 28,000*l.*, and an outlay of 160,000*l.*, there are still 429 Lunatics unprovided for, to be maintained by their parishes. We have stated our reasons for thinking that the Hanwell Asylum ought not to be enlarged. The original cost of Hanwell for 300 patients was 124,000*l.* Supposing a similar outlay for the 429 patients, and the cost of maintaining each of these persons to be the same as that of a Lunatic in the present Asylum, the annual charge on the parishes and county, for the Pauper Lunatics (besides an additional outlay of 124,000*l.*, making altogether 284,000*l.*) will be 36,000*l.* And, should the magistrates enlarge their accommodations and continue their present system of admission, they will, apparently, but increase the accumulation of incurable cases, without extending the resources of cure.

An extension of the establishment likely to increase the accumulation of incurable cases, without extending the resources of cure.

Serious attention of the Legislature called to the state of Middlesex with respect to Pauper Lunatics.

We have called attention to the state of the County of Middlesex, with respect to its Pauper Lunatics, because, although the evils which exist there, prevail to a very great extent in other counties, they have risen up in the county of Middlesex with a rapidity which has not been equalled elsewhere, and to a magnitude which appears to us to require the serious attention of the Legislature.

Condition of County of Lancaster.

The condition of the county of Lancaster shows that the evils, which we have pointed out as existing in Middlesex, are not confined to the last-mentioned county. In 1816, the Lancaster Asylum was opened for 160 patients. It now contains 600 patients, and there are more than 500 Pauper Lunatics in the county, for whom it has no accommodation; and the information obtained at this Asylum is, that nearly all of them have been brought from Workhouses, where they have been detained so long as to diminish the probability of their recovery. The counties of Middlesex and Lancaster have a large class of patients, which are not met with, in the same numbers, in other counties. The county of Middlesex had, in 1841, 108, in 1842, 116, and 1843, 126, county Pauper Lunatics, or Lunatics whose settlement had not been ascertained. The county of Lancaster had, in 1842, 118 county Pauper Lunatics.

Peculiar condition of Counties of Middlesex and Lancaster as regards Pauper Lunatics.

The Asylum for the county of Surrey was opened in June 1841, and the Visiting Physician went round to the different licensed Asylums in which the pauper Lunatics were distributed, and selected from them 299 cases, which were thereupon removed to the county Asylum. At the period of our visit in 1843, there were 385 cases, including those which had been removed from Licensed Houses. All these 385 persons, with the exception of only thirty-seven cases, had been insane more than twelve months. There were (according to the Poor Law returns for 1843,) 591 pauper Lunatics belonging to the county of Surrey; and the number in the Asylum, on the 1st January, 1844, was 382, of whom 362 were reported incurable. We inquired at this Asylum if any steps had been taken by the Visiting Magistrates to secure recent cases being sent there, but we were informed that no measures had been adopted for that purpose, and we fear that the condition of the county of Surrey, with an excellent Asylum, will soon, as regards the cure of its insane poor, be similar to that of the county of Middlesex, unless patients be sent to the Asylum in an earlier period of their disorder, and some plan be devised for disposing of such of the incurable cases as it may be necessary, in that event, to remove.

Establishment of Asylum for county of Surrey.

These remarks lead us to another and most important cause, which operates to fill Lunatic Asylums with incurable patients, and to prevent the public from deriving any considerable benefit from them as Hospitals for the cure of Lunacy ; and this must continue to operate and neu- tralise all other efforts for the benefit of the insane, unless means are adopted to relieve the Asylums, from time to time, from the pressure of incurable patients, and to provide for such patients in some other Establishment.

Lunacy essentially different from other maladies.

The disease of Lunacy, it should be observed, is essentially different in its character from other maladies. In a certain proportion of cases, the Patient neither recovers nor dies, but remains an incurable lunatic, requiring little medical skill in respect to his mental disease, and frequently living many years.

Patients beyond reach of medical skill should be removed from Asylums, instituted for cures.

A Patient in this state requires a place of refuge ; but his disease being beyond the reach of medical skill, it is quite evident that he should be removed from Asylums instituted for the cure of insanity, in order to make room for others whose cases have not yet become hopeless. If some plan of this sort be not adopted, the Asylums admitting Paupers will necessarily continue full of Incurable Patients ; and those whose cases still admit of cure, will be unable to obtain admission, until they themselves become incurable; and the skill and labour of the physician will thus be wasted upon improper objects.

Places of Refuge should be provided for Incurable Lunatics.

Under all these circumstances, it seems absolutely necessary that distinct places of refuge should be provided for Lunatic Patients who have become incurable. The great expenses of a Lunatic Hospital are unnecessary for Incurable Patients : the medical staff, the number of attendants, the minute classification, and the other requisites of a Hospital for the cure of disease, are not required to the same extent. An establishment, therefore, upon a much less expensive scale would be sufficient.

In illustration of these remarks we call to your

Lordship's notice the rapidity with which the accumulation of patients has taken place at the Asylum for the County of Lancaster:—From the 25th June, 1842, to the 24th June, 1843, 267 patients were admitted into this Asylum. The discharges during the same period amounted to 103, and the deaths to 71, and thus were added, in that year, 93 persons, whose chance of recovery was diminished by the circumstance of it not having been effected within the first twelve months. A similar accumulation is taking place, although not to the same extent, in nearly all the county Asylums; so that a certain and progressive increase of chronic or incurable cases is produced, in all houses which have no outlet for them, a circumstance which seems never to have been contemplated by those who have the management of these large public Asylums, and for which no relief or remedy has hitherto been provided.

Rapid accumulation of Patients in Lancaster Asylum.

Similar accumulation in other Asylums.

We are glad to remark that the Visiting Justices of the Asylums for the West Riding of the county of York, and for the counties of Nottingham and Stafford, permit the substitution of recent for old cases.

Substitution of recent for old cases permitted in certain places.

The disposal of incurable patients, however, although a very serious and difficult question, is certainly of less moment than the exclusion of curable cases from Lunatic Hospitals, which have been erected at great public cost, and are fitted up with every convenience for the purpose of cure.

Disposal of Incurable Patients.

As far as we can learn, the admission of patients appears, for the most part, to be either indiscriminate or matter of accidental arrangement, and has no reference to the urgency of each case. In reference to the length of time during which incurable Patients remain in Asylums, and the great importance therefore of early admissions, with the view of diminishing their numbers, it may be observed, that those who recover generally do so within the first year after their attack, and

Admission of Patients indiscriminate or accidental.

that those who do not recover within the first two years after their attack, seldom regain the use of their reason. In reference to this subject, we may state that the Superintending Physician of the Hanwell Asylum has published a Table, showing the length of time during which each patient who was in that Asylum in the year 1842 had been confined there. The duration of the confinement of the patients in Hanwell, however, varies at different times, and may also differ from that in other similar establishments. It will be seen, by reference to the Table,* that there were, in 1842, 936 patients in the Hanwell Asylum, of whom 696 had been there more than two years, and were reported incurable. The average duration of the confinement of these 696 patients had been upwards of six years and nine months. The yearly cost of each patient at Hanwell, at the rate of 7s. a week, and adding 4l. per annum, paid by the county for repairs and furniture, is 22l. 4s.: Each patient, therefore, who has been confined during that period, will have cost his

Marginal note: Table published by Superintending Physician at Hanwell.

* Table showing the length of time during which 936 Patients, remaining on September 30th, 1842, had been in Hanwell Asylum.

			1841.			1842.		
TIME.			M.	F.	T.	M.	F.	T.
Not exceeding 1 Month	.		9	6	15	..	..	.
"	3	"	14	17	31	7	7	14
"	6	"	14	34	41	15	15	33
"	9	"	21	31	52	34	34	53
"	1 Year		8	7	15	13	13	26
"	2	"	61	57	118	72	72	114
"	3	"	34	43	77	49	49	97
"	4	"	53	99	152	39	39	71
"	5	"	12	15	27	95	95	143
"	6	"	30	18	48	14	14	26
"	7	"	15	24	39	18	18	47
"	8	"	13	16	29	24	24	39
"	9	"	26	42	68	14	14	25
"	10	"	47	70	117	37	37	62
"	11	"	30	52	82	65	65	107
"	14	"	..	..	..	50	50	79
Total . . .			387	531	918	390	546	936

parish 140*l*. In reference to this calculation, it should not be forgotten, that many pauper lunatics have families, who, would no longer be thrown on parishes for support, if their mental maladies could be removed, or even materially ameliorated.

Another fact connected with the condition in which the insane poor are sent to Asylums is, we think, calculated to have a very prejudicial effect. The Poor Law Commissioners, in their printed orders and regulations, have adverted to the 45th section of the Poor Law Amendment Act, which enacts that " no-" thing in this Act contained shall authorise the deten-" tion in any Workhouse of any dangerous Lunatic, " insane person, or idiot, for any longer period than " fourteen days ; and every person wilfully detaining in " any Workhouse any such lunatic, insane person, or " idiot, for more than fourteen days, shall be deemed " guilty of a misdemeanour." They remark upon this clause, " The words dangerous lunatic, insane person, or " idiot, in this clause, are to be read dangerous lunatic, " dangerous insane person, or dangerous idiot, according " to the opinion of the Law Officers of the Crown, given " to the Poor Law Commissioners." The following extract is taken from the printed directions of the Poor Law Commissioners, as to the detention of lunatics in Workhouses, dated the 5th of February, 1842. " From " the express prohibition of the detention of dangerous " persons of unsound mind in a Workhouse, contained " in the clause just cited, coupled with the prevalent " practice of keeping insane persons in the Work-" houses before the passing of the Poor Law Amend-" ment Act, it may be inferred that persons of un-" sound mind, not being dangerous, may be legally " kept in a Workhouse. It must, however, be remem-" bered that with lunatics, the first object ought to be " their cure, by means of proper medical treatment. " This can only be obtained in a well-regulated Asy-

Extracts from printed orders of Poor Law Commissioners.

" lum; and therefore the detention of any curable
" lunatic in a Workhouse is highly objectionable, on the
" score both of humanity and economy. The Commis-
" sioners, indeed, believe that most of the persons of
" unsound mind detained in Workhouses, are incurable
" harmless idiots. But, although the detention of per-
" sons of this description in a Workhouse does not
" appear to be liable to objection on the ground of
" illegality, or of defective medical treatment, they
" nevertheless think that the practice is often attended
" with serious inconveniences, and they are desirous of
" impressing upon the guardians the necessity of the
" utmost caution and vigilance in the management of
" any persons of this class who may be in the Work-
" house."

Opinion of Poor Law Commissioners as to Lunatics in Workhouses.

We entirely concur in the opinion expressed by the
Poor Law Commissioners, " That the detention of any
" curable lunatic in a workhouse is highly objectionable,
" on the score both of humanity and economy." We
think, however, that they must be under some miscon-
ception as to the condition of lunatics in Workhouses,
when they represent them as being in general incurable
harmless idiots, and their detention not objectionable
on the ground of defective medical treatment.

The Poor Law Commissioners have, in their return of
Pauper Lunatics in England and Wales for the year
1842, returned the numbers of Lunatics belonging to
Parishes formed into Unions, at that time, at 6451,
and of Idiots 6261. In these Returns, the word

Use of the term "Idiot" in Poor Law Commissioners' returns of Lunatics in Unions.

"Idiot," is used in a more extensive sense than that
in which it is usually employed by medical men, and
we think that the term ought to be confined to cases
of congenital idiocy. This will account for the very
large numbers which have been returned under this
description, and which, in point of fact, includes a
large number of lunatics of every class. The return
would represent that the lunatics of all descriptions

belonging to Parishes in Unions, throughout England and Wales, exceeds that of the idiots only by 190.

In the year 1843, there were in the Chester Asylum 167 patients, of whom 39 (an unusually large proportion) were idiots; in the Bedford County Asylum there were 140 patients, of whom 15 were idiots; in the Cornwall County Asylum there were 147 patients, of whom 7 were idiots; in the Dorsetshire County Asylum there were 105 patients, including 2 idiots; in the Kent County Asylum there were 253 patients, of whom 4 were considered idiots. The above instances are given by way of example, and there will be found to be a very small proportion of idiots compared with other lunatics in the other public Asylums in England.

As idiots are considered less dangerous than other lunatics, and may be regarded as being beyond the means of cure, there is, perhaps, a larger proportion of them in Workhouses and elsewhere, than is usually met with in County Asylums. Idiots, however, are by no means to be considered as persons always harmless. Two male idiots of the age of 18 were lately found in an Union workhouse committing an unnatural offence. They were taken before a magistrate, and were by him sent back to the Workhouse as irresponsible persons. Such individuals should be deemed dangerous, not only in the ordinary but in a moral acceptation of the term, and ought not, we think, to have been sent back to the Workhouse. In the Leicester Workhouse, we found (in Oct. 1843) a dangerous female idiot who had knocked out the teeth of a child. There are constantly instances of idiots exhibiting the most depraved as well as the most dangerous propensities. *Idiots often dangerous.*

The Metropolitan Commissioners are directed by the act of the 5th & 6th Vic. c. 87, to visit houses licensed by Justices of the Peace for the reception of insane persons, and also County Lunatic Asylums. The *Workhouses visited by Commissioners.*

H

act does not direct any visits to Workhouses. In the year 1842, however, we availed ourselves of all opportunities to visit such Union and other Workhouses as lay in our road. We obtained also your Lordship's authority to visit, in the course of the last year, the Union Workhouse at Bath, the Infirmary Bethel at Norwich, and the Workhouses at Birmingham, Manchester, Sheffield, and at Portsea; and in consequence of special information which we received, we were induced to visit the several Union Workhouses subsequently noticed.

Appendix (C.) gives Reports concerning Idiots and Lunatics in Workhouses.

The reports given in the Appendix (C.) of the Workhouses which have been visited by us, will show that some of them contain not only incurable harmless idiots, but numerous maniacal and dangerous lunatics of every class.

Particular instances specified.

In the Union Workhouse at Redruth, in Cornwall, there were forty-one insane paupers, of whom six were idiots. Several of them were violent, and at times required restraint. In the Union Workhouse at Bath, there were twenty-one insane persons, of whom one female was constantly under restraint; another was under excitement, and secluded in a cell; and one man had been in the house four months without any medicine, although his case appeared susceptible of benefit from medical treatment. In the Leicester Union Workhouse, there were thirty insane persons, of whom three males, and nine females, were dangerous lunatics, in the strict sense of the word, and most unfit inmates of the place in which they were confined, and where, as we were informed, they had been long detained, in spite of the remonstrances of the visiting Surgeon, and some of the Magistrates. In the parish Workhouse at Birmingham, there were seventy-one insane persons, subject to insanity in various forms; several of them being epileptics, liable, after their paroxysms of epilepsy, to fits of raving madness, during which they were usually excessively violent, and some of them occasionally under great excitement, and furiously maniacal.

Whilst we feel it our duty to state to your Lordship the condition in which we have found numerous lunatics in the Workhouses which we have visited, we thoroughly appreciate the great difficulties which those who administer the Poor Law have to encounter in the disposal of pauper lunatics, by reason of the insufficient provision made for their reception in proper Asylums. We think, however, that the detention in Workhouses, not only of dangerous lunatics, but of all lunatics and idiots whatsoever, is highly objectionable.

The clause which is supposed to sanction the confinement in Workhouses of lunatics, without adverting to the probability of their being curable or not, provided they be not dangerous, is, in our opinion, impolitic, and open to serious objection. Although a patient may not be violent or raving, he may require medical treatment, and it is at the beginning of attacks of insanity, when the causes of the disease are in most powerful operation, and the symptoms are developing themselves, that the skill of a medical officer experienced in this disease is most required. Our objection to the clause of the Act to which we have referred is,-that it has a tendency to impress upon those who have the care of the poor, the belief that there is no harm in keeping lunatics away from Asylums so long as they are not dangerous, and thus to combine with the other causes which we have pointed out in producing that incurable condition in which pauper lunatics are so often sent to Asylums. The clause seems, moreover open to this observation,—if it really sanctions the detention of harmless lunatics,—namely, that the Parish Authorities may take advantage of it to deprive persons of their liberty, although they would do no harm if at large.

If, notwithstanding these objections, a necessity

Confinement in Workhouses of Lunatics, objectionable.

exists for detaining any of the insane poor in Workhouses, care should be taken to secure for them proper
treatment, by persons experienced in the diseases of the
insane. The law has provided that all houses licensed
for the reception of lunatics, shall be regularly visited
by a medical man, and that such medical man shall
make and sign a statement of the health of all the
patients once in every week. The ordinary medical
attendants, however, of Union and other Workhouses,
are not always persons conversant with the treatment
of insanity. Even for harmless incurable lunatics,
proper means of exercise and occupation ought to be
provided, and experienced attendants ought to be employed. Yet, at the Bath Union Workhouse there
were nine Insane females under the care of an aged and
feeble woman, who was stated to be upwards of ninety
years old. One woman under her charge was always
confined in a strait waistcoat, and another was in a state
of great excitement, and secluded in a solitary cell.
When this feeble woman was unable to manage the
female patients, her practice had been to call in the aid
of an old man who had the charge of the male lunatics.
In the Leicester Workhouse, there were nineteen female
lunatics, some of whom were extremely dangerous.
Some of these persons were found shut up in a small
refractory ward, without any attendant. We were told
that it was the duty of a female servant to look in upon
them once an hour, but that she feared to remain with
them.

Exercise and occupation should be procured for harmless Idiots.

It will be seen from the foregoing statements, to what
a formidable extent the number of incurable patients
have increased in many of the public Asylums. And
this seems to have arisen principally from two causes,
viz. :—1st. The detention of patients in Workhouses or
elsewhere, until they were past the chance of recovery;
and 2ndly. The want of any separate Establishment
to which patients could be sent when they became
incurable.

Formidable increase of Incurable Patients.

It is manifest, indeed, either that County Asylums must, in their original construction, have been made inadequate for their purpose; or that, from some cause, insanity has since increased. And there can be no doubt, we apprehend, but that there has been a great increase in the numbers of lunatics, and that this is to be ascribed, in some measure, to the system of admissions and general arrangement which prevails in the large Asylums, and which has prevented the poor and the public from obtaining the full benefit intended to be afforded by those Institutions. Should the system of detaining curable patients from Asylums until they are beyond cure, and sending thither those only who are incurable, still continue, it is difficult to foresee the extent to which the numbers of incurable Lunatics may increase, especially in some of the populous Counties.

Increase to be ascribed in some measure to system of admission in large Asylums.

If incurable Lunatics should be allowed to reside in Unions or Workhouses, it is indispensable that they should have separate Wards and Airing-grounds, together with proper Diet and superintendence, and that these Wards should be visited regularly, like other Lunatic Asylums. We think, however, that it would be far better that they should be provided for at a distance from the ordinary Poor, to whom they might be a subject of annoyance, and who might themselves become a source of irritation to the Lunatics. And there can be no doubt, we apprehend, but that the comfort and proper treatment of Lunatic Patients would be secured much more effectually in a distinct Establishment. Whether the existing Asylums, which contain a very large number of Patients, can be rendered efficient Hospitals for the treatment of curable Patients only; or whether they may not be exclusively appropriated advantageously to the use of incurable Lunatics, is a question that may deserve future consideration.

Question whether existing Asylums can be rendered efficient Hospitals for curable Patients.

When we call your Lordship's attention to the fact that the number of Pauper Lunatics in England

and Wales appears to be about 17,000, and that there is accommodation in county Asylums for not more than 4500, we do not recommend the providing public Asylums for such a number of persons upon the expensive scale on which county Asylums have hitherto been erected. We submit, however, that it is the duty as well as the interest of the public to provide suitable places, in every county or within certain districts, where recent cases may be received without delay.

Suitable places for reception of recent cases should be provided without delay.

III.

FORMS OF DISEASE, MEDICAL TREATMENT, DIET, AND CLASSIFICATION.

Principal forms of Insanity distinguished.

WE have thought it expedient in this place to distinguish the principal forms of Insanity which are usually met with in Lunatic Asylums, in order to render more clear and intelligible the statements which we are about to make respecting the classification and treatment of their inmates. They may also be useful in illustrating the Statistical Tables which will be found in the Appendix.

The principal forms are comprehended, in the Tables which accompany this report, under the following heads :—

I. Mania, which is thus divided :
    1. Acute Mania, or Raving Madness.
    2. Ordinary Mania, or Chronic Madness of a less acute form.
    3. Periodical, or Remittent Mania, with comparatively lucid intervals.

II. Dementia, or decay and obliteration of the intellectual faculties

III. Melancholia.

IV. Monomania.

V. Moral Insanity.

The three last mentioned forms are sometimes comprehended under the term Partial Insanity.

VI. Congenital Idiocy.

VII. Congenital Imbecility.

VIII. General Paralysis of the Insane.

IX. Epilepsy.

To these heads may perhaps be added "Delirium Tremens," since it is mentioned, as a form of Insanity, in the Reports of some Lunatic Asylums.

A few brief descriptions of the disorders to which these terms are appropriated, may be deemed requisite by way of explanation.

I. *Mania.*—This term is used to designate a particular kind of madness, as affecting all the operations of the mind. Hence the term Total or General Insanity is used as synonymous with Mania. Maniacs are incapable of carrying on, in a calm and collected manner, any process of thought; their disorder for the most part betraying itself whenever they attempt to enter into conversation. It likewise affects their conduct, gesture, and behaviour, which are absurd and irrational; their actions being characterized by great restlessness, appearing to be the result of momentary impulses and without obvious motives. Mania is also accompanied by hurry and confusion of ideas, and by more or less excitement and vehemence of feeling and expression. When these last symptoms exist in an excessive degree, the disorder is termed *Acute Mania* or Raving Madness.

1. Acute Mania or Raving Madness is the first stage of the disease, which often becomes gradually milder in its character, and is then termed Chronic Mania or

General definition of Mania.

Acute Mania.

simply Mania. In other cases, the disposition to high excitement or raving continues through the whole course of the disease, which sometimes becomes fatal through the exhaustion occasioned by perpetual agitation and want of rest. It is also generally attended with considerable disturbance of the vital functions.

Chronic Mania.   2. The Chronic Form of Madness is attended with less excitement of the passions, less rapidity of utterance, and less violence of action. In this stage, the disorder of the mind is not always immediately perceptible; but it soon becomes apparent that the patient is incapable of continued rational conversation or self-control, and that his acts are the results of momentary caprice, and not governed by rational motives. A great proportion of Maniacs labour under *Illusions* and *Hallucinations*, or false impressions as to matters of fact, but in these illusive notions there is no consistency or permanence. Patients labouring under this chronic form of Mania are often tolerably tranquil and harmless. Many of them are capable of being employed in agricultural and other active pursuits, and of amusing themselves by reading, music, and various entertaining games. A great proportion of the inmates of Lunatic Asylums belong to this class. However quiet and manageable they may appear to be under the authority and supervision to which they are subjected in an Asylum, they are quite unfit to be at large and to mix with ordinary society.

Intermittent Mania.   3. Intermittent Mania or Madness attended with lucid intervals is by no means so frequent as might be inferred from the writings of authors on medical jurisprudence. Some medical writers, of considerable note, have denied the existence of lucid intervals altogether. The fact is, that in all large Asylums, there are patients subject to occasional paroxysms of raving madness, but who have intervals of comparative tranquillity and rest. It generally happens that after the alternations of raving fits and periods of tranquillity have continued for some time, the intervals become less clearly marked, and the mind is found to be weakened, the temper more irritable, and both the feelings and the intellectual faculties more and more disordered.

Recurrent Insanity differs from *Intermittent* Mania, though often confounded with it. ' In Intermittent Mania paroxysms occur either after regular or irregular periods, and this is the ordinary character of the disease. Recurrent Insanity is a name applied to any form of mental disorder, when the patient recovers perfectly, but suffers from relapses after considerable periods of time.

Distinction between recurrent Insanity and Intermittent Mania.

II. *Dementia.*—Chronic and protracted mania is frequently the prelude to a decay and final obliteration of the mental faculties, which is termed Dementia.

Dementia.

Dementia differs from all other forms of insanity. It differs from Mania, in which the intellectual powers still exist, though they are exercised in a confused and disordered manner. It differs from Idiocy, in which the powers of the mind have never been developed, while in Dementia they have been lost.

Dementia is, in some instances, the primary form of mental derangement, and its phenomena make their appearance in the first onset of the disease. Cases of this kind are chiefly from causes of a depressing nature, such as deep and overwhelming grief, extreme poverty, destitution, and old age. In those instances in which dementia is the sequel of protracted mania, it is not easy to determine the point at which mania ends, and dementia begins. It is sometimes, also, the sequel of epilepsy, apoplexy, paralysis, and other affections of the brain.

In most large Asylums the prevailing forms of insanity are Mania and Dementia. In the collective numbers of Patients in the Lancaster County Asylum,

Mania and Dementia prevailing forms of Insanity in large Asylums.

the Superintendent has furnished the following statement, viz., Out of 619, reduced to 580 by the omission
of 39 doubtful cases, there were labouring under mania
235, and dementia 183=418, which is about two
thirds of the whole number of the Patients.

Melancholia.

III. *Melancholia.*—A considerable proportion of the
inmates of all extensive Lunatic Asylums, are the
Melancholics; among whom there are several degrees
and varieties. Some patients display merely lowness
of spirits, with a distaste for the pleasures of life,
and a total indifference to its concerns.—These have no
disorder of the understanding, or defect in the intellectual
powers, and, however closely examined, manifest no delusion or hallucination. This state often alternates with an
opposite condition of the mind, namely, one of buoyancy
of spirits, and morbid activity. It is thus frequently very
difficult to determine in what degree Melancholy, when
it exists without delusions, constitutes insanity. A
great number of persons whose disorder is precisely
that which is above described, and who betray no
particular error of judgment or hallucination, are confined in Lunatic Asylums as a precaution against suicide,
to which they are prone, in many instances, from a
disgust of life.

Another class of Melancholics derive their grief and
despondency from some unreal misfortune, which they
imagine to have befallen them. Many are convinced
that they have committed unpardonable sins, and are
doomed to eternal perdition. Others believe themselves
to be accused or suspected of some heinous crime, of
which they are destined to undergo the punishment;
and of this they live in continual dread. Some
fancy that they have sustained great pecuniary losses,
and are utterly and irretrievably ruined. A numerous
class of melancholy patients live under the impression
that they labour under some terrible bodily disease.
Many of them have, in reality, some complaint of

which they magnify the symptoms : they fancy every trifling sensation of a painful kind to be certain indications of their incurable distemper, which they often attribute to some fantastical cause.

Melancholy patients require particular care and constant inspection, on account of the frequency of suicides among persons of this class. In the Report of the Patients admitted into the Northampton Asylum from August 1838, to November 1843, out of 118 cases of Melancholia, a suicidal propensity had been discovered in sixty-four.* The suicidal propensity is not, however, restricted to this class of patients. In a late annual Report of the Lancaster County Asylum, there are only forty-five cases of Melancholia mentioned, while it is stated that a suicidal propensity had been manifested by 105 out of the total number of 619. *Particular care required by melancholy patients to prevent suicide.*

IV. *Monomania.*—Monomania, properly so termed, is a form of Insanity, which, from the attention given to it, might be supposed to be of more frequent occurrence than it really is. The term is professedly given to cases in which the intellectual faculties are unimpaired, except with relation to some particular topic. Instances, indeed, are continually occurring in which some particular impression of a delusive and insane kind, occupies the attention of the patient and is uppermost in his mind, but unless the power of reasoning correctly on subjects unconnected with the illusion, is retained, the disorder is not a case of Monomania, or " Partial Insanity." *Monomania.*

A frequent illusion of Monomaniacs is, that they hold conversation with supernatural beings.

In most instances of Partial Insanity Melancholy

---

* It is remarkable that the excess of suicidal cases prevailed in the pauper part of the establishment. Thus, in forty-two cases of Melancholia, occurring among private patients, there were only eighteen suicidal cases, while in seventy-six among the paupers, forty-six were suicidal.

connects itself with the subject of delusion. These cases properly belong to Melancholia.

Moral Insanity.

V. *Moral Insanity.*—This term is used to designate a form of mental disease in which the affections, sentiments, habits, and, generally speaking, the moral feelings of the mind, rather than the intellectual faculties, are in an unsound and disordered state. The common distinctive character of all these cases is of a negative kind, viz.—that the faculties of the understanding remain apparently unimpaired, and that no delusive impression can be detected in the mind of the patient, which may account for the perversion of his moral dispositions, affections, and inclinations. Cases of this description were formerly looked upon as unaccountable phenomena. They are, however, now recognised as a distinct form of mental disorder in nearly all the public Asylums. They are characterized by a total want of self-control, with an inordinate propensity to excesses of various kinds, among others habitual intoxication. This is often followed by an attack of Mania, which, however, speedily subsides when the patient is confined, but is generally reproduced, by the same exciting cause, soon after he is discharged.

Among the Female Inmates of Asylums, there are many whose disorder principally consists in a moral perversion connected with hysterical or sexual excitement.

Congenital Idiocy and congenital Imbecility.

VI. & VII. *Congenital Idiocy, and Congenital Imbecility.*—Congenital Idiots are persons whose intellectual faculties have never been developed.

Congenital Imbecility is the result of some original defect, which renders the mind feeble in all its operations, though not altogether incapable of exercising them within a limited sphere. There are many degrees of Imbecility, but the examples chiefly found in Lunatic Asylums are persons labouring under this weakness in an extreme degree. It is evident that more discrimination ought to be used than has hitherto been practised

in selecting from persons of this class proper objects for
confinement.

VIII. *General Paralysis of the Insane, and other* General Para-
forms of Paralysis complicated with Insanity. Insane.

· Paralysis is not unfrequently complicated with Insanity, and is almost an invariable indication that the
case is incurable and hopeless, marking the existence of
organic disease in the brain.

In some instances, Insanity is the consequence of an
attack of apoplexy, or of hemiplegia. This happens
more especially in aged persons.

In others, apoplexy or paralysis supervenes on protracted mania or dementia.

The most strongly marked case of the complica-
tion of paralytic symptoms with those of mental
disorder, is the disease termed General Paralysis of the
Insane. This is more properly to be considered as an
affection distinct both from ordinary paralysis and from
insanity. The paralytic symptoms in this affection
are sometimes observed to precede those of mental
disturbance ; and others they follow. General paralysis
of the Insane seldom occurs in females, but mostly
in men, and is the result almost uniformly of a
debauched and intemperate life. Its duration is
scarcely ever longer than two or at most three years,
when it generally brings its victim to the grave. The
onset of the disease is distinguished by an impediment
in the articulation, an effort is required in speaking,
and the words are uttered with a sort of mumbling,
and stammering. At this period, there is no other
perceptible sign of paralysis, and the mobility of the
limbs is not at all impaired. In a second stage, the
patient is observed to have a tottering gait : the limbs
are weaker than in health, especially the lower extremities, while the functions of the organs of sense are
likewise enfeebled. In the progress of time, a third
stage appears, during which the victim of this malady

loses not only the power of locomotion, but can neither feed himself nor answer the calls of nature. He becomes more and more weak and emaciated, but generally perishes under some secondary disease, such as gangrene, sloughing of the surface of the body, or diarrhœa, unless he be cut off at an earlier period by an apoplectic or epileptic attack, to which these patients are very liable. The disorder of the mind is peculiar in this affection. It is generally a species of monomania, in which the individual affected fancies himself possessed of vast riches, and power.

This specific form of Insanity has been known for some time in France, by the Physicians of which country it was first described: its existence has been more recently recognised in the English hospitals, and some instances of it are reported in the enumeration of cases transmitted from most of the County Asylums. The proportions which these cases bear to the whole number of admissions is very different in different Asylums; as will appear by reference to the following Table:

CASES OF GENERAL PARALYSIS.

In 213 admissions into Hanwell Asylum, . 32
In 120   „   „   Surrey .   . 16
In 619   „   „   Lancaster . . 13

Epilepsy.

IX. *Epilepsy.*—In most of the Lunatic Asylums there are some, and in the large Asylums many persons confined among the insane who are subject to epilepsy. For this disease, unfortunately, is often complicated with insanity. There are, however, some Epileptics in these Asylums who are not insane, or in any way disordered in mind during the intervals of their paroxysms.

Epilepsy is complicated with defects or disorders of the mind, in various ways.

Epileptic Idiots.

1. Epileptic Idiots.—Persons whose intellectual faculties have never been developed. They are not mate-

rially different, as regards their mental deficiency, from
idiots not subject to Epilepsy; but they require greater
care, on account of the accidents to which this disease
renders them liable.

2. Epileptics who are imbecile or demented.—When
paroxysms of Epilepsy are very frequent and severe, and
the disease is of long duration, it generally impairs the
intellectual faculties. Torpor, weakness and imbecility
come on, which, if the patient survives under his disease for many years, terminate in fatuity, similar in every
respect to the fatuity which ensues in protracted Mania.

3. Epileptic Mania.—Some persons subject to severe
paroxysms of Epilepsy without suffering obliteration of
their intellectual faculties, and even without obvious disorder of the mind during the intervals of their paroxysms,
are nevertheless subject to occasional fits of a maniacal
character. It is an observation frequently made by the
attendants of Asylums, that when the Epileptic fits are
coming on, such persons are irritable, morose, malicious,
and sometimes exceedingly dangerous. During these
periods, Epileptics are prone to violence, and sometimes
perpetrate the most atrocious acts. Many instances are
upon record of such persons, at a time when their disorder had been in abeyance, or even supposed to have
ceased altogether, having been seized with a sudden
impulse to commit homicide, infanticide, suicide, or to
set fire to houses.* In other instances, the mental
disorder of Epileptics has the form of acute mania, or
rather of raving* delirium. The patient, generally a
day or two after the attack of Epilepsy, sometimes

Imbecile or demented Epileptics.

Epileptic Mania.

* Shortly before the second visit of the Metropolitan Commissioners
to the Asylum at Gateshead Fell, a man had escaped, who it was
thought had become nearly convalescent, and who was accordingly
employed in the grounds belonging to the house. He was apparently
so far recovered, that the Parish Officers (without reference to the
Medical Visitor) determined to leave him at large. On the third night
after his escape, he murdered his wife and daughter. His case was one
of epileptic mania.

immediately after it has ceased, is seized with a sudden fury, during which he sings, roars, shrieks, or resembles a man in a violent fit of intoxication. The species of madness which is complicated with Epilepsy is one of the most mischievous and dangerous forms of the disease. But the instances of this affection bear a very small proportion to the cases of Epilepsy in general.

Epileptics whose intellects are unimpaired.

A great number of instances of Epilepsy, however, are well known to exist without any considerable disorder of the mind. Persons subject to occasional paroxysms, or those of infrequent occurrence only, are, during the intervals, in a tolerably perfect possession of their intellectual faculties, and are capable of following their ordinary pursuits.

Adult persons of this description are scarcely to be found in Lunatic Asylums, but we have been informed that boys and girls, when they have become a source of anxiety and trouble to their parents, as well as dangerous to themselves, have sometimes been sent by Boards of Guardians to Asylums for protection. We do not, however, consider this a sufficient reason for associating this class of epileptics with the Insane. Where a proper classification exists, the Epileptics are placed in wards by themselves, or are separated from the insane; but there are many Lunatic Asylums where this regulation is entirely neglected.

The proportion of Epileptics to the other inmates is very considerable in some Asylums, as may be seen by the following statement.

	Numbers in House.	Epileptics.	
		M.	F.
Hanwell	975	80	63
Bethnal Green . . .	562	40	19
Hoxton House	396	24	20
Lancaster	611	40	23
York W. Riding . . .	433	23	16
Kent	249	15	14
Chester	164	12	6

X.—*Delirium Tremens.* — Instances of Delirium Tremens are occasionally, though not often, seen among inmates of Lunatic Asylums. The disorder is well known. It is the result of intemperance, and frequently supervenes on a fit of intoxication. It is named from the muscular tremor and agitation which accompanies it, and the peculiar affection of the mind, resembling the delirium of fever rather than the phenomena of Insanity. It is not a disease of long duration, but terminates, for the most part, in a short period, either in death or in recovery. Hence, there are comparatively few cases of this description in Lunatic Asylums.

MEDICAL TREATMENT.

Having thus described the different forms in which Insanity manifests itself, we now proceed to consider the Medical Treatment to which the Patients confined in Lunatic Asylums are subjected.

In our visits to these Asylums, both public and private, we have been careful to make inquiries as to the methods of medical treatment adopted by the proprietors or superintendents, or by those persons to whom the medical care of the patients has been confided. We have occasionally found some difficulty in obtaining information on this subject. In some instances, we have not seen the medical officers, and we have derived our information, in such instances, from the proprietors, superintendents, and the inmates of the respective Asylums. Yet, on the whole, we have obtained a tolerably correct knowledge of the state of these establishments, with regard to the manner and degrees in which the resources of medicine are applied in them to the cure and alleviation of mental diseases.

A great difference prevails, in this respect, in the different classes of Lunatic Asylums. The licensed houses, containing fewer than 100 patients, in which the residence of a Medical Officer is not required, by the

Act 2, 3, Will. IV. cap. 107, within the walls of each Establishment, and which, in some instances, are under the management of persons entirely without medical education, are visited generally by medical practitioners in the neighbourhood. These visits to the Asylums are usually made twice in a week, and in some instances more frequently.

In some Asylums, the whole system of management appears to have been constituted less with regard to the cure of insanity, and to the restoration of lunatics to health and society, than to their seclusion and safe custody. Occasional doses of medicine are administered, when incidental deviations from bodily health or any contingency calls for their use, but the application of medicine and other restorative means, on any determined plan, with a view to promote recovery, and to restore the mental faculties to a sound state, appears in some Asylums never to have been contemplated. To accomplish this object, the residence of a Medical man on the spot, or in the immediate vicinity, is very essential; and here we cannot but notice the following extract from a Report of the Commissioners who visited the Norfolk County Asylum in August, 1843, which will point out the evils likely to be contingent on this arrangement.

Report of Commissioners on Norfolk Asylum.

" The most serious defect in this Institution, and one " which may be attended with the most mischievous, " if not fatal, consequences, is the want of a Resident " Medical Officer. On this subject, we cannot but " notice, as a singular anomaly in the law, that, whilst " it is required in every Licensed House, containing " 100 Patients, that there shall be a Resident Physician, " Surgeon, or Apothecary, there is no similar provision " as to County or Subscription Asylums, or public " Hospitals. The liability to apoplexy, and the pos- " sible occurrence of cases of suspended animation from " strangling may be mentioned as among the many " reasons calling for the constant attendance or immediate

" vicinity of a Medical man. We put some questions to
" the Superintendent, as to what he would do in cases
" such as we have described. His answer was that he
" would not venture upon the responsibility of acting or
" applying remedies, that he could not bleed, and had
" no knowledge or experience, medical or surgical.
" Upon asking, then, what steps he would take in
" such cases, we were told that he would immediately
" send to Norwich, the nearest place, three miles dis-
" tant, for one of the Medical visitors. He subsequently
" directed our attention to a pony on the lawn,
" which he informed us was constantly ready to be
" saddled as occasion required."

It must be observed, that of several private Asy- General charac-
lums the proprietors are physicians, who reside within ter of Medical
men attached
their own establishments. Many of them are able to Asylums.
and well-informed men in their profession, and appear to treat their patients with judgment and skill.
Many of the Superintendents of County Asylums, and
some of the Medical Officers in those licensed houses
which, from their containing one hundred patients
require the residence of such an attendant, are men
intelligent, and active in doing all that is practicable
towards the restoration of their patients.

The Medical Officers residing in the Asylums have
been led by personal observation and experience, nearly
to the same conclusions, as to the most efficacious treatment of Insanity; or, to speak more precisely, of administering the aids of medicine and regimen to those classes
and descriptions of persons who are principally the
inmates of public Lunatic Asylums. Amongst the Causes of In-
most frequent causes of Insanity in Paupers, are sanity in Paupers.
habitual intemperance, poverty and destitution, grief,
disappointment; and, we fear, in some instances want
of sufficient sustenance. These causes act with different degrees of influence on different individuals,
according to the various states of their constitution,

but they have all a tendency to bring the body into a state of weakness and exhaustion. This is greatly aggravated by the insane poor being very generally sent in the first place to workhouses and other improper receptacles, instead of to Asylums, where they might be immediately subjected to medical treatment, at a time when the disease is known to be curable in a large proportion of cases.

Curative treatment of Pauper Lunatics.

It is the general opinion of the best-informed medical attendants on Lunatic Asylums that the most successful method of attempting the cure of pauper lunatics in public hospitals, exhausted and destitute as they often are, is to obviate the state of body which poverty and distress have a tendency to induce. This is best effected by a restorative plan, and by means calculated to reproduce a vigorous state of bodily health. For this purpose a nutritive and tolerably full diet is allowed, consisting of a considerable proportion of animal food, wholesome digestible bread, milk porridge, or milk thickened with various farinaceous substances, and good broth. To these a moderate quantity of malt liquor, ale, or porter, is added in most cases, and in some extreme instances, wine and other stimulants. Warm clothing and bedding, and a moderately warm and dry atmosphere, are indispensable auxiliaries for promoting the comfort and cure of lunatics, in whom the circulation is languid, and who for the most part are chilly, and suffer much from exposure to cold and damp air. Exercise in the open air in cheerful airing-grounds; baths, either warm or cold, according to the state of the circulation and the habitual temperature of the skin; frictions promoting cleanliness and dryness of the surface of the body, and tending to keep up the action of the blood-vessels to a certain healthy standard, are generally found to promote the restoration of patients whose cases are of a curable description.

The whole of this plan is said to prove beneficial only in those cases which are free from the ordinary signs of congestion in the brain, and from tendencies to epilepsy and paralysis. When these exist, they must be treated by appropriate remedies, such as topical bleedings and counter-irritations. In the cases before alluded to, tonic and stimulant medicines, and all the remedies which promote healthy digestion and a due circulation of blood to the extremities, are said to be productive of beneficial results. The tonic remedies most in use are carbonate of iron, cinchona, sulphate of quina., gentian, combined with aloetics when required by the state of the natural functions, or with astringents, when, in cases of great debility and exhaustion, there is a tendency to diarrhœa, or dysentery. A moist or relaxed state of the skin, with cold extremities; a shrunk and shrivelled surface, with a livid and blotchy, or pale and yellow complexion and feeble circulation, are well known to frequently co-exist with insanity, and are especially noted in those cases which are the result of depressing agencies. In this state of the system, great advantages are said to arise from the use of carbonate of ammonia, given in frequent doses, and continued for a considerable time. Emetics and powerful purgatives are said to be rather injurious than useful, in the forms of disease now described, except where any temporary complaint indicates the necessity of having recourse to them. It is the testimony of the best-informed among the Medical Superintendents of Asylums, that the restoration of bodily health is frequently accompanied by a marked improvement in the state of the mental faculties. We must not omit the fact, that although a very general agreement exists among the intelligent Medical Officers of Lunatic Asylums, as to the most efficient method of treatment for the cure or relief of the class of patients above described, there are some remarkable

Regulations as to treatment in some Asylums at variance with general opinion;

exceptions, and that the regulations of some Asylums are quite at variance with the general opinion.

DIET.

first, as to diet;   In the first place as to diet. We have remarked that nothing is more important than a sufficient and appropriate diet in the treatment of lunatics. It is indeed evident, that nothing can be effected without an ample supply of·proper food, in the restoration of the patients from that state of physical weakness and exhaustion, which is the condition of the majority among the inmates of pauper asylums.

It is worthy of remark, that in two of the County Asylums, viz. those of Middlesex and of Dorset, the diet of the patients was sometime since improved by an increased allowance of food, and that in both of these asylums, there was recorded after this' alteration an increase in the number of recoveries. Complaints have been made of the too great use of broths and gruel: in consequence of which, at Hanwell, a meat dinner has been substituted for pease-soup, on one of the two days on which the latter was previously given. It has been suggested to us, that regard should be paid to the nature of the food to which the patient was accustomed before his confinement.

In the private Asylums admitting pauper patients, there is considerable diversity with respect to the allowance of food. In many of these establishments (and this is the case even in some which are defective in other particulars), a tolerably good and liberal diet is furnished to the patients. In many asylums a fixed quantity of beer is furnished to the patients, and in all these asylums it is the opinion of the proprietors that this allowance is beneficial. There are other asylums where beer is allowed to those who will employ themselves chiefly in out-door labour. In many in-

stances no malt liquor is furnished to the patients : this
is observable in many of the large asylums in the North
of England. In the Asylum of Lincoln it was thought
advisable, sometime since, by the Committee of Management, to increase the quantity of nutritious food allowed
to the patients, as a substitute for fermented liquors formerly allowed to the patients. In the Leicester Asylum we were informed that the diet was varied with regard to the different classes of patients ; a poorer or
lower diet being laid down for the Epileptics and Incurables than for others.

The supply of a sufficient quantity of proper food ap- proper diet an
important aid to
pears to us one of the most important aids towards the cure or relief;
relief or cure of insanity. We have received assurances
from various intelligent superintendents of Asylums,
that this disease has been frequently alleviated, and
repeatedly cured, solely by increasing the quantity of
wholesome food. The want of food is considered by
the Superintendent of the Lancaster Asylum to have
been the exciting cause of insanity in many cases which
have come under his care. In some private Asylums,
where a low scale of diet prevails, the small sum
allowed for each patient has been pointed out, by which
it appeared that the proprietor of the Asylum would
have been scarcely remunerated for a more liberal supply
of food. It is our opinion that the amount of food
allowed to pauper lunatics, and the rate of payment
made for them in private Asylums, should be under
the control of official visitors. The Dietaries of the
Pauper Patients in the several county and principal
other Public Asylums, and a selection from the Dietaries of the private Asylums receiving Paupers, will
be found in Appendix E to this Report.

The next subject to be noticed is that of temperature. second, as to
temperature.
A most important aid towards the restoration of debilitated Insane patients to bodily health, and therefore
towards their ultimate recovery, is afforded by a pure, dry,
and warm atmosphere. External warmth is required by

the general state of circulation and of the skin, in a great
majority of cases, and patients are known to suffer
much from being in a cold or damp atmosphere.* In
the Lincoln Asylum the lower galleries were found
cold at our different visitations, and we were surprised
to observe, among the standing regulations of the Committee of Management, an express prohibition to the
admission of heated air, although in the galleries no
means existed of raising the temperature to a proper
degree. It was quite evident to us that much needless
suffering must be occasioned to the patients by this prohibition.

In some of the smaller private Asylums, the apartments are not only cold, but extremely damp. These
defects are calculated to occasion the prevalence of
diarrhœa, dysentery, and pulmonary complaints, which
are among the most frequent causes of death in Lunatic Asylums.

Means of exer-
cise.

The means of exercise in the open air are very defective in many of these Asylums. Even where there are
extensive pleasure-grounds around the houses, pauper
patients are in some instances prohibited from availing
themselves of these advantages, and are shut up in small
and cheerless yards.

Use of opiates in
Insanity.

The utility of opiates as a remedy in cases of insanity,
is a question on which we have found some diversity
of opinion among the Medical Superintendents of Lunatic
Asylums. Some abjure the use of all narcotic medicines, while others look upon sedatives as a most valuable resource in cases of agitation and excitement, and
have recourse to them on all occasions, when want of
sleep and restlessness produce debility and exhaustion.
This last practice seems to be gaining ground. Preparations of opium and other sedatives, given in repeated
and sufficient doses, are thought by the best-informed
practitioners, who conduct the medical treatment in

* This subject is adverted to farther in the section on Warming and
Ventilation.

the large Asylums, to be of great efficacy in subduing excitement and agitation, and conjoined with the use of baths, cold applications to the head, and the use of anti-spasmodics and aperients, are said to promote the cure of Mania in the early and acute stages. Several instances are recorded, at the Licensed Houses of Bethnal Green, of Patients having been restored to reason, in a very short time, by the skilful administration of opiates. The Committee of Management of the Lincoln Asylum, among other regulations for the guidance of their Medical Officers, have established the following rule,—that " the process of " subduing violence by the use of tartarised antimony, " or of narcotics, the practice of enforcing sleep by " opiates and courses of drastic medicines, are hereby " interdicted, except in special cases otherwise medically " requiring the same."

The foregoing remarks upon the medical treatment practised in various Asylums must be understood to apply principally to recent cases. In chronic forms of the disease, although medicine alone is found to be of less efficacy, much is still accomplished by skilful medical superintendence, combined with judicious moral treatment.

Pursuant to the Act 5 & 6 Vict. c. 87, sect. 8, we have inquired whether any medical treatment was in any of the Asylums substituted for coercion. It has been reported to us that no such system prevailed in any of the Asylums: but that the use of emetic tartar, of sedatives combined with aperients, and cold applications to the head in recent cases of high excitement, has occasionally rendered mechanical restraint unnecessary.

Medical treatment not substituted on coercion.

CLASSIFICATION OF LUNATICS.

One of the most important ameliorations, introduced during late years into the treatment of the insane in Lunatic Asylums, consists in the proper classification

Classification of Lunatics.

and distribution of patients into different departments. In former times the inmates of these houses, if not confined in solitary cells, were seen crowded together indiscriminately; tranquil, and often timid and sensitive patients being assembled in the same apartments with violent and noisy maniacs. If any classification existed, it was little more than a separation of persons according to their various grades in society; the poorer classes being divided from those who, by reason of larger payments, were considered to be entitled to greater personal comforts. The classification of lunatics, now generally adopted in well-regulated Asylums, is founded on a different principle. It consists in the distribution of patients with reference to their mental disorders, and in associating those persons whose intercourse is likely to be mutually beneficial, and in separating others who are in a state that renders their society a source of mutual irritation and annoyance.

Most beneficial in curable, requisite in incurable cases.

The distribution of lunatics, on this principle, is found to have a most beneficial influence in promoting their recovery, when their cases admit the hope of cure, and in incurable cases it is equally requisite, with a view to the personal security of the patients, as well as their comfort and tranquillity. The rules desirable to be observed, in order to obtain the most advantageous system of classification, have been mainly founded upon experience. They have been, as yet, carried into effect by no means sufficiently or generally in Lunatic Asylums. This has been abundantly manifest to us in our visits of inspection. We shall endeavour to point out to your Lordship the several advantages and defects of these Institutions, in the particular to which we have now adverted, and to show how far the arrangements adopted in them answer to the requisite conditions of a complete and proper system of classification.

Separation of dangerous Lunatics from others.

The first object is the separation of dangerous Lunatics from others. Wherever a considerable number of

Lunatics are assembled, there are found some who are subject to paroxysms of violent excitement, during which they are apt to assault other patients, or any persons within their reach. Others who are more dangerous, suddenly and without any previous sign of mischievous intention, inflict serious injuries, on slight provocation, or without any apparent motive, or they are prone to set fire to houses, and display various destructive and malicious propensities. These persons would be sources of perpetual danger and alarm, and would sometimes occasion serious calamities if they were left at large in the midst of other patients, without being carefully watched. It is desirable for the complete security of the rest, to keep such dangerous persons, as far as practicable, in one or more separate divisions, where they may be surrounded by a sufficient number of vigilant and experienced attendants. There is in this particular a deficiency in many Lunatic Asylums which we have visited.

In the second place, restless, noisy, and agitated Noisy Patients. lunatics, who would annoy and irritate the more tranquil, by shouting and screaming, require on this account, separate wards and airing grounds, removed as far as possible from the places appropriated to patients of a different description. Where these arrangements have not been adopted, which is the case in many of the private and in some of the public Asylums, the presence of noisy and turbulent maniacs is a source of perpetual irritation to the quiet patients; and it must tend materially to aggravate their disorder, and in many instances to retard or prevent their recovery. We have particularly noticed the inconveniences arising from the absence of adequate means for separating the noisy from the tranquil patients, in our visits to the public Asylums at Lincoln, Suffolk, and in the licensed houses of Hoxton, Box, and Bailbrook House. The defect now pointed out occasions great disquiet, and an appearance of restless agitation through the whole of those establishments.

Dirty Patients. A separate department is obviously required for that class of patients, a very numerous one in many Lunatic Asylums, whose state or conduct is such as to render them disgusting and offensive to others. Fatuous persons or those who have sunk into the last stage of Dementia, and who are insensible to the calls of nature, **Ill effects of want of such separation.** are of this description. In most of the Lunatic Asylums of which the extent is sufficient to admit of an adequate separation of patients from each other, attention has been paid to their comfort in this particular, but we have in some instances had occasion to observe great disquietude arising from the want of such an arrangement, particularly at Lainston House, Bailbrook House, and the private Asylums at Derby and Plympton. It is right to state that the present proprietor of the Derby Asylum, is about to discontinue the Pauper part of his Establishment.

Melancholic Patients especially affected. Melancholy or dejected patients often retain sufficient power of observation and reflection to render them aware of the state of others, and of their own condition, and they contemplate with horror the prospect of being reduced to the miserable plight of demented persons, or violent maniacs, when they are associated with such patients as they often are in Lunatic Asylums. On this account melancholics suffer more than any other class of insane persons from confinement in ill-regulated Establishments. **Treatment of Suicidal Patients.** Patients labouring under Melancholia, on account of the frequent instances of a suicidal tendency which are known to occur among them, require greater vigilance than any other description of persons. The classification of these patients calls for much care and discrimination. Their despondency would be aggravated if they were placed in the same apartments with individuals whose intellects are more deeply injured. They occasionally derive benefit from the comparison and contrariety of

their several illusions, and some melancholics are cheered
by being associated with patients of a lively and ex-
citable habit of mind. In the Lancaster Asylum, the
suicidal patients are associated with the cheerful, and
this arrangement appears to be judicious, and attended
with advantageous results. During an entire year, no
actual instance of self-destruction had occurred, though
there were upwards of a hundred cases in that Asylum
in which a suicidal tendency had been ascertained to
exist, and though no individual had been subjected to
personal restraint.*

There are many reasons which point out the impro- Separation of
priety of keeping persons subject to attacks of epilepsy in Patients.
the same apartments with the other inmates. The
sudden paroxysms to which these patients are liable
are very distressing and alarming to timid persons, such
as are many of those who labour under the less severe
forms of insanity. On the other hand, the frequent
noises and causes of excitement which happen in wards
inhabited by maniacs, with whom epileptics are often
placed, are very injurious to the last-mentioned patients,
whose state requires that they should be kept free from
all disturbance and sources of irritation. In reference to
epileptic, and also to suicidal patients, an arrangement Arrangement
is adopted in the Lincoln Asylum, which we have coln Asylum.
observed in no other institution, but which we think
deserving of imitation. These patients are placed in
dormitories, where they are constantly watched throughout the night by an attendant, who sits up and is so
placed as to have a complete view of the apartments in
which the patients sleep.

Another class among the inmates of Lunatic Asylums

* It must be noted that four instances of suicide had occurred
during the preceding year within a short time, a fact which had been
attributed by the Superintendent, principally to the temptation and
opportunity occasioned by the existence of iron bars in the patients'
rooms.

Separation of
tranquil and
convalescent
patients. are the tranquil and convalescent patients. In this
department all those persons may be placed who, though
insane, are capable of conducting themselves quietly,
and occasion no annoyance to others.

Deviations from
rule to be deter-
mined by cir-
cumstances. Deviations from the above method of separating
patients, are occasionally introduced with advantage,
by mixing individuals of one class with those of a
different description, when the particular state of such
patients is likely to be improved by that arrangement.
The propriety of such deviations from a general rule
must be determined by particular circumstances. It
will be seen that a somewhat mixed classification has
been adopted in the Lancaster Asylum.

We have not thought it necessary to specify all the
instances in which we have found classification imperfect. These may in a great degree be collected from
the other parts of our Report, in which the excess of
restraint, and the defective construction of Asylums,
have formed the subjects of particular animadversion.

Classification in
Lancaster Asy-
lum the most
complete. The method of classification adopted in the Lancaster
Asylum, is the most complete of any that has fallen
under our observation. The outline of this is subjoined.

LANCASTER COUNTY ASYLUM.

CLASSIFICATION AND NUMBER OF ATTENDANTS BEFORE AND SINCE THE SYSTEM OF NON-COERCION WAS ADOPTED.

On each side of the Establishment are ten Wards.

1. Cases of Dementia, associated with active, orderly,
and quiet cases, who have been some time in the
house, and are capable of rendering assistance to
the cases of Dementia.

2. Recent cases, associated with the orderly, active
and quiet cases of longer standing.

3. Patients who have not manifested a tendency to
violence, to the commission of suicide, or to escape
from the Establishment.

4. Convalescent cases, a few old cases, and one or two
   suicidal cases.

5. Refractory and excited cases.

6. Suicidal cases, associated with cheerful and watchful
   cases.

7. Refractory Patients, and violent Epileptics.

8. Epileptic Patients who are not violent.

9. Aged quiet cases, who have been a considerable
   time in the Establishment, and a few suicidal
   cases.

10. Infirmary.

The classification adopted in the Gloucester County
Asylum is on a more simple plan, and it seems to be
productive of good effects, since that establishment
presents the appearance of comfort, tranquillity, and
good management. Excepting in what regards the
separation of epileptics—an arrangement, as we have
remarked, not frequently met with elsewhere—the system
of the Gloucester Asylum may be considered as a fair
specimen of the classification adopted in County
Asylums. The patients are there distributed as follows:
one class consists of quiet patients and those approach-
ing to convalescence; a second comprises the epileptics;
a third, the fatuous patients; a fourth, the dirty and
noisy; and a fifth, the working class, forming a distinct
body, which varies in number, and consists of the con-
valescents, and of some incurable patients, who, however, are capable of employment, and are occupied in
cultivating the garden and grounds.

Classification in Gloucester County Asylum.

IV.

OCCUPATION, AMUSEMENTS, AND EXERCISE.

———◆———

By the Acts 2 & 3 Will. IV. c. 107, s. 37, and 5 & 6 Vict. c. 87, ss. 10, 34, we are directed to inquire what occupations and amusements are provided for Insane Patients; and (by the latter Act) to state the effect thereof, in-door and out-door respectively.

Beneficial effects of occupations and amusements.

The answers which we have received to our inquiries have been generally, that occupations and amusements, especially such as take place in the open air, are beneficial to the bodies as well as to the minds of the Patients. Indeed, all intelligent persons who are well acquainted with the disease of Lunacy, by having seen it in its different stages and varieties, and can therefore form some opinion as to the chance of its relief or ultimate cure, are strenuous in advising that insane patients should be employed as much as possible. From the observations which we have been enabled to make on the subject, in the course of our visits through the several public and private Asylums of this country, we are disposed to concur fully in this opinion. It appears to us that employment should be afforded to all patients, whether pauper or private; and that they should be induced to occupy themselves as much as is consistent with their bodily health: not, however, with the view of deriving any profit from their labour, but solely for the purpose of relief or cure. There can be little doubt but that by amusing the mind of a patient, and diverting his attention from any idea, either painful or delusive, which occupies it, that much good may be effected. The longer a delusion is dwelt upon, the stronger and more inveterate it becomes. It is important, therefore,

129

that it should be displaced (though only for a time) as soon as possible, by a fresh and healthy train of thought, and by occupations which may improve the patient's bodily condition, with which his state of mind is often connected, especially in the early stages of insanity. Employment, therefore, in cases of long standing, tends to the tranquillity, and in recent cases contributes materially to the recovery, of the patient.

In most instances, it is desirable to place at the disposal of the patient, the same species of occupation that he has been accustomed to follow, previously to his entering the asylum; and if he has not been brought up to any profession or trade, it may be even proper that he should be instructed in some regular pursuit, in order fully to engage his attention. It is at all times important, that as much exercise and employment as possible, in the open air, should be afforded, and that for this purpose, gardening and agricultural labour should be provided.

Without reference, however, to any pecuniary advantage that may result to the rate-payer, or to the proprietor of the Asylum, we deem it most necessary that employment should be provided for the lunatic. In fact, the labour of a Patient neither can, nor ought to, be reckoned upon as a regular source of profit. In the first place, it is uncertain; depending upon his health, temper, and disposition. A Lunatic, moreover, is a person afflicted with a positive malady, which frequently circumscribes his physical powers, and at other times exhibits itself in the shape of dangerous or violent excitement, suspending for a time, the capability of making himself useful. The object of employing a patient is not that he should make a return in value for the money expended upon him, but that his tranquillity and comfort should be promoted, and the disease with which he is afflicted, consequently mitigated or even removed. For this purpose, moderate labour only should be resorted to, and that as much as

Labour of patients not to be reckoned on as a source of profit.

K

possible in the open air, in order to strengthen without fatiguing the body; and it should be of such a nature as will afford amusement, without any risk of harassing the mind.

Spacious yards and pleasure grounds should be provided.

With a view to these objects, spacious and cheerful yards, and also pleasure-grounds, should be provided, for the purposes of exercise, and of yielding the patient opportunities, at all seasonable times, of occupation and amusement in keeping them in order. But as, by these means only, sufficient employment cannot at all times be afforded to any considerable number of persons, it seems necessary that a farm, or extensive gardens, (proportioned to the number of patients), should be attached to every large Asylum, and that a variety of in-door employments should also be provided. In order to promote exercise and occupation, it is also advisable that some trifling indulgencies should be given to such patients as are willing to perform a moderate quantity of labour.

Music, dancing, &c.

Music, dancing, and various games (as many as possible in the open air) may be resorted to with advantage, in most cases, except where the patient is too exciteable. No Asylum should be without a library. Books, judiciously chosen, especially such as will not encourage any morbid ideas already existing, are an important help in promoting a happy and serene state of mind. In cases of great depression, and particularly of religious melancholy, books of a cheerful character should be placed, to a much greater extent than is generally done, at the disposal of the patients. In most of the Asylums that we have visited, we have found an abundance of religious publications, and in some few of them little else. However useful such works may be, we have frequently urged upon the various proprietors and superintendents, the duty of their also procuring books and publications of an entertaining character, adapted to the capacity of the patients under their care.

In the better-conducted Asylums, these views are apparently acted upon to a considerable extent. Books are procured and placed at the disposal of the patients; the exercise of trades and other in-door employments is encouraged,—in some cases rewarded; and out-of-door occupation is provided by means of large gardens or farms, in which patients regularly labour in the proper seasons.

In the Wakefield Lunatic Asylum, to which are attached a garden of three acres, and a farm of forty acres of land, we were informed (on our visit in September, 1842) that 120, out of 208, male patients, and 135, out of 190, female patients, were employed in various ways. These patients belonged to a manufacturing district, and occupied themselves in woollen and cotton weaving, and all the clothes, including the shoes, used throughout the establishment were made by the inmates. They made fancy articles also for sale, and performed all the gardening and agricultural labour. A variety of amusements was provided for them, and the effect both of occupation and amusement was considered to be highly beneficial.

In the Kent Asylum, containing 253 patients, we were informed (September, 1843) that about half the patients of each sex were induced to work; the men in gardening and field-labour, and in cleaning the yards of the establishment; the women in knitting, sewing, washing, and household work. The land attached to this Asylum consists of thirty-seven acres, fourteen of which (laid out in gardens and airing-grounds) are inclosed by walls.

In Dr. Warburton's Asylum, at Bethnal Green, a library of very considerable extent has been purchased, from time to time, for the use of the patients, who are also encouraged to employ themselves in various ways; some in making shoes, clothes, and mats; and others

Provisions for employment, &c., in better-conducted Asylums;

In Wakefield Asylum;

Kent Asylum;

Bethnal Green;

in the kitchen and laundry, and in needle and household work, and in and about the yards of the Asylum.

Dorset County Asylum ;

In the Dorset County Asylum, (containing, in October, 1842, 109 pauper patients), a considerable proportion are employed in the garden, laundry, in plaiting straw, and in needle and household work ; and they are encouraged thus to occupy themselves by an extra diet. A few books, and various amusements, are provided for them ; and they are allowed to take exercise in the neighbouring fields.

Gloucester County Asylum ;

At the Gloucester County Asylum, besides the extensive and cheerful yards and grounds in the midst of which the buildings stand, there are twenty acres of garden ground without the walls, which are entirely cultivated by patients. On our visit to this establishment (in September, 1842), a number varying from sixteen to twenty-six were thus employed, and a considerable proportion of the other patients were occupied in various ways, and always, according to the superintending physician's report, with beneficial effect.

Deficiency in respect of employment, &c. in many Asylums ;

But, in a considerable number of asylums, (not excepting even some of the county asylums) there is a great deficiency in respect to employment, and this deprives the lunatic of his fair chance of that benefit which these establishments were intended to afford. It appears to us that no means of cure or relief should be left unattempted, in hospitals where the professed object is to restore to health all who are still susceptible of cure, and to relieve those who are incurable, as far as is practicable.

West Auckland;

At the West Auckland Asylum, there was at our first visit only one, and there are now only two very small yards, (each measuring about twelve yards wide by thirteen yards long) for the thirty-one patients confined there. There is, indeed, half an acre of garden ground, and six acres of grass land, but these are available only at certain seasons of the year for the purpose of employing the male patients. Very little exertion appears to be made at this asylum for the employment of any of the patients. They were all, with the exception of one, unoccupied when we visited the place in August, 1843. We saw no books, and no means of amusement.

At St. Peter's Hospital, in Bristol, the only place where the female patients, forty in number, can take exercise, is a small passage or paved yard at one end of the hospital. It is, in fact, part of a lane or road, and is the only road through which carts and other carriages have access to the house. Upon the approach and return of every vehicle, the female patients are removed into the House, in order that the gates at each end of the road may be opened. It is right to state that every exertion has been used to render the place commodious, but this, from want of space, is quite impracticable. St. Peter's Hospital, Bristol;

At the Hilsea Asylum near Portsmouth, containing, in June, 1843 twenty-nine patients, there is one yard of tolerable size, for the male patients, adjoining the high road, and a small one at the back of the house, which appears, from its being overgrown with grass, to be little used, for the women. We could not ascertain that any of the patients occupied themselves, with the exception of two or three of the women, who, we understood, were occasionally employed in needle and household work. Hilsea Asylum;

At the Leicester County Asylum, in which there were, in August, 1842, 117 patients, there are only three acres used as garden ground and pasture, besides the yards attached to the buildings, which last are inclosed within high walls. Leicester County Asylum;

At the Nottingham County Asylum, in which there were, in Oct. 1842, 159 patients, there are good Nottingham County Asylum;

yards; but the premises are nearly surrounded by adjacent buildings, and there are only a small garden and three acres of land (rented) to afford employment for the patients. Every endeavour, however, which the space will allow, is made to occupy them.

Norfolk County Asylum; At the Norfolk County Asylum, which contained, in August, 1842, 165 patients, there are less than five acres of ground, including the sites of the buildings.

Haverfordwest Asylum; At the Haverfordwest Asylum, in the county of Pembroke, which contained eighteen patients (in September, 1842) there was no place for exercise, except two small yards, surrounded by walls; and there was neither garden, pleasure-ground, nor field, to afford any opportunity whatsoever for the patients to employ themselves. There were no books, nor any means of amusement. The consequence was, that every patient in the Asylum was listless and unoccupied. Most of these, however, were apparently incurable.

Hoxton House; At Hoxton House, containing nearly 400 patients, of both sexes, there are only yards—some of them, indeed, not deficient in space, but surrounded by high walls, and (partly) by adjacent buildings,—for the purpose of exercise. Being in the suburbs of London, there are no means, of course, except at a very great expense, of obtaining any considerable quantity of additional ground.

Lancaster Asylum; The land immediately attached to the Lancaster Asylum, where there were, in October, 1842, 621 patients, then, and until recently consisted, of five statute acres, including the sites of the buildings and offices. There were also ten acres (separated from the Asylum by a public road), which are cultivated as a farm; but the entire quantity of land was quite inadequate to provide sufficient employment for so large a number of patients, many of whom belong to the agricultural class. This caused a considerable proportion of them to remain unoccupied. * The superintendent, appears to use his best endeavours to promote in-door employment, in the shape of plaiting, straw, household work, and the exercise of various trades.

At the Asylum, called the Refuge, near Hull, in which there were (in September, 1842) 100 patients, there are only yards of moderate dimensions for exercise. The proprietor has no land for agricultural purposes; but there is a garden of some extent, in which the patients (the males and females alternately) take daily exercise, when the weather will permit. Refuge, near Hull;

The Devonport Workhouse, situate in the poorest and most populous part of Devonport, with narrow streets and high adjoining buildings on every side, is licensed as an Asylum for lunatics. But there is only a very small paved yard, in which the patients, amounting to twenty-three, can take exercise. It is quite insufficient for the purpose. The lunatic wards, however, in this establishment, appeared to us to be under excellent management. Devonport Workhouse;

At the Asylum at Duddeston (near Birmingham), there are extensive grounds, but the pauper lunatics, amounting to 60, (in January, 1844), are generally (if not always) confined within very small yards, quite insufficient for the purpose of exercise. Asylum at Duddeston;

The Bailbrook Asylum, near Bath, is situate on an eminence, but it is without the means of affording out-of-door labour to the patients, amounting to 94 in number, and almost all of the poorer class.—The yards at Kingsdown Asylum, near Box, in Wiltshire, where there is a large body of pauper lunatics, are small and bad, and quite insufficient for the purpose of exercise. Bailbrook Asylum.

We have selected the foregoing instances, in order to General remarks.

* The County Magistrates, as has been elsewhere stated, have lately added 30 acres to the Asylum, by purchase, under the powers of a Local Act.

show the nature of the defects inherent in several of the Asylums; and in order also that previously to the future erection of any establishments (especially public Asylums), the subject may receive fair and full consideration. We are fully satisfied of the great value of occupation to the lunatic, and we think that no public Asylum should be sanctioned without first ascertaining that ample space exists, and that proper arrangements will be made, for carrying this desirable object into complete effect.

Insufficient provision for exercise in Workhouses.

We have not here animadverted upon the small space afforded to lunatics, for the purposes of exercise, in the various Workhouses wherein they are confined. In the Workhouse situate in the middle of the town of Birmingham, there were, in September, 1843, seventy-one insane patients of both sexes, and the only place allotted to eighteen of the females, was a yard, common to them and the other inmates of the Workhouse, in which they were permitted to walk from ten till eleven o'clock in the morning, and from three to four in the afternoon. The remainder of the patients, fifty-three in number (nearly thirty-three males and twenty females), took exercise in a confined court or yard, not more than sixty-six feet long by forty-five in width; one corner (twenty-three feet by twenty) being railed off for the females. Both yards are surrounded by high buildings. In the other unlicensed Workhouses which we have seen, the space for exercise assigned to Insane poor, is generally less in proportion to their numbers, even than in those Licensed Houses to which we have adverted, as especially deficient in this respect.

V.

RESTRAINT.

——◆——

WE are directed by the Act 5 & 6 Vic. c. 87, to inquire in every Licensed House whether any patient is under restraint, and why ; and to report whether there has been adopted, either in the whole or in part, any system of non-coercion, and the result thereof. By section 32, a similar report is required to be made as to every county Lunatic Asylum.

In every licensed house and county Lunatic Asylum; and also in every public hospital, and other place containing insane persons, which we have visited, we have made minute inquiries as to the particulars of every person found under restraint, and as to the system adopted in the establishment in this respect.

In some Asylums, both public and private, the superintendents and proprietors state that they manage their patients without having recourse to any kind of restraint whatever. In other Asylums, it is affirmed that the disuse of restraint is their rule and system, and that its use, in cases of necessity or expediency, forms the exception to the rule. Those who profess the entire disuse of restraint, employ manual force and seclusion as parts of their method of management, maintaining that such measures are consistent with a system of non-restraint. It is said by these persons that when any of the limbs (as the legs or hands of a patient) are confined by the strait-jacket, the belt, or by straps or gloves, he is under restraint. But in cases where he is held by the hands of attendants, or when he is for any excitement or violence forced by manual strength into a small chamber or cell, and left there, it is said that

General remarks on the use or disuse of restraint.

restraint is not employed, and the method adopted
in these cases, is called " the non-restraint system."
In those cases where the patient is overpowered by
a number of keepers holding his hands or arms during
a paroxysm of violence, it is said that there is no
mechanical restraint. Here restraint of some sort or
other is manifest; and even in those cases where the
patient is forced into a cell by manual strength, and
prevented from leaving it until his fit of excitement shall
have passed, it is difficult to understand how this also
can be reconciled with the profession of abstaining from
all restraint whatever, so as to be correctly termed 'Non-
restraint.' It seems to us that these measures are only
particular modes of restraint, the relative advantages of
which must depend altogether on the results.—The advocates of these two systems, to which we have called your
Lordship's attention, appear to have been actuated by a
common desire to improve the condition of the insane.
Those who employ, as well as those who do not employ
mechanical restraint, adopt an equally mild and conciliatory method of managing their Patients. The usual
forms of mechanical restraint are strong dresses, strait-
waistcoats, gloves, straps or belts made of linen-cloth or
leather.

The Retreat, at York. The Retreat, at York, was established in the year
1796, and introduced a milder system of managing the
insane, than any then previously practised. This ad-
mirable institution has from its foundation up to the present time steadily pursued the same humane and benevolent method of treating its patients with which it
commenced, and Mr. Samuel Tuke, so well known in
connexion with this Asylum, and who accompanied us
in going over it, said that no considerable change in
regard to the system in use at the Retreat had recently taken place.

Attention of Commissioners directed to abo- In the year 1828, the licensing and visiting of Houses
for the reception of the Insane in the Metropolitan dis-

trict was entrusted to this Commission; and we have since that period constantly directed our attention to procure the abolition of restraint, in all cases in which we have considered that its use could be avoided with benefit, and without danger, and to its modification and diminution in those cases in which we have thought it to be still necessary.

Whatever may be the means or forms of control exercised over the persons of patients, or whatever the degrees in which the application of this control may be varied in different Asylums, we have the gratification of reporting to your Lordship that in every public and private Asylum in the kingdom, which is well managed, bodily restraint is not permitted, except in extreme cases, and under the express sanction of a competent' superintendent. The unanimous opinion of the medical officers and superintendents of these public and private Asylums is, that the diminution of restraint in the treatment of lunatics has not only lessened the sufferings, but has improved the general health and condition, as well as promoted the comfort of the insane. We entirely concur in this opinion. Bodily restraint not permitted in well-managed Asylums, except in extreme cases.

Before noticing the distinctions that we have found in the different public and well-conducted Asylums, upon the subject of restraint, we feel it to be our duty to direct your attention to that excessive and highly censurable degree of restraint, which we found in practice at the licensed Asylums at West Auckland, Wreckenton, Lainston, Plympton, Box, Nunkeeling, and some other houses which we have elsewhere made the subject of especial notice. In' the present state of some of these establishments, restraint is rendered more necessary than in a well-constructed Asylum, but all such places are, in our opinion, unfit for the proper care of the insane. With respect to these Asylums, in which the restraint in use has been so improper and unjustifiable, we hope that the day is not distant when Censurable restraint practised in certain Asylums.

they will either wholly cease to be licensed for the reception of insane persons, or will be put upon an entirely improved system in this and in other respects.

Results of the non-restraint system.

The non-restraint system* appears to have been established at Lincoln in 1838, and to have been adopted at Hanwell in 1839, and at Lancaster in 1840. The same system has been in operation for some years in the Suffolk Asylum, and is now in practice at Gloucester, and has been pursued at Northampton from its opening in 1838; and at the Haslar Hospital it had been in operation fifteen months at our visit in 1843. The superintendents of these Asylums have all steadily pursued this system since its introduction, and, as they consider, with great advantage to their patients; but they still think that it is necessary to restrain the limbs during surgical operations. We found the Asylums at Gloucester, Lancaster, Northampton, and Haslar, very well managed, and their patients tranquil and comfortable and the superintendents of these Establishments, consider that the comfort of the patients, and the general condition of the Asylums, have been improved since the adoption of this system. No inconveniences whatever have been experienced at Gloucester or Northampton. In the year ending the 30th of June, 1842, there were four deaths by suicide at the Lancaster Asylum. The superintendent of this Asylum has stated that had mechanical restraint been in practice in the Asylum, it would not have been resorted to in any of these cases, and that these lamentable events are not fairly to be attributed to the absence of such restraint. The present Medical Officers at the Lancaster Asylum have carried out the system of non-restraint to its fullest extent. By every expression of kindness, by appearing to sympathise in the patient's imaginary

---

* By the non-restraint system is understood the system which does not employ restraint, by dresses, gloves, belts, or other similar contrivances.

sufferings, and by taking a deep interest in all his concerns, they endeavour to soothe morbid irritation, and thus allow an opportunity of restoring the healthy action of the mind. By this method, in several recent cases the Superintendent has been successful in curing the disease, or at all events in preparing the frame for the reception, and favourable operation of medicines, and other means calculated to promote a cure. We found unusual excitement prevailing in the disorderly ward on the female side of the Asylum at Lincoln ; and in one of our visits to Hanwell and at both our visits to the Suffolk Asylum, we witnessed, amongst the worst class of females, outbreaks of violence and excitement, which we have not met with elsewhere. At the Lincoln Asylum, a register of accidents and bruises, &c., is kept, which seem frequent.

The system of non-restraint at Hanwell has been carried on by mild and kind treatment of the patients, by an increase in the numbers of attendants, and by adopting seclusion or solitary confinement, sometimes in darkened cells, in lieu of mechanical restraint. At our visit to this Asylum in 1843, there was no patient under mechanical restraint ; but we saw a violent female lunatic, who had been endeavouring to bite other persons as well as herself, seized by four or five of the nurses, and after a violent and protracted struggle, forced with great difficulty into, and fastened in, one of the cells. During this scene, there was much confusion in the ward, and the great efforts of the patient to liberate herself, and (after her seclusion) the violence with which she struck the door of the cell, and threw herself against it, must have greatly exhausted her. In another case, a female, secluded in a darkened cell, had contrived to tear off considerable quantities of a woollen rug, which she formed into balls and swallowed ; one of these stuck in her throat, and, but for prompt assistance, accidentally rendered at our visit, she might have been suffocated.

System at Hanwell.

In another case, a female patient rushed against an elderly female with all her weight, striking her at the same time violently on the loins, and precipitating her forwards. The person thus struck, being quite unaware of the attack, fell forwards on her head and neck in such a way as to cause apprehension lest a dislocation of the neck might have taken place; fortunately she did not receive any serious damage. Another woman was seen by us with the skin of her arm torn nearly from the wrist to the elbow, and bleeding from a severe cut which she had just received, by thrusting it through the window of the cell in which she was confined. Besides these acts of violence, we observed on the bodies of several other patients various cuts and bruises, which we were told had been inflicted by their insane companions, and which we rarely meet with in other Asylums. During the short interval between the first and last days of our visit to this Asylum in June, 1843, one of the male patients was killed by another.— On our visit to Hanwell in the year 1844, we found the Asylum in good order, and the patients, with one or two exceptions, tranquil and comfortable ; and not one under mechanical restraint.

The Suffolk Asylum.

In the Suffolk Asylum, the patients, with the exception of those of the worst class of females, were tranquil. At our first visit, however, in the ward occupied by refractory females, and in the airing-court attached to it, there were a great number of violently-excited patients, who attacked, abused, and struck at the other patients, and rendered the whole place a scene of distressing turbulence and confusion. At our second visit, the matron expressed a fear of the consequences, in the event of our going into the female refractory yard. We found some of the Patients half naked, from having destroyed their clothes ; one was, during the whole time we were in the yard, struggling with a nurse ; two of the most violent were removed from the yard before we entered it, and the fury of those who remained was excessive.

We do not offer any opinion as to whether the acts of excitement and violence which we met with in the Lincoln, Hanwell, and Suffolk Asylums, were the result of mechanical restraint being dispensed with. It is to be observed, that at the Lincoln and Suffolk Asylums, there is a great want of proper classification, to which the scenes which we witnessed were no doubt partly to be attributed.

Want of classification may lead to excitement and violence.

With respect to the public Hospitals and County Asylums which still occasionally employ mechanical restraint, we found the following numbers of persons under such restraint at the periods of our visits.

Tabular view of numbers under restraint at Commissioners' visits to Public and County Asylums.

PUBLIC HOSPITALS AND COUNTY ASYLUMS USING MECHANICAL RESTRAINT.

Hospitals.	Number Confined.	Numbers under restraint.	Hospitals.	Numbers confined.	Numbers under restraint.
Retreat, at York .	99	0	Radcliffe . . .	42	0
York Asylum .	159	1	Liverpool . . .	73	1
St. Luke's . .	222	1	Exeter	48	1

County Asylums.	Numbers confined.	Numbers restrained.	County Asylums.	Numbers confined.	Numbers restrained.
Bedford	140	4	Nottingham . .	159	0
Chester	157	1	Norfolk	164	0
Cornwall . . .	147	0	Stafford	244	1
Dorset	105	0	Surrey	344	1
Kent	253	1	Wakefield . . .	398	10
Leicester . . .	114	2			

At the Retreat, at York, at our first visit, one female was under restraint. She was sitting at table dining with the other patients, and had only one hand confined. Another patient was secluded in a room. At our second visit, no one was under mechanical restraint, and there had been no one so restrained for nine months. We

Case of restraint at the Retreat, York.

found the patients in the Retreat tranquil, cheerful, and clean, and apparently enjoying every comfort of which they were capable.

System of Restraint at York Asylum, &c.

The York Asylum, the Hospital of St. Luke, the Radcliffe (now the Warneford) Asylum), and the Asylums at Liverpool and Exeter, have for many years pursued a mild system of treatment, and have not resorted to restraint except in cases of emergency, and under medical authority. Some of these Hospitals are more commodious and have better accommodations and conveniences than others, but in all of them we found the patients kindly and judiciously treated, and, as far as their circumstances would admit, comfortable.

Practice pursued in County Asylums.

In the County Asylums, in which mechanical restraint is still occasionally resorted to, the system pursued is that of dispensing with it in every case, unless either the cure, or the security of the patient, or others, is considered to render it necessary. The single patient found under restraint at the Chester Asylum was a most violent and dangerous maniac, who had been convicted of murder, and would, if at liberty, instantly attack any person near him, in the most savage manner. The only person under restraint at the Kent Asylum, in which was a large proportion of most violent female patients was a powerful and dangerous man, who is disposed to strike and injure the other patients, and especially those who are not so strong as himself. At the Nottingham Asylum, when visited in 1843, no restraint had been used during the previous year, except in four cases, for surgical purposes. We have in general found the patients confined in these Asylums tranquil and comfortable. At the Wakefield Asylum there were ten patients under restraint. This may be considered a large number: this Asylum, however, is in general very well conducted.

Restraint in Licensed Houses.

We feel that it is more difficult for us to convey to your Lordship an accurate view of the state of licensed houses, than of public Hospitals and County Asylums in respect to the subject of restraint. There are ninety-nine licensed houses in the provincial districts, of which thirty-nine receive paupers; and forty-three licensed houses in the Metropolitan district, of which four admit paupers. At the licensed houses at Denham-Park and Fairford, restraint is stated not to be employed, under any circumstances; and these houses are both well managed. We were, however, sorry to see a female, in 1843, at Fairford, permitted to gnaw her fingers into sores. The proprietors of almost all the best-managed Asylums for private patients, in the provincial and Metropolitan districts, employ restraint only in extreme cases. Although we believe that the two houses above-mentioned, are nearly the only Licensed Houses in which mechanical restraint is entirely suppressed, yet out of 60 Houses receiving only Private Patients in the Provincial Districts, we found, in 37 that there was not one person, and in 15 only one person in each, under restraint. In the Metropolitan District at our last visit in the year 1843, out of 32 houses receiving only Private Patients, in 22 there was not one, and in 6 we found only one under restraint. At the White and Red Houses of Dr. Warburton, at Bethnal Green (the one for males and the other for females) there are 575 patients, the larger part of whom are paupers, and many of the females are of the worst and most hopeless and violent class. In these houses, we seldom find more than one or two persons under bodily restraint, and in four out of our last eight visits, not one. At Hoxton, containing upwards of 400 patients, there are frequently eight or ten persons restrained: but in the present defective accommodations of this house more restraint is employed than would be necessary in a well-constructed Asylum.

Those who profess wholly, and those who profess in part only, to dispense with restraint, employ seclusion or solitary confinement; but the former resort to and advo- *Seclusion or solitary confinement.*

cate this mode of treatment more extensively than the latter. Seclusion or solitary confinement is now getting into general use in the treatment of the insane, and great numbers of the superintendents of public, and of the proprietors of private Asylums throughout the country are fitting up and bringing into use solitary cells, and padded rooms for violent and unmanageable Lunatics. Lincoln Asylum is the only place in which even seclusion is not resorted to. Seclusion (or solitary confinement) is found to have a very powerful effect in tranquillising, and subduing those who are under temporary excitement or paroxysms of violent insanity. As solitary confinement is coming into more general use, as a remedy in Asylums, and as persons who have been subjected to its operation for long periods, have become insane, we feel that we ought to notice the practice so far as it may be employed in the treatment of lunatics. As a temporary remedy, for very short periods, in cases of paroxysms and of high excitement, we believe seclusion to be a valuable remedy. We are convinced, however, that it ought to be used only for short periods, and that it should not be permitted as a means of managing and treating those persons who are permanently violent and dangerous. Long solitary confinement of any person in a cell, is calculated to destroy his bodily health.

Register should be kept where solitary confinement employed.

If solitary confinement is to be employed in Asylums, every institution, whether public or private, which uses it, should be required to keep a register of every person who shall be in such confinement, and of the duration of every separate term of confinement. If it has been deemed necessary by the legislature to require a register of restraint, it is equally necessary, in our opinion, to have a register of seclusion or solitary confinement, which is more liable to abuse, and less capable of detection, than those means of bodily coercion, which are visible, and are in ordinary use. At Hanwell this precaution has been wisely adopted, and was found in practice at our last visit, being required by the printed rules of the Asylum. It is obvious that seclusion, or confinement, with the limbs all at liberty, is not a protection against the indulgence of certain dirty and disgusting practices, which are very injurious and not uncommon, but very difficult to overcome in the insane. Mechanical restraint has succeeded in some, but by no means in all cases, in removing them. At the Middlesex Asylum, it has been attempted to defeat dirty habits by the administering of aperients. At the Lancaster Asylum, good effects have been produced in obviating, and in many cases in entirely removing, such habits, by assiduously endeavouring to invite due attention to the calls of nature. Dirty habits.

With a view to lessen the necessity for bodily coercion, we have enjoined, in the Metropolitan district, the division of patients into classes, and the separation of those, whose habits or temporary excitement render them dangerous, from others who are inoffensive; we have also urged an increase of attendants on the former classes. We have further recommended the erection of separate rooms for the temporary seclusion, during short periods only, of those who are subject to paroxysms of excitement or violence. Means employed in Metropolitan district to obviate restraint.

In the month of July last, we found, at Whitmore House, a gentleman sitting in a room with a number of other patients, who had a short time previous bitten the hand of one of the attendants, so as to cause serious apprehensions that it would have been necessary to amputate the arm. This patient had been secluded in a padded room some portion of the day on which we saw him, and at the time of our visit was unrestrained, but under the watch of two keepers, who were in the apartment for that purpose. The medical superintendent and keeper both stated that notwithstanding the precautions then in use, they were appre- Danger of total disuse of mechanical restraint, illustrated by cases.

hensive of a similar injury being inflicted by him upon some other patient or attendant; but in deference to the popular opinion on the subject, they did not apply mechanical restraint, although they thought that it was necessary. We recommended that bodily restraint should be employed. Shortly after giving this recommendation, we found at the Asylum of Mr. Scales, near Portsmouth, the widow of a former superintendent, whose hand had a few months previous been bitten by a dangerous patient, who was in the house at the time of our visit. The superintendent died from the effects of the bite, within twelve days after the injury. In the County Asylum, at Bodmin, we found two patients, one of whom had lost an arm, and another a thumb from amputation, in consequence of the bites of other patients.

In the Asylum for the county of Dorset, we found a patient whose suicidal propensities were so determined that he had once attempted to drown himself, twice to hang himself, once to cut his throat, and also to choke himself by thrusting his sheets down his throat, and to strangle himself by twisting his handkerchief round his neck. The restraint of muffs was resorted to; and, although previously restless and trying continually to get out of bed, this person began to sleep comfortably, and was, when we saw him, tranquil and apparently convalescent. Restraint had only been used in six cases in this Asylum during twelve months. The particulars of four of these cases are unfit for publication. Of these six cases, three had been discharged cured, and another was recovering.

At Great Foster House, near Egham, a gentleman had been brought to the house in a state of violent excitement. For seven successive nights he had no bodily restraint, but had two attendants in his bed room, and neither he nor they had had any sleep. He was continually getting out of bed and struggling with the attendants. The attempt to do without bodily restraint had been carried to this extent, in some degree, in deference to the popular opinion, but it was then thought right not to continue it any longer; and on the eighth night muffs were put on the patient, and he soon after fell asleep, and slept throughout the night. On the next night, he recommenced his violence, but the muffs being produced, he became tranquil and went to sleep, without its being necessary to put them on. This gentleman was discharged much improved, but not cured. The superintendent stated his opinion to be, that the struggling with the attendants irritated, but the application of the muffs tranquillized the patient.

The proprietor of the Asylum at Fish Ponds, near Bristol, stated that he believed that a patient in his house recovered entirely owing to his having bodily restraint. He had been previously watched by attendants. and was very much excited by it; when put under such restraint he fell asleep and gradually became tranquil.— The same good effect was produced, at Mr. Taylor's Asylum, near Bristol, on a female Patient, who was exceedingly irritated at being watched, but became quiet when placed under some slight mechanical restraint. —At Moorcroft House, Hillingdon, a patient was continually striking himself with great violence, and we were informed would have produced serious, if not fatal injuries, unless he had been restrained.—In the Bethnal Green Asylum, a male patient, with dangerous propensities, was allowed to go unrestrained, and during this period assaulted a keeper, and kicked him so violently in the abdomen, that an abscess ensued, and the keeper was for some time in danger of losing his life.—At Northumberland House Asylum, a powerful maniac, one of whose hands it is now considered advisable to restrain by a strap, was permitted to go at large, during which period he struck the pointed end of a pair of snuffers into a keeper's head, and endangered his life.—We have, at different times, received numerous assurances that the use of mild mechanical restraint has had the effect of making the Patients tranquil and comfortable.

Remarks on the practice of restraint.

It is possible, that cases such as those which we have instanced, may be managed without mechanical restraint. The question, however, in which the humane and intelligent medical practitioner is interested, is not whether it be possible, but whether it be preferable,' in all cases, to dispense with such restraint altogether, and to substitute, in its stead, manual coercion and solitary confinement. It is necessary to observe, that a system of management which may be eligible under some circumstances, may not be equally so under others. That which may be practicable in large Asylums, may not be feasible in smaller Establishments. These and other circumstances must be taken into consideration, in estimating the practicability of adopting or rejecting a system, entirely interdicting the use of mechanical restraint.

Additional expense for Paupers in Private Asylums, if restraint dispensed with.

In Private Asylums which receive paupers, if it be desired that the Visitors shall require an entire absence of mechanical restraint, the public must be prepared to pay an additional sum for their care and maintenance of the patients, otherwise they must either suffer long-continued solitary seclusion, which will destroy their health, or the attendants and other patients will be exposed to constant peril.

Safety of attendants endangered by absence of restraint.

Attention to the safety and comfort of Attendants is a very important part of the duty of the proprietors of Asylums for the insane. It is a great object to secure the services of respectable and superior persons as attendants and nurses; but if such persons are to be induced to take charge of the insane, it is necessary to assure them that they are not to lead a life of ceaseless anxiety and to be in continual apprehension of violence.

On visiting the Asylum of Mr. Phillips, at Devizes, we found that there were 153 patients in the House, and that one woman only was restrained, who had just been quarrelling with some other patients. In the yard where she was, and which contained the worst class of females, there were more than twenty most violent and dangerous women, who, but for the presence of two experienced and very clever nurses, would probably have injured each other. Whilst we were taking down the names of the patients, in one of the men's yards, an athletic male Patient suddenly came up and struck the resident medical attendant a blow on the head, with all his force. Another keeper was sent for, and, with our sanction, a strap was put round the man's body, and one of his hands was fastened to it.

Within the last few weeks, at Dr. Philp's House, at Kensington, the male patients had all been taken out to walk in the garden. A very powerful and dangerous male patient asked permission of the attendant to go into the house, to the closet. In a minute or two, shrieks were heard, and upon the servants rushing into the house, they found that he had seen the matron at a window, (who, in the absence of the patients, had gone to look over the men's rooms,) had attacked her in the most savage manner, and had knocked out seven of her teeth, and otherwise severely injured her. Her life was for some time afterwards in imminent danger.

To these must be added the cases, already mentioned, of the superintendent at Hilsea, and of the attendants at Whitmore House and Bethnal Green.

The mild system now adopted in all the county Asylums which do not profess to do entirely without restraint, has required the employment of an increased number of attendants and nurses. In some of these Establishments, it is considered that, although the comfort of the patients has been promoted, the attendants have been subjected to greater risks, by the diminution of restraint. In order, however, to carry into effect, with perfect safety to the patients and attendants, a

Additional number of attendants and nurses required by adoption of mild system.

system of entire abstinence from bodily or mechanical restraint, there ought to be a greater number of yards than some Asylums, such as those of Lincoln, Suffolk, and Hanwell, possess, in proportion to the numbers of their patients. In Hanwell, for instance, the yards, which are of triangular shape, are comparatively small, measuring about 195 feet at the sides, and 120 at the base. One of these yards is open to two wards containing 90, another to four wards containing 197, and a third to five wards containing 124 patients. If, instead of only 30, there were a large number of curable and recent cases in this Asylum, we think that, with the present accommodations, even more attendants than are now employed would be absolutely necessary. Any additional yards must be attended with some increase of expense; but if the entire disuse of mechanical restraint, and the substitution of solitary confinement, be more humane towards the insane, and more conducive to their cure, than the use of such restraint, the increase of expense will assuredly not be considered a sufficient justification for its continuance. Magistrates, however, before they decide upon adopting a system of managing their pauper lunatics, which will necessarily impose a considerable additional expense upon parishes and counties, will, of course, previously satisfy themselves that the advantages to be derived from it are real and sufficient to justify the additional cost.

Opinions of Medical Superintendents of Asylums on restraint.

During our visits to the different Asylums, we have endeavoured to ascertain the opinions of their Medical Superintendents in reference to the subject of restraint; and we will now state, in general terms, the result of our inquiries. Of the Superintendents of Asylums not employing mechanical restraint, those of the Hospitals of Lincoln, Northampton, and Haslar, and of the County Asylum at Hanwell, appear to consider that it is not necessary or advisable to resort to it in any case whatever, except for surgical purposes. On the other hand, the Superintendent at Lancaster hesitates in giving an opinion decidedly in favour of the non-restraint system : he thinks that although much may be done without mechanical restraint of any kind, there are occasionally cases in which it may not only be necessary, but beneficial. The Superintendent of the Suffolk Asylum considers that in certain cases, and more especially in a crowded and imperfectly constructed Asylum, like the one under his charge, mechanical restraint, judiciously applied, might be preferable to any other species of coercion, as being both less irritating and more effectual.—The Superintendent of the Gloucester Asylum states that he has adopted the disuse of mechanical restraint, upon the conviction which his experience has given him during a trial of nearly three years.— Of the Superintendents of Asylums who employ mechanical restraint, those of the Retreat at York, of the Warneford Asylum, and of the Hospitals at Exeter, Manchester, Liverpool, and of St. Luke's, consider that although the cases are extremely rare in which mechanical restraint should be applied, it is, in some instances, necessary. Similar opinions are entertained by the Superintendents of the County Asylums of Bedford, Chester, Cornwall, Dorset, Kent, Norfolk, Nottingham, Leicester, Stafford, and the West Riding of York.— At the Retreat at York, mechanical or personal restraint has been always regarded as a "necessary evil," but it has not been thought right to dispense with the use of a mild and protecting personal restraint, believing that, independent of all consideration for the safety of the attendants, and of the Patients themselves, it may in many cases be regarded as the least irritating, and therefore the kindest method of control. Eight of the Superintendents employing bodily restraint have stated their opinion to be that it is in some cases beneficial as well as necessary, and valuable as a precaution, and a remedial agent; and three of them have stated that they consider it less irritating than holding with the hands, and one of them prefers it to seclusion.

Practice in Houses receiving only Private Patients. In all the Houses receiving only private Patients, restraint is considered to be occasionally necessary. In the large and very well conducted Houses, where the Proprietors are persons of great experience, and where they have every means of separating and managing their Patients, and have large numbers of attendants and nurses, the application of restraint is considered at times not only necessary, but beneficial to the Patient. In several instances, Patients have been named to us who, apprehensive of their attacks coming on, have requested to be restrained for their own security. At the Cornwall Asylum, we found a man who voluntarily wrapped his arm round with bands of cloth from the fear of striking others. He untied the cloth himself at our request. We know the case of one lady, who goes home when she is convalescent, but voluntarily returns to the Asylum, when she perceives that her periodical attacks of Insanity are about to return, in order that she may be placed under some restraint.

We have thus endeavoured to state with accuracy the difference between the methods of treatment adopted by those who wholly disuse, and those who occasionally employ mechanical restraint; the condition in which we have found the Public Hospitals, County Asylums, and Licensed Houses which are conducted according to these systems; and lastly, the opinions which have been expressed to us by the Medical Superintendents of these Institutions, as to the employment or disuse of mechanical restraint. We have explained to your Lordship that, in our visitations to Lunatic Asylums, we have witnessed, without remonstrance, such measures of mechanical restraint as, in the opinion of the Superintendents, sufficed to prevent dangerous or disgusting propensities, when assured that it was deemed necessary in the one case and expedient in the other; and that we have, in more than one instance, recommended the application of some mechanical restraint in cases of extreme violence, when the Medical Superintendent has told us that he scrupled to use it, out of deference to what he considered to be the public opinion upon the subject, although he thought it necessary.

Of the Asylums entirely disusing restraint, in some of them, as we have stated, the patients have been found tranquil and comfortable, and in others they have been unusually excited and disturbed. Without, however, attaching undue importance to the condition of the Asylums at the time of our visits, or to accidents that may happen under any system of managing the Insane, it is nevertheless our duty to call your Lordship's attention to the fact, that since the Autumn of 1842 a Patient and a Superintendent have been killed; a Matron has been so seriously injured that her life was considered to be in imminent danger; another Superintendent has been so bitten as to cause serious apprehensions that his arm must have been amputated; and two keepers have been injured so as to endanger their lives. These fatal and serious injuries and accidents have been caused by dangerous patients, and some of them in Asylums where either the system of non-coercion is voluntarily practised, or is adopted in deference to public opinion.

Having stated, in general terms, the opinions prevailing in the principal Asylums, for and against the system of absolute non-coercion; it may be desirable, with the view of enabling your Lordship to judge more accurately of the value of each, to add the reasons (as far as we have been able to collect them) which the several advocates adduce, for adopting or continuing their respective modes of managing or controlling the Insane.

Arguments of Medical Officers and Superintendents advocating absolute non-coercion.

The Medical Officers and Superintendents who adhere to the system of absolute non-coercion, never using mechanical restraint, even in cases of extreme violence, argue—

1st. That their practice is the most humane, and most beneficial to the Patient; soothing instead of coercing him during irritation; and encouraging him when tranquil, to exert his faculties, in order to acquire complete self-control.

2. That a recovery thus obtained, is likely to be more permanent than if obtained by other means; and that in case of a tendency to relapse, the Patient will, of his own accord, be more likely to endeavour to resist any return of his malady.

3. That mechanical restraint has a bad moral effect that it degrades the Patient in his own opinion; that it prevents any exertion on his part; and thus impedes his recovery.

4. That experience has demonstrated the advantage of entirely abolishing restraint, inasmuch as the condition of some Asylums, where it had been previously practised in a moderate and very restricted degree, has been greatly improved, with respect to the tranquillity and the appearance of cheerfulness among the Patients in general, after all mechanical coercion has been discontinued.

5. That mechanical restraint, if used at all, is liable to great abuse from Keepers and Nurses, who will often resort to it for the sake of avoiding trouble to themselves; and who, even when well-disposed towards the Patient, are not competent to judge of the extent to which it ought to be applied.

6. That the Patient may be controlled as effectually

without mechanical restraint, as with it; and that the only requisites for enabling the Superintendents of Asylums to dispense with the use of mechanical restraint, are a greater number of Attendants, and a better system of classification amongst the Patients; and that the additional expense thereby incurred ought not to form a consideration where the comfort of the Patients is concerned.

On the other hand, the Medical and other Superintendents of Lunatic Asylums, who adopt a system of non-restraint as a general rule, but make exceptions in certain extreme cases,—urge the following reasons for occasionally using some slight coercion. They affirm—

Arguments of Medical Officers and Superintendents who admit restraint in extreme cases.

1st. That it is necessary to possess, and to acquire as soon as possible, a certain degree of authority or influence over the Patient; in order to enforce obedience to such salutary regulations as may be laid down for his benefit.

2. That, although this authority or influence is obtained in a majority of cases by kindness and persuasion, there are frequent instances where these means entirely fail. That it then becomes necessary to have recourse to other measures, and, at all events, to show the Patient that, in default of his compliance, it is in the *power* of the Superintendent to employ coercion.

3. That a judicious employment of authority mixed with kindness (and sometimes with indulgence) has been found to succeed better than any other method.

4. That the occasional use of slight mechanical restraint has, in many instances, been found to promote tranquillity by day, and rest by night.

5. That it prevents, more surely than any supervision can effect, the Patient from injuring himself or the other Patients.

6. That, particularly in large Establishments, the supervision must be trusted mainly to the attendants, who are not always to be depended on, and whose pa-

tience, in cases of protracted violence, is frequently worn out. That in such cases mild restraint ensures more completely the safety of the attendants, and contributes much to the tranquillity and comfort of the surrounding patients.

7. That in many cases mild mechanical restraint tends less to irritate, and generally less to exhaust the Patient, than the act of detaining him by manual strength, or forcing him into a place of seclusion, and leaving him at liberty to throw himself violently about for hours together.

8. That the expense of a number of attendants,—not indeed more than sufficient to restrain a Patient during a violent paroxysm, but nevertheless far beyond the ordinary exigencies of the Establishment,—is impracticable in Asylums where only a small number of Paupers are received.

9. That the occasional use of slight coercion, particularly in protracted cases, possesses this additional advantage; that it gives the Patient the opportunity of taking exercise in the open air, at times when, but for the use of it, he would necessarily be in a state of seclusion.

10. That the system of non-restraint cannot be safely carried into execution without considerable additional expense; a matter which will necessarily enter into the consideration of those who are desirous of forming a correct opinion as to the precise benefits likely to arise from the adoption or rejection of such a system.

11. That the benefit to the Patient himself, if indeed it exist at all, is not the only question ; but that it ought to be considered, whether the doubtful advantage to himself ought to be purchased by the danger to which both he and his attendants and other Patients are exposed, when restraint is altogether abolished.

And 12thly. That, when a Patient is forced into and secluded in a small room or cell, it is essentially coer-

cion, in another form and under another name; and
that it is attended with quite as bad a moral effect, as
any that can arise from mechanical restraint.

VI.

RELIGIOUS SERVICES.

In respect to Devotional Exercises, and Religious Instruction, we have the satisfaction of reporting to your Lordship, that proper attention appears to be very generally paid by the Proprietors and Superintendents of Asylums to these important duties; that the service of the Church is, for the most part, regularly performed every Sunday; and that Prayers are, in many cases, read on other days of the week, where there are Patients in a condition to benefit by them. We may state also, as the result of our inquiries, that the effect is tranquillizing, and productive of good order and decorum, in a remarkable degree, and in some instances permanently beneficial.

Proper attention generally paid to religious observances.

The Patients are said frequently to look forward to the service with pleasure, and to consider exclusion from it as a privation.—Considering Religious Exercises in Lunatic Asylums merely as medical aids, and conducive to good order, they are of most important use. So long, at least, as the Service lasts, they occupy the Patient's mind, and set before him an example of quiet and decorum. The Prayers of the Church are eminently calculated to produce a soothing influence upon even the insane hearer. Instances of misconduct or disturbance are said to be very rare; and when they do occur they seem to produce much less effect upon the other Patients present than they would do upon persons not

Effect on Patients.

accustomed, as the inmates of a Lunatic Asylum are, to scenes of noise and confusion, and to the occurrence of epileptic fits, or maniacal paroxysms, from day to day.

Difference of opinion among Medical Officers, &c.

In the opinion above expressed as to the tranquillising effect of Religious Exercises,—the Medical Officers and Superintendents of Asylums—with whom we have conversed, are, almost without exception, agreed; they differ, however, somewhat, in their views with respect to any permanent or lasting benefit being produced thereby upon the minds of the Patients. The experience and observation of many Superintendents have led them to the conclusion that the temporary effect ceases with its cause; and that after the conclusion of the Service, little or no trace is left of its soothing influence. They all concur in saying that Religious Instruction injudiciously imparted, and Controversial Discourses, are positively injurious.

Appointment of Chaplains desirable.

Without entering into the question whether or not Religious Exercises are of greater or more lasting benefit to the Patient than is commonly attributed to them, it is, we think, desirable, when practicable, to procure the assistance of the Incumbent of the Parish, or of a Clergyman in the neighbourhood, who should visit the Asylum regularly, in the capacity of a Chaplain, and who should be required to enter minutes of his visits in a book to be kept for that purpose; and that entry should be made of the number of Patients attending Prayers, from time to time.

Practice adopted at various Asylums.

We have found, in some instances, that the Proprietor of the Asylum, or one of his Superintendents, or Keepers, or even one of the Patients, has been the only person in the habit of reading the Church Service, or other Prayers, to the Inmates. In one House (at Box) a Patient, obviously Lunatic, was permitted to exhort his fellow-Patients every Sunday, in reference to their Religious Duties, in an extemporaneous address. In other places, a Keeper or Nurse (without any apparent qualifications for rendering the subject as impressive as it ought to be) has been the only person delegated to read the service to the assembled Patients.

The Proprietors of some Private Asylums have made arrangements, such as those to which we have adverted, with the Clergy in their respective neighbourhoods. At Gateshead Fell Asylum, the Rector of the Parish attends once in a month, on Sunday evenings, and performs Divine Service, which is read on the intermediate Sundays by the Proprietor. At Nunkeeling, the Incumbent of a neighbouring Parish has recently been licensed as Chaplain to the Asylum; and at Gate Helmsley, a Clergyman from an adjoining Parish attends regularly every Wednesday, and reads the Evening Service, and delivers a short discourse to the Male and Female Patients assembled together. He also visits the sick. Similar arrangements have for some years been in operation in some of the larger Houses within the Metropolitan District. We adduce these cases, to which we might add others, as examples of those arrangements made voluntarily by Proprietors of Asylums, which we think desirable, wherever there are any considerable number of Patients capable of benefiting by the assistance of a Clergyman.

We will now briefly notice the County and other Public Asylums; in the first of which we found, with one exception, Chaplains appointed, or the duties performed, (as at the Dorset and Cornwall Asylums,) by the Chaplain to the County Gaol. At Chester there was no Chaplain, and the Service was read on Sundays by the Head Keeper and Matron respectively, on the Male and Female sides. We were informed that a Chaplain was about to be appointed; and this was found, upon our second visit to that Asylum, to have been done. In some County Asylums, a large proportion of the Patients attend the Service. This is the case at Chester, where the Service is now read, and a Sermon delivered every Sunday evening. The effect is stated to be generally tranquillizing, and some of the Inmates appear to derive consolation from joining in it. At Leicester, the proportion of Patients who usually attend Chapel is about two-thirds of the whole; at Bedford, Bodmin, and Stafford, one-half; at the Dorset Asylum, one-third; and at Lancaster, one-fourth. The smallest proportion which we have found attending Chapel was at the Suffolk Asylum, viz., about 36 in 216, or one-sixth. The Medical Superintendent of this Asylum stated as his opinion, that the beneficial effect of the Service was doubtful, the number of those capable of understanding it being very small.

We had an opportunity of observing the quiet and orderly demeanour of the Patients during Service on a Sunday, at Lancaster; and of witnessing the effect apparently produced upon about seventy of each sex, by the appropriate and impressive discourse of the Chaplain. At the Northampton Asylum also, we availed ourselves of an opportunity to attend the Morning Daily Prayers, which were read by a Chaplain, who visits the Asylum daily, and has keys of the wards. The conduct of the Patients was orderly and decorous.

The Chaplain to the Bedford Asylum, with whom we had some conversation, expressed very decided views as to the comfort and benefit derived by Patients from Religious Services; and mentioned the case of a female who, upon recovering her reason, described the pleasure she had experienced, whilst Insane, in attending Prayers.

The average number attending Chapel at the Hanwell Asylum is 300, and the Holy Communion is administered to those who are considered in a fit state of mind to receive it. The practice adopted at Hanwell in regard to the selection of Communicants, is that, one fortnight before the quarterly administration of the Lord's Supper, the Keepers and Nurses are directed to give.

notice to the Patients in their several wards, and to inquire whether any of them desire to attend. Usually
about fifty of each sex ˙express a wish to do so. Their
names are taken down, and from their number the Chaplain selects those whom he thinks in a fit state to
receive the Communion. These are on an average fifty
in number; namely, about thirty males, and twenty
females. Their demeanour is said to be uniformly suitable to the occasion.

There is no Chaplain at the Lincoln Asylum. Prayers
are read daily, and twice on Sundays, by the House-
Surgeon, who considers the effect very beneficial,
as tending, amongst other things, to revive devotional
feelings. The result of our inquiries at St. Luke's
Hospital was, that Prayers had never been read to the
Inmates of that Institution; but that a Chapel was in
progress of being fitted up, and a Chaplain about to be
appointed. At the Warneford Asylum, near Oxford,
a Chapel has been recently built, for the use of the
inmates.

VII.

ON THE ADMISSION AND LIBERATION OF PATIENTS.

The law has required that no person, not being a
Pauper, shall be received into any Licensed House for
the reception of Insane Persons, without an order,
under the hand of the person by whose direction he is
sent, and without the Certificates of two medical men.

Order and Certificates required for admission of Patients, not Paupers, into Licensed Houses.

The order is to contain a full description of the Lunatic, and the name, place of abode, and degree of rela-
tionship, or connexion with the Lunatic, of the person
signing the order. The medical men signing the Certi-

ficate are to examine the Patient separately, and are to comply with other particulars required by the Act of 2 & 3 Will. IV. c. 107. These Orders and Certificates, and the different particulars which they require, have been framed for the protection of the liberty of the subject, and for the prevention of abuse in improperly confining those who are not insane.

Visitors to examine Orders and Certificates. The persons who are appointed to visit Licensed Houses are required to examine these Orders and Certificates. We consider this duty to be one of great importance, and are careful in our visitations to call attention to any irregularity which we discover in these documents. They enable us, in cases of difficulty, to communicate with the family of the Patient, and with the medical men who have signed the Certificates. Copies of the Orders and Certificates are sent to our Board, and enable us to give information of any person who has been placed in confinement.

Orders and Certificates not required by Public Hospitals; By 9 Geo. IV. c. 41, Public Hospitals were required to have Orders and Certificates of Insanity in the same form as Licensed Houses, but the clause requiring such Certificates was omitted in the Act of 2 & 3 Will. IV. c. 107. Private Asylums are not only required to have Orders and two Certificates previously to admission, but are subjected to visitation, whereas Public Hospitals may not only receive Private Patients without any Order or Certificate, but are not subject to any visitation. In 1815, the then Commissioners in Lunacy recommended to the Committee of the House of Commons on Madhouses, that the exemption of Public Hospitals for the Insane from the law for the regulation of Licensed Asylums, " should be confined to Pauper Lunatics admitted into such institutions as objects of charity, and not extended to those who pay, and sometimes largely, for their accommodation." All the Lunatic Hospitals, by their own private regulations, require Certificates, before the admission of Patients, and gener-

ally in the same form as those which are required by law
for Licensed Houses. This shows the opinion of the
governing bodies of these institutions as to the propriety
of requiring them.

It is to be regretted that any difference has been
made in the forms of admission of Private Patients into
any description of Asylum. No person ought to be
placed in confinement except under the strongest sanction for its necessity, and under the written authority
either of relatives or other persons, who may be applied
to in case of doubt or difficulty. There is at least as much
reason for requiring Orders and Certificates on the admission of Insane persons into Public Hospitals, as into
County Asylums. *Orders and Certificates desirable in all cases.*

A gentleman who was a Private Patient in the County
Asylum at Leicester, complained to us that he was con-
fined upon the Certificate of one medical man, who was
a relation. It has been the practice of the Visiting
Physician of the County and Subscription Asylum at
Nottingham to sign Certificates for the admission of
Private Patients into this Asylum. As regards Licensed
Houses, such Certificates would be deemed irregular.
In the Lunatic Asylum at Northampton, a Private
Patient was pointed out to us by the Physician who was
not insane, but had been sent there because her habits
were a source of annoyance to her family. At the
Public Hospitals, as well as at other Asylums, we meet
with cases of persons who are termed morally insane,
about the propriety of whose detention there are fre-
quently great doubts. *Irregularities consequent upon the system of admission in Public Hospitals.*

The provisions of the law respecting Certificates and
Orders for the admission of Insane persons into Asylums,
require some notice. As regards Private Patients, Certificates of their insanity from two medical men are
required for their admission into a Licensed House, and
from only one medical man for their admission into a
County Asylum. As respects a Pauper Lunatic, the *Remarks on provisions of the law for admis- sion into Asy- lums.*

Certificate of his insanity must be signed by one medical man, and the Order for his admission into a County Asylum must be signed by two Justices, if for a pauper belonging to the county, and by one Justice if for a pauper of another county; and by one Justice, or by the officiating Clergyman of the parish and one Overseer, if for his admission into a Licensed House. It appears to us to be desirable to have one form of Orders and Certificates for the admission of all Private Patients, and one form also for the admission of all Pauper Patients, into Asylums of every description.

Practice at St. Luke's Hospital;

At St. Luke's Hospital, the Governors are in the habit of permitting Patients to go to their friends upon trial, and of re-admitting them as old Patients, without requiring any fresh Certificate. Hospitals are enabled to do this, because they are not required by law to have any Certificates for the admission of Patients. The subject has been frequently mentioned to us by the Proprietors of Private Asylums, and it may deserve consideration whether or not a power to permit the temporary removal of Patients, on trial visits, or for change of air, can be safely conceded to the keepers of Licensed Houses. If such temporary removals, or trial visits, are to be permitted, we think they should be allowed only under the express sanction and authority in each case of Visiting Justices or Commissioners, after due inquiry.

At the Gloucester Asylum.

At the Gloucester Asylum, as has been stated to us, the Superintending Physician permits Patients, before they are discharged, to go home to their own families, and receives them again without requiring fresh Orders and Certificates; and ten or twelve Pauper Lunatics appear to have ingress and egress from the Asylum at all times, at their own discretion. This practice is contrary to law, and appears to us to be open to serious objections.

Act 2 & 3, Will. IV. c. 107, ss. 46 & 47, disregarded.

By the Act 2 & 3 Will. IV. c. 107, it is a misdemeanor to receive to board, or lodge, in any house not

licensed, any Insane Person, Pauper, or otherwise,
without having the usual Order and Certificates
required for Private Patients confined in Asylums, and
copies of such Order and Certificates are directed to be
transmitted to the Clerk of the Metropolitan Commissioners in Lunacy. The law in this respect appears to
be wholly disregarded as respects Paupers, and very
much evaded as respects Private Patients. No Orders
or Certificates whatever, authorizing the reception
of Paupers, are ever sent to our clerk, and those
relating to Private Patients are so few in number as
to render it manifest that the most culpable negli-
gence exists. The 47th section of the above Act does
not require the Orders and Certificates to be sent until
within twelve months after a Patient has been received.
The length of time allowed to send in the Orders and
Certificates has, we incline to think, been one cause of
the provisions of the Act being evaded. We have
reasons for believing that the Proprietors of Licensed
Houses receive Private Patients in lodgings, without
ever making any return of the Orders and Certificates,
which they are required to receive and to transmit to
our clerk.

The object of the Law in requiring these Orders and
Certificates is, that the place wherein every Lunatic is
confined, may at all times be known, with the view of
ascertaining his condition in reference not only to his
state of mind, but also to the treatment which he receives from the person with whom he is resident.
From the information which we have obtained from
various quarters, there can be no doubt but that Pauper
Lunatics have been, and still are, subject to very severe
and unjustifiable restraint, in cases where they are singly
confined, or boarded out in the houses of persons who
receive them for small sums. In the County Asylum
at Leicester there is a man now daily at work, and
apparently cheerful and in good bodily health, who, for

Object of Orders and Certificates.

Pauper Lunatics subject to un-justifiable re-straint.

seven years previously to his admission, was kept chained night and day in a small back room at Peckleton, in the same County. In the Asylum of Plympton St. Mary, there is a Male Lunatic who was formerly a Boarder for eleven years in a Private House, and during the whole of that time he was constantly chained. We found him without any restraint, and at work in the grounds of the Asylum. A poor woman was removed from the Asylum at Northampton to board with another Patient; but it was found absolutely necessary to send her back (twice) to the Asylum, because she was kept upon so low a diet that relapses of her disease were brought on by want of more liberal food. We have elsewhere stated our reasons for thinking that the condition of Pauper Lunatics, who are placed out as Boarders, deserves the attention of the Legislature.

Liberation of Patients.

The Liberation of a patient once properly certified to be Insane, manifestly requires the greatest caution. In almost every case, in which we have interfered to promote the liberation of a person confined as a Lunatic, we have considered it advisable, in the first instance, to recommend that the patient should be removed by his friends; and it has been only on the refusal of the friends to act on our suggestion, that we have resorted to the power vested in us by the Acts of Parliament. In numerous cases, we have found, that the mind of the patient, even where he has derived benefit from having been confined in an Asylum, retains a feeling of animosity towards the persons who originally authorised his confinement, and an impression that he has been injured by them. We have, therefore, thought it right that these persons should have the opportunity, at a proper time, of doing an act which would, in all probability, tend to remove or lessen this unjust feeling; and indeed it is not unimportant to the future well-doing of the patient himself, that he should recommence his career in society with as few hostile prejudices and unfounded opinions, and in general with as little recurrence to his past state of mind, as possible.

Instances are, besides, perpetually occurring in which a patient, although not completely recovered, is nevertheless in such a state of convalescence or improved health, as to render it desirable that he should have a certain amount of liberty allowed him, without possessing entire freedom. The transition from strict seclusion to complete liberty of action should, in many cases, be gradual. This is material, not only for the sake of tempering the patient, and inuring him, by a regular process, to unrestrained intercourse with society; but also as a test whereby his fitness for liberation may be ascertained, before he is made absolute master of his own actions. Endeavours, it is true, are made, in some of the better conducted Lunatic Asylums, to effect this object, by classifying the patients, and regulating the degree of freedom allowed, by their advance towards recovery; but there are cases where it may be preferable to remove the patient altogether from an Asylum, and from the presence of companions of disordered intellect, and to accustom him (under the supervision of a single attendant) to associate only with persons who are perfectly sane. This plan, by leaving in the hands of the patient's friends a certain power, which they themselves may gradually relax, invests them at once with the means of control, so long as it may seem necessary to exert it, and a considerable moral influence afterwards, when they have of their own accord restored the patient to the full enjoyment of his liberty.

Suggestions as to a plan of gradual liberation.

In reference to cases of this sort, where great improvement, short of perfect recovery, has taken place in the health of a patient, it may be observed, that by the Acts 2 & 3 Will. IV. c. 107, and 5 & 6 Vict. c. 87, under which our authority is derived, we are empowered to liberate patients altogether; but that we have

Commissioners not empowered to grant partial liberty.

no power to direct the continuance of any control or management after they have quitted an Asylum. The liberation of a person, confined as a Lunatic, if it be effected by the exertion of our statutory powers, must be complete.

Difficulty in deciding on liberation in certain cases.

Besides the cases last adverted to, there are others, not of partial or incomplete recovery, but where the amount or character of the disorder is of such a nature as to present great difficulties in the exercise of our discretionary power of liberation. These are chiefly cases, 1st, of drunkenness; 2d, of epilepsy and periodical excitement; 3d, of weakness of intellect; and 4th, of what has been termed moral insanity.

Without laying down any precise rule on the subject, we have assumed, as a general principle for our guidance, that wherever a man of ordinary intellect is able so to conduct himself, that he is not likely to do injury, in person or property, to himself or others, he is unfit to continue as the inmate of a Lunatic Asylum. In judging, however, of this likelihood to do injury,—in anticipating, in short, the future good conduct of a person who has been once insane, from the present abated state of his malady, or from his apparent recovery, there is frequently extreme difficulty and, always the most serious responsibility. In some cases, insanity may have been produced by temporary causes, which being removed, little probability exists of a return of the complaint. But the majority of cases proceed either from congenital causes, or from some organic defect in the system, inducing periodical returns of the disorder, in each of which cases there is little chance of complete cure; or else from the depraved or imprudent conduct of the patient, against the repetition of which there can be no security, that he will not relapse: there are cases also where the intellect possessed by the patient is so feeble or limited as to render it exceedingly perplexing to decide, whether he is or is not fit to be intrusted with the management of his own affairs : and there are others, which modern writers class under the head of Moral Insanity, many of which are scarcely distinguishable from cases of ordinary crime. It appears to us that these last, if admissible as instances of actual disease, should be admitted only after the most careful and severe scrutiny ; and that the shelter of a Lunatic Asylum should not be furnished, except upon incontrovertible grounds, to persons *primâ facie* liable to be dealt with by the criminal law of the land.

In all cases, whether of these or other species of insanity, it is clear that the patient, who apparently has claims to be liberated, should be examined and liberated only by persons familiar with the disease, and as a consequence accustomed to observe the peculiar habits and moods of mind of the insane. *Patients should be examined by competent persons, previous to liberation.*

So far as respects the exercise of the power of liberation by the County Magistrates, we believe that a patient has very rarely been discharged by them until he has been in a fit state to be restored to society ; there have been one or two instances, however, in which they appear not to have acted with their usual discretion. At the Witney Asylum, the Visiting Justices (with their medical attendant), examined a patient, who was confined there, and had been guilty of violence, twice in one day, and thereupon expressed their desire that the proprietor of the Asylum (a respectable medical man), would open his doors and let the patient out at once. He refused to do this without an order. The Justices urged this liberation, on the advice of their medical attendant, who had never seen the patient until that day ; and they soon afterwards brought the matter before our consideration, and two members of our body accordingly investigated the case; but they, after repeatedly examining the Lunatic, and hearing the evidence of various persons respecting his conduct and general habits, whilst out of the Asylum, *Exercise of power by County Magistrates.*

did not feel themselves justified in liberating him. It is right to add that this Lunatic, although somewhat abstracted and moody, did not present very obvious marks of disease. The testimony, however, corroborative of his disordered state of mind, which was given by several persons, apparently unbiassed, was very strong.

At the Licensed House at Nunkeeling, near Beverley in Yorkshire, the Visiting Justices liberated a dangerous Lunatic under unusual circumstances. We were informed by the brother-in-law of the Lunatic, and by the Proprietor of the House, that the Lunatic had been in a state of continued drunkenness for many weeks; that he had threatened the life of his wife and child, under a delusion that he was not the father of the child; and that two of the Lunatic's brothers had died insane. We found the following entry made by the Visiting Justices in the Visitors' Book, Dec. 19, 1842. " We have this day made a special visit to the Asy- " lum in order to examine into the case of P. H." (the Lunatic referred to), " who has been placed here " at the instance of his wife. He appears to be per- " fectly sane at the present, and unless sufficient cause " for his further detention be shewn to the Magistrates " assembled in Petty Sessions at Leven, on Thursday " next, the 22nd instant, we order that he be dis- " charged from the Asylum on Friday, the 23rd." This Lunatic had been confined under proper certificates, and the Proprietor of the House remonstrated; but the man was discharged, and afterwards threatened the life of his wife, who was obliged to leave her home, and he was then placed under the custody of the constables. The Justices, according to the act empowering them to liberate, ought to have visited this Lunatic three times (instead of once), and the real power of liberation belonged not to them, but only to the Justices assembled in Quarter Sessions: and we entered a statement to that effect in the Visitor's Book, and pointed out the great risk of liberating a dangerous Lunatic under such circumstances. Cases of this sort, however, are, as we have said, extremely rare.

But liberations or removals at the instance of the patient's friends, or parish officers, are continually taking place; generally, indeed, only when the patients are reported convalescent, but frequently without the sanction of any visitors, and sometimes even against their remonstrances. With respect to patients who have ever been guilty of violence, it appears to us very questionable, whether their friends, or parish officers ought, in any case, to have the power of authorising or procuring their discharge without the previous sanction of the Commissioners, or Visiting Justices, or other competent authority. At present, a violent Maniac, confined in a licensed Asylum, may, as it appears, be liberated and thrown back upon society, by the mere order of the relative, or other person, who originally placed him there. Now, whether this liberation be obtained by the importunities of the patient, or take place in order to save the expense attending his confinement in a Lunatic Asylum, or proceed from any other cause, short of the deliberate judgment of persons accustomed to observe cases of Insanity, it is, or may be, equally injurious to the public welfare. This power of liberating dangerous Lunatics, vested in or assumed by incompetent and irresponsible persons, is a subject that we think deserving of grave consideration.

Frequency of irregular liberations.

In reference to this part of the subject, we beg to state, that on our visiting the Refuge, at Hull, we found an entry made by the Visiting Justices, disapproving of the removal of certain paupers by parish officers. From the inquiries we there made into the matter, we were induced to concur in opinion with the Justices, and we accordingly made an entry in the Visitors' book to that effect. Three cases were subsequently brought under

Cases of irregular removals.

our notice by the clerk of the Visiting Justices of this Asylum. One was that of a quarrelsome Idiot, who had been confined for threatening to stab another person. The other two were Imbeciles; one having been admitted for obscenity of conduct, and the other being subject to fits of great excitement, and of considerable duration. Of these patients, one was removed by the Overseer, and the other two were discharged by two Justices of the county, who were not the Visitors. The letter accompanying the order for the removal of the Idiot, stated that she was not to be placed in the Union House, but with some quiet old woman. Two of these patients were dangerous, and all were removed uncured, in opposition to the opinion of the Visiting Justices, and of the proprietor of the Asylum. A fourth patient had been confined because she had taken a violent and unfounded dislike to her husband, and had threatened to poison him. She was removed on the day of our visit, by her husband, against the remonstrances of the proprietor of the Asylum, and notwithstanding that she had still the same dislike and expressed the same threat as formerly. We found in the same Asylum, a patient (a young man) who had been twice previously discharged; the second time contrary to the opinion of the superintendent, who did not consider him convalescent. Shortly after his second discharge, he met a relation whom he passed and afterwards followed and stabbed dangerously in the side with a knife. He is now confined as a criminal Lunatic. The superintendent considered that this outrage would have been avoided, if he had had power to delay for a short time the patient's discharge.

In the Asylum, at Newcastle-upon-Tyne, there was an extremely dangerous man, who had threatened the lives of his wife and children. When we saw him, he appeared perfectly rational, and we were informed that he was staying in the Asylum in the hope of escaping the consequences of legal proceedings, commenced against him for some offence. The resident Physician was of opinion that this man had sought shelter in the Asylum from the proceedings, and that (although a dangerous Lunatic) he would obtain his liberation as soon as all danger should have passed.

It will be observed, that one of the cases which we have adverted to; as involving great perplexity, is that of a patient whose insanity has arisen from drunkenness, and who has apparently recovered. Such a person, at the commencement of his disease, is generally in a state of violent excitement, and likely to do injury to himself or others. Cases of this description have frequently come under our consideration, within the Metropolitan district and elsewhere; and the difficulty which we have experienced has been to determine for how long a period the patient ought to be detained in confinement after his malady has apparently ceased. We have thought it desirable that he should not be exposed too soon to the temptation of again indulging in strong liquors; it having been almost invariably found that patients of this class, if liberated without having undergone a sufficient probation, are very liable to resort to their former practices, and to relapse. At the same time, we have considered that a Lunatic Asylum is not a place for the permanent detention of persons who have recovered the use of their reason, and are not obnoxious to the charge of unsoundness of mind, otherwise than on account of their liability afterwards to run into their former excesses, when restored to liberty. It has been our practice, in cases of this sort, to liberate the patient after a short confinement, if it be the first attack of Insanity from this cause, and if he appear to be aware of his misconduct, and to have a desire to reform his habits. In the event, however, of his being confined a second time owing to the same cause, we

Difficulty of dealing with cases of drunkenness.

have felt that his probation ought to continue for a much longer period; and indeed we have felt that great responsibility has rested upon us in such a case, and have at all times very reluctantly,—and only after vainly endeavouring to induce the patient's friends to take charge of him,—resorted to our power of liberation.

Instances of sane persons being sent to Asylums, rare.

In reference to the subject of liberating patients, it is right to state that, in the course of our experience, we have rarely found any patient confined in a Lunatic Asylum, who, as far as we could judge, had been sent there whilst in a decidedly sane state. Occasionally, the reasons for confining a patient at a great distance from his home, or for affording him an allowance apparently incompatible with his means, have required explanation, and this has not perhaps always proved satisfactory; but there have been very few instances where the condition or conduct of the patient has not been sufficient to justify or extenuate his confinement.

Confinement frequently too much prolonged.

At the same time, it must be added that confinement has in many cases been too far prolonged, and we have not unfrequently encountered a reluctance, on the part of the patient's relatives or parish officers, to remove him when he has been considered convalescent, and when in our opinion he might have been removed from the Asylum without danger. In the case of Private Patients, the reluctance of the relatives has often proceeded from timidity, and occasionally perhaps from a wish to conceal the fact of the patient's insanity; whilst the reluctance of parish officers has, without doubt, frequently arisen from a desire of saving expense, or from the circumstance of the patient having been found troublesome in the workhouse or union. In many of these cases, the parties have evidently been anxious to throw all the responsibility of the Act of Liberation upon the Metropolitan Commissioners.

Power of liberation should be vested in some

It is under circumstances of this nature, and also where the person originally signing the order for the patient's confinement dies or goes abroad, (such person's consent being required previously to the patient's discharge,) that we have felt our power of liberation to be of the highest importance and utility; and we think that some such authority should always, under the sanction of the Legislature, be vested in some persons, in order to ensure due protection to the subject.

persons under sanction of the legislature.

VIII.

STATISTICS OF INSANITY.

· THE importance of Statistics of Insanity, and their intimate bearing upon the more immediate subjects of our inquiry, have induced us to resort to all accessible sources of information, for the purpose of estimating the actual numbers of the Insane, of all ranks, in England and Wales; and of presenting, in one view, the numbers, with the several classes and conditions, of those confined in Asylums. Our inquiries have also comprised the prevailing forms and causes of Insanity, and causes of death, with the results of treatment, as far as they are deducible from the records of admissions and discharges. We have thought it expedient to confine ourselves, upon this occasion, to a few important heads, reserving others for future investigation. One reason for thus limiting our inquiries was, that, whilst it was desirable to collect the information from the various Asylums, public and private, in a uniform shape, many of those Persons by whom it was to be supplied were not in possession of sufficient data to enable them to furnish all the required details.

General observations.

The subject is one upon which, from the scanty and uncertain nature of the materials for computation, the

Erroneous notions formed on the subject.

N

178

most erroneous notions have been formed by several writers who have treated upon the Statistics of Insanity By one writer, the number of the Insane in England was, in the year 1810, estimated at one in 7,300 of the population; by another, in 1820, the number was estimated at one in 2,000; by a third, in 1829, at 16,500, altogether, in England and Wales. It will be seen, in a subsequent part of this Report, how very far these estimates were from the truth.

Returns of Pauper lunatics.

The means of arriving at a nearer approximation to the real numbers of the Insane in this Kingdom, have been furnished by certain returns of Lunatics and Idiots chargeable to Unions and Parishes, in the years 1836, 1842, and 1843. Abstracts of these Returns have been prepared by the Poor Law Commissioners, and a copy of the last of these Abstracts will be found in Appendix F

Reports of County and Public Asylums.

to this Report. The printed Reports of the various County and other Public Asylums, and the Statistical Tables drawn up by the Medical Officers of those Institutions, supply most valuable information. They are, however, plainly insufficient for general deductions. These circumstances, and the importance of the subject, led us to undertake the inquiry, the results of which we now present to your Lordship. Our acknowledgments are due to the Superintendents and Proprietors of Asylums, generally, for the readiness with which they supplied the information requested, and the labour bestowed by them upon their several Returns.

Commissioners, inquiries extended to Scotland and Ireland

We have (as will be observed) extended our inquiries, in a certain degree, to Scotland and Ireland; in regard to which, we availed ourselves of the best private channels to request information from the principal Institutions in Scotland; the several District Asylums of Ireland; Swift's Hospital, Dublin: and the large and important Pauper Asylum, at Cork. Our request was met most cheerfully by the Managers and Medical Officers of those Institutions, who have favoured us with Returns for the most part full, and complete, which will be found at the end of the Separate Appendix. We have thought it due to the Parties furnishing the Returns, as well as desirable in other respects, to append to them extracts from the several communications by which they were accompanied, so far as the same appeared necessary for their elucidation.

We come next to speak of the materials for the statistics of Insanity, which exist in the shape of Returns required by Law. We shall, in the concluding portion of our Report, submit to your Lordship our views as to the propriety of prescribing certain forms of Registers and Medical books, to be kept in all Asylums, with a view to the preparation of Statistical Returns, at stated and uniform periods. The absolute want in some cases, and the deficiency, and variety in form generally, of such Registers, have tended much to enhance the difficulties we have had in procuring the necessary information, and to render it a work of much labour to the several Superintendents to supply it in the shape that we requested. The circumstance also of several of the Public Asylums making up their Annual Statements to a period of the year other than the 31st of December, has been a source of much additional trouble and inconvenience to some to whom we have been indebted for Returns applicable to the 1st of January, 1844.

Registers, &c. in Asylums, should be kept in a prescribed form.

To revert to the subject of the Returns now required by Act of Parliament. The visitors of each County Asylum are bound by the Act 9 Geo. IV. c. 40, s. 56, to make annual Returns,* in the month of June, of the patients confined therein, or who shall have been confined

Returns required by law;

---

* The Lists of Patients in County Asylums are directed to be sent to the Clerk of the Metropolitan Commissioners, appointed under the Act 9 Geo. IV. c. 41, who is to enter the same in a Register. The last-mentioned Act having been repealed, and the Metropolitan Commissioners being now appointed under the Acts 2 & 3 Will. IV. c. 107, and 5 & 6 Vict. c. 87, some County Asylums make no Returns to this Board.

therein within the twelve months preceding; and similar Returns are required by the Act 2 & 3 Will. IV. c. 107, s. 63, from Public Hospitals and Charitable Institutions.*

not regularly made. These Returns, if universally made, would supply much useful information under the several heads to which they relate, more especially as to the Occupation and Profession of the patients. It appears, however, by the collection of Returns, relating to County Asylums, printed by order of Parliament in 1842, that they are not universally made, and that some of those made apply only to the Patients admitted during the year.

Return by Visiting Commissioners; The Visiting Commissioners are directed by the Act 5 & 6 Vict. c. 87, s. 36, to require and transmit to this Board, a List, according to the form in Schedule B to that Act, of Admissions, Discharges, and Deaths, during the year ending the 31st December preceding. No one, however, is named in the Act to furnish the List.†

by proprietors of Licensed Houses. As respects Licensed Houses, the Proprietors are required by the Acts 2 & 3 Will. IV. c. 107, ss. 30, 31, and 3 & 4 Will. IV. c. 64, ss. 3, 4, within two days after the Admission, Discharge, or Death of Patients, to transmit to the Clerks of the Peace, in the case of Provincial Asylums, and to this Board in all cases, copies of the Orders of Admission, and Medical Certificates, and Notices of Discharge, or Death, as the case may be, to be entered in a Register, by reference to which, the fact and also the place of confinement of any Inmate of a Licensed House may be ascertained.‡ Similar Notices are also required by the Act 5 & 6 Vict. c. 87, s. 27, to be given of escapes. It is very important that materials should be furnished for the formation of a correct and complete Register of Insane persons,

* The Act does not specify the person whose duty it shall be to make the Return, which is in fact made by one Public Hospital only.

† The Superintendent of the Nottingham Asylum, on this ground, declined to furnish the List when required so to do.

‡ The Commissioners have power to permit searches to be made for this purpose.

wherever confined; and that regular Returns should be made, with this view, from all Asylums, Public and Private, in a uniform shape.

The next class of Returns to which we shall advert, and which is a most important one, as containing the only authentic information upon the subject, furnished to Parliament and the Public, applicable to the whole Kingdom, is that of Lunatics and Idiots chargeable to Unions and Parishes. The Enactments upon this subject are the 9th Geo. IV. c. 40, and the new Poor Law Amendment Act, 5 & 6 Vict. c. 57. The first-mentioned Act is now confined to Parishes not comprised in Unions, the Overseers of which are still required, annually, in the month of August, to transmit to the Clerks of the Peace "lists of all Insane persons chargeable to their respective Parishes." These Returns, it is believed, are not very regularly made.

The principal Returns of Pauper Lunatics are those made by the Clerks of Boards of Guardians, under the New Poor Law Amendment Act. These last Returns contain a variety of details, not supplied by the former; and, if filled up with care, and by competent persons, would be more valuable, in a medical point of view, than they now are. It is plain, from these Returns, that a large number of Insane persons, returned under the head of Idiots, are not Idiots properly so called, namely, Idiots from birth or infancy. The Returns, however, may be generally relied upon as regards the aggregate of Lunatics and Idiots chargeable to Unions. These, it is to be observed, probably, in many cases, do not comprise the Insane members of families chargeable as Out-door Paupers, of the numbers of which no means exist to form an estimate. There is also another class of Pauper Lunatics not included in the Returns; viz.—those maintained in Asylums at the charge of the several *Counties*.

The only remaining Returns which we shall notice

Returns of Pauper lunatics and idiots.

are those required by the Act 2 & 3 Will. IV. c. 107;
sect. 47, in the case of single private Patients, and de-
nominated in the Act " Private Returns." They apply,
however, to those patients only who have been under
the charge of the same individual for the space of one
year. Of patients who have been under private care
for shorter periods than a year, no Return is required ;
so that a large class of Insane persons *under certificate*
exists, in respect to whose number there are no materials
for calculation. As regards also those of whom Returns ought to be made, it is believed that in a very
small proportion of instances is the law complied with.
This is abundantly manifest from the number, so far as
it could be ascertained, in the month of January, 1844,
and which was furnished to us with your Lordship's permission. This number was 37 only ; viz.—24 Males, and
13 Females. It is to be observed, also, that no notice is
required to be given of removal or death ; so that whilst,
on the one hand, a large number of certificated single
Patients may, and no doubt does exist, of whom no
Returns have been made, either from ignorance or neglect
of the provisions of the Act on the part of the Persons
having the charge of them, or because such Patients
have not been under the care of any one Person con-
tinuously for so long a period as a year; on the other
hand, those of whom Returns have been regularly made
may have subsequently died, or been discharged, or
removed by their friends. For these reasons, we have
not taken the Class last mentioned into account, in our
estimate of the present numbers of the Insane. Even
if these Returns were complete, and all *certificated* single
Patients were comprised in them, there would still
remain a considerable class of Insane persons, of all
ranks of life, under the care of Guardians or Relatives, *without certificate*, of whose probable number
there are no means of forming an estimate. These
considerations, as well as those suggested as to

the numbers of the Insane Poor, are necessary to be borne in mind, in all calculations relative to the amount and prevalence of Insanity in this Country.

With these remarks upon the existing materials for the Statistics of Insanity, we proceed to state to your Lordship the course we pursued, and the nature and objects of the Tables which we issued to the several Superintendents of Asylums. Copies of the Returns received, with a Tabular View of the state of the Patients in each Asylum on the 1st of January, 1844, will be found in a Separate Appendix. *Course pursued by Commissioners in their inquiry.*

This Tabular View, to which we allude first in order, as forming (with information derived from other sources) the basis of a Census of Insanity, contains, as will be seen, a Statement of the Total Numbers of each sex, pauper and private, confined in Asylums on the 1st of January, 1844; their state as to probability of recovery; the number of Epileptics and Idiots; of those with homicidal or suicidal propensities; the condition of the Inmates as to marriage; their several classes of life, and previous occupations; the number of Criminal Lunatics (commonly so called); and of the Patients found Lunatic by Inquisition. It is only necessary to observe, in respect to the Returns from which the Statement last mentioned has been compiled, that the greatest pains have been taken to insure accuracy, by repeated communications with the various Superintendents of Asylums, and by obtaining from them, whenever necessary, explanations and corrections of their several Returns.

The following Table exhibits the general results, in which the numbers found Lunatic by Inquisition have been corrected, by a statement furnished to this Board by the Board of Visitors of Chancery Lunatics. To this we subjoin a more detailed Abstract of the Returns made to this Board from the several Classes of Asylums.

184

GENERAL STATEMENT OF INSANE PERSONS CONFINED IN ASYLUMS
ENGLAND AND WALES, 1 *Jan.* 1844.

			Males.	Females.	Total.
Private Patients			1989	1801	3790
Paupers			3532	3950	7482
	Total		5521	5751	11,272
State as to probability of recovery.	Curable	Private	492	553	1045
		Pauper	687	787	1474
		Total	1179	1340	2519
	Incurable	Private	1497	1248	2745
		Pauper	2834	3157	5991
		Total	4331	4405	8736
Epileptics			575	376	951
Idiots			347	251	598
Homicidal Patients			180	98	278
Suicidal Patients			303	393	696
Civil State.	Married		1501	1664	3165
	Single		3346	2982	6328
	Widowed		340	798	1138
	Not known		212	197	409
Class of life, and previous occupation.	Upper and Middle Classes		1389	1315	2704
	Agricultural		1183	469	1652
	Artisan, and In-door		1640	2228	3868
	Others		1187	1629	2816
Criminal Lunatics			202	55	257
Found Lunatic by Inquisition			146	87	233

	County Asylums			Mily. & Naval Hospitals			Bethlem Hospital			St. Luke's Hospital			Other Public Asylums			Metrop. Licensed Houses			Provincial Licensed Houses		
	M.	F.	Tot.	M.	F.	Tot.	M.	F.	Tot.	M.	F.	Tot.	M.	F.	Tot.	M.	F.	Tot.	M.	F.	Tot.
Private Patients	130	115	245	164	4	168	106	159	265	72	105	177	249	287	536	520	453	973	748	678	1426
Paupers	1962	2282	4244	—	—	—	70	20	90	16	15	31	177	166	343	360	494	854	947	973	1920
Total	2092	2397	4489	164	4	168	176	179	355	88	120	208	426	453	879	880	947	1827	1695	1651	3346
Curable — Private	29	32	61	18	—	18	72	109	181	34	59	93	63	64	127	69	84	153	207	205	412
Curable — Pauper	297	354	651	—	—	—	—	—	—	10	6	16	28	31	59	46	65	111	306	331	637
Curable — Total	326	386	712	18	—	18	72	109	181	44	65	109	91	95	186	115	149	264	513	536	1049
Incurable — Private	101	83	184	146	4	150	34	50	84	38	46	84	186	223	409	451	369	820	541	473	1014
Incurable — Pauper	1654	1922	3576	—	—	—	70	20	90	6	9	15	149	135	284	314	429	743	641	642	1283
Incurable — Total	1755	2005	3760	146	4	150	104	70	174	44	55	99	335	358	693	765	798	1563	1182	1115	2297
Epileptics	296	215	511	7	—	7	—	—	—	—	—	—	13	16	29	97	56	153	162	89	251
Idiots	179	114	293	4	—	4	—	—	—	—	—	—	18	11	29	51	61	112	95	65	160
Homicidal Patients	94	58	152	5	—	5	22	15	—	2	—	2	4	1	5	14	6	20	44	18	62
Suicidal Patients	152	189	341	—	—	—	13	34	47	5	17	22	31	28	59	36	44	80	61	81	142
Married	689	781	1470	35	2	37	37	31	68	23	42	65	103	126	229	175	206	381	449	466	915
Single	1165	1209	2374	102	—	102	37	48	85	57	58	115	290	245	535	594	491	1085	1101	931	2032
Widowed	151	314	465	11	2	13	1	11	12	8	17	25	21	52	73	44	171	215	104	231	335
Not known	76	87	163	16	—	16	—	—	—	—	3	3	12	5	17	67	79	146	41	23	64
Upper and Middle Classes	152	123	275	50	—	50	17	19	36	11	19	30	138	138	276	391	394	785	630	622	1252
Agricultural	535	222	757	—	—	—	10	6	16	8	4	12	89	44	133	108	35	143	432	158	590
Artisan and In-door	877	1121	1998	—	—	—	35	60	95	33	42	75	99	100	199	158	429	587	424	431	855
Others	497	880	1377	114	4	118	3	15	18	36	55	91	100	146	246	223	89	312	209	440	649
Criminal Lunatics	76	20	96	—	—	—	70	20	90	—	—	—	10	4	14	18	6	24	38	9	47
Found Lunatic by Inquisition	2	5	7	—	—	—	—	—	—	—	—	—	—	—	—	48	32	80	71	45	116

The numbers as respects the Hanwell Asylum apply to the 30th of September, 1843, to which the Return from that Asylum was made up. The total numbers were on that day, 412 males and 563 females, total 975; whilst on the 1st Jan. 1844, the total number was 982: viz., 416 males and 566 females.

Patients in Bethlem;

In the absence of any specific information upon the subject, we have entered the Criminal Lunatics in Bethlem Hospital, viz. seventy Males and twenty Females, as Paupers. We have also assumed that the remainder of the Patients in Bethlem generally, are of the Private class, although we have reason to believe that some of them are maintained, wholly or in part, at the charge of Unions or Parishes. Seven male, and nine female, curable Patients, entered in the last printed Report, as " out on leave," have been added to the numbers returned as in the Hospital on the 1st of January, 1844.

at Haverford-west.

The Return from the Asylum for the County of Pembroke, at Haverfordwest,* as to the Patients confined therein on the 1st of January, contained merely a statement of absolute numbers, viz. eleven male, and six female Paupers. These Patients, consequently, are only found in the first Division of the Table.

" Civil state," and "Class of life and previous occupation."

With respect to " Civil State," and " Class of life and previous occupation:" 232 Patients; viz. 122 Males, and 110 Females (including those above mentioned in the Pembroke Asylum) do not appear under either of those Heads, the Returns received not having supplied the necessary information. The numbers omitted under the Heads to which we have last alluded are as follows, viz.;

	Males.	Females.	Total.
Haverford West Asylum.	11	6	17
Bethlem Hospital			
Out on leave	7	9	16
Incurables	34	50	84
Criminals	70	20	90
Guy's Hospital		25	25
Total.	122	110	232

It is necessary to state this, in order to account for

---

* No notice whatever was taken of any of the repeated applications made for information ; nor was any answer received from this Asylum, until after the interference of the Chairman of Quarter Sessions, to whom a letter was addressed upon the subject.

187

the apparent inaccuracy of the general statement in the above respects.

The condition of Pauper Patients in Asylums, as to probability of recovery, being made the subject of frequent observation in other parts of this Report, and being matter of great public interest, we have drawn up from the Returns the following Synopsis, which shews at one view the state, in this respect, of the Pauper Patients confined in the several Classes of Asylums, on the 1st of January, 1844 :—

Curable patients.

STATE OF PAUPER PATIENTS IN ASYLUMS, AS TO PROBABILITY OF RECOVERY, 1 *Jan.* 1844.*

Where Confined.	Total Number of Pauper Patients.			Curable.			Proportion per cent. of curable to total Number.
	M.	F.	Tot.	M.	F.	Tot.	
County Asylums . .	1951	2276	4227	297	354	651	15$\frac{2}{5}$
Other Public Asylums.	177	166	343	28	31	59	17
Licensed Houses :—							
Metropolitan . .	360	494	854	46	65	111	13
Provincial . .	947	973	1920	306	331	637	33$\frac{1}{6}$
Total . .	3435	3909	7344	677	781	1458	19$\frac{4}{5}$

The following Table exhibits the proportions per cent. of Curable to Total Numbers of Paupers, in the several County Asylums, on the 1st Jan., 1844, according to the Returns made to this Board :—

Date of Opening	County.	Per Centage.	Date of Opening	County.	Per Centage.
1814	Norfolk . .	65$\frac{2}{5}$	1829	Suffolk . .	13$\frac{1}{10}$
1837	Leicester . .	50	1818	York W. Riding	11$\frac{8}{10}$
1829	Chester . .	30$\frac{1}{4}$	1816	Lancaster . .	10$\frac{3}{5}$
1812	Notts. ..	29$\frac{3}{4}$	1833	Kent . .	8$\frac{4}{5}$
1823	Gloucester .	21$\frac{3}{8}$	1820	Cornwall . .	9$\frac{3}{4}$
1812	Bedford . .	19$\frac{1}{2}$	1831	Middlesex .	6
1818	Stafford .	19$\frac{1}{8}$	1841	Surrey . .	5$\frac{1}{4}$
1832	Dorset . .	17$\frac{3}{4}$			

* Under the head County Asylums is included St. Peter's Hospital, Bristol, which is made, by a Local Act, subject to the provisions of 9 Geo. IV. c. 40. The numbers in the Asylum for the County of Pembroke, at Haverfordwest, for the reasons before mentioned, are not included. St. Luke's Hospital is omitted, because of its particular constitution, recent cases only being admitted in the first instance ; and Epileptics, Paralytics, and Idiots, also aged and infirm Patients, and those previously discharged uncured from other Asylums, being inadmissible:

General observations on remaining Tables.   'The remaining Tables require few observations. They were prepared with all practicable simplicity, and in a form which was considered best calculated to obtain the desired information. The Returns apply, as will be observed, for the most part, to the period of five years, ending in 1843, and, with few exceptions, on the 31st of December.

Some of the Returns of Admissions, Discharges, and Deaths, extend back to the dates of the opening of the Asylums, thus supplying the entire numbers of Patients who were in the Asylums at any time during the whole period. In other cases the numbers in the several Asylums, as they existed at the commencement of the periods included in the Returns, only have been given. For the purpose of Statistical deductions, the Returns last-mentioned are the same, in substance, as the former; inasmuch as the Patients in each Asylum, at the time from which the statement of events commences, may be considered as having been then admitted, and the Asylum as having been then opened.

With respect to the Per-centages of Cures and Deaths, contained in the Table to which we shall next advert, a difference of opinion prevails as to the true principle upon which they should be calculated. Some persons are of opinion that they should be estimated upon the average numbers resident in the Asylum during a given period; others upon the total number of discharges and deaths; and a third class upon the total number who have been under care. We conceive that, for the purpose of instituting a comparison between the systems of treatment pursued in various Asylums, the first and second methods should be employed. It is hardly necessary to state that the greater the number of years over which the calculation extends, the more accurate will be the deductions drawn. It was our intention, in framing the Table, that the Per-centages of Cures and Deaths should be estimated upon the average numbers resident during each year.

The Returns appear to have been made, for the most·
part, upen this principle. In some, however, other
methods have been adopted.

The following Table exhibits the per-centages of Cures
and ·Deaths in the several County, and principal other
Public Asylums, as deduced from the Returns made to
this Board. Some trifling errors appear in those Returns,
but not of a· magnitude to affect the calculations in this
Table.

PER CENTAGES OF CURES AND DEATHS IN COUNTY AND PRINCIPAL OTHER PUBLIC ASYLUMS.

ASYLUM.	Date of opening.	On average number resident in Asylum during last 5 years.		On total number of cases discharged (including deaths).			
				Since opening.		During last 5 years.	
		Annual Cures.	Annual Deaths.	Cures.	Deaths.	Cures.	Deaths.
COUNTY ASYLUMS.							
Bedford	Aug. 1812 .	15·9	10·5	39·7	23·3	44·3	29·3
Chester	Aug. 1829 .	30·1	11·8	59·0	30·0	63·2	24·7
Cornwall*	Aug. 1820 .	13·4	7·9	—	23·8	47·6	28·2
Dorset	Aug. 1, 1832	15·6	12·2	58·5	36·1	52·9	41·4
Gloucester	July 24, 1823	31·7	10·7	65·5	13·7	61·7	20·8
Kent	Jan. 1, 1833	7·5	10·7	38·3	47·3	35·0	50·0
Lancaster	July 28, 1816	16·6	13·2	48·2	46·0	52·4	41·5
Leicester . . . '. .	May 10, 1837	36·1	11·3	18·1	60·0	60·7	19·0
Middlesex	May 16, 1831	6·7	9·1	37·4	55·7	38·7	52·9
Norfolk	May 18, 1814	13·3	19·1	52·3	45·4	37·9	54·4
Nottingham	Feb. 12, 1812	24·6	9·2	15·8	14·5	58·4	21·8
Stafford	Oct. 1, 1818	21·0	13·7	—	—	42·7	27·9
Suffolk	Jan. 1, 1829	16·1	10·8	50·4	33·7	52·6	35·3
Surrey	June 14, 1841	—	—	47·8	50·9	—	—
York, West Riding . .	Nov. 23, 1818	17·1	13·6	50·1	36·9	48·0	38·2
St. Peter's Hospital, Bristol	Incorp. 1696	20·3	19·7	46·0	27·3	33·0	32·0
OTHER PUBLIC ASYLUMS.							
Exeter	July 1, 1801	47·6	12·4	54·1	9·2	47·6	12·4
Lincoln	April 6, 1820	17·9	15·0	42·2	21·9	33·1	27·8
Liverpool	April 6, 1792	62·7	16·7	41·2	11·1	31·4	8·3
Northampton	Aug. 1, 1838	30·3	14·0	58·6	28·3	59·6	27·5
Warneford, near Oxford	July, 1826 .	22·4	7·5	54·7	12·8	60·0	20·0
York Asylum . . .	Sept. 20, 1777	7·9	6·8	36·0	21·7	35·6	30·6
Friends' Retreat, York	Midsm. 1796	8·2	5·7	54·6	26·7	45·6	31·7

The Superintendents of some large Asylums have,
in addition to the Returns requested, favoured us with

* The Return from the Cornwall Asylum gives the Average numbers and annual discharges and deaths, for the last three years only.

some valuable statements which we have appended to
their several Returns. As respects Bethlem Hospital,
we have selected, from the printed Report of that Institution, some of the most material Tables upon the
several subjects embraced in the Returns from other
Asylums.

Total numbers
of Insane.

We proceed, in conclusion, to state, as far as circumstances admit and materials for computation exist,
the total numbers of Insane persons, Pauper and Private,
in England and Wales, on the 1st of January, 1844.
This statement, for the reasons we have given, can be
considered only as the nearest practicable approximation
to the truth. It may be depended upon, however, as
exhibiting the minimum amount of Insanity, ascertained, or estimated upon authentic data.

It was first necessary to compute the entire number of
Pauper Lunatics and Idiots on the day to which the
Census of Insanity applies. The means of doing so were
furnished by the Abstract, to which reference has been
made, of the Returns from the Clerks of Boards of
Guardians, in August, 1843.

The following Tables formed the basis of our calculations :—

Number of Lunatics and Idiots chargeable to Parishes included in
Unions, in the years 1842 and 1843, according to Returns made
under the New Poor Law Amendment Act, 5 & 6 Vic. c. 57.

		Population of the Unions, according to Census of 1841.	Lunatics and Idiots.		
			M.	F.	Total.
589 Unions, Aug., 1842.	England Wales	12,978,377 884,173	5803 507	6909 651	12,712 1,158
591 Unions, Aug., 1843.	England Wales	13,152,341 884,173	6248 523	7367 654	13,615 1,177

Total number of In-door and Out-door Paupers relieved
during the Quarter, ending Lady Day 1843 . . 1,539,490
Lunatics and Idiots, as above 16,641
Proportion per cent. to number relieved . . 1.08

The two Unions which were formed, as appears by the above Table, between the years 1842 and 1843, were those of Oldham and Ashton-under-Line, the former containing a Population of 72,394, and the latter 101,570; together, 173,964.

Upon the assumption that the aggregate number of Pauper Lunatics chargeable to Unions, bore the same proportion to that of Pauper Lunatics belonging to Parishes not in Union, which the aggregate Population of the Unions, according to the census of 1841, bore to that of the Parishes not comprised in Unions, the total numbers of Pauper Lunatics in England and Wales, in the month of August of the years 1842, and 1843, respectively, were as follows :—

		POPULATION of England and Wales.	LUNATICS AND IDIOTS.			Proportion per cent. to Population.	ONE Lunatic or Idiot, to Persons Living.
			Males.	Females.	Total.		
August, 1842.	England	15,253,890	6705	7983	14,688	·096	1039
	Wales	927,335	523	671	1194	·129	777
	Totals	16,181,225	7228	8654	15,882	·098	1019
August, 1843.	England	15,457,529	715	8399	15,522	·100	1000
	Wales	939,7123	539	674	1213	·129	777
	Totals	16,397,244	7562	9073	16,735	·102	980

It appears from the last Table that the number of Pauper Lunatics, in proportion to the Population, had slightly increased from August, 1842, to August, 1843.

We have taken the Population from the Enumeration Abstract, presented to Parliament in 1843. We mention this, in order to account for a trifling difference which appears between the above estimate and that of the Poor Law Commissioners, who made use of the Population Returns as first received, which were rendered more perfect by some subsequent corrected Returns. *fourth*

It is stated, by the Registrar General, in his report for ~~1842~~, that " the increase of Females," " in the ten years, 1831—1841, was 14.17 per cent, or at the rate of 1.334

per cent annually;" and he assumes, for the reasons he gives, that the Male Population increased at the same rate; and that the increase, in both cases, was " uniformly at that rate throughout the ten years."

The computation which we have made in the last Table, of the Population in August 1842 and 1843, respectively, and in that which follows, on the 1st January 1844, has proceeded upon the hypothesis that the Population has increased at the annual rate above mentioned, since the 6th of June, 1841, the date of the last Census. It has also, in the Estimate given of the actual number of Pauper Lunatics on the 1st of January, 1844, been assumed that their numbers increased, from the date of the Poor Law Returns of 1843, in proportion to the Population.

With this explanation, we present to your Lordship the following statement, to which we have added a Table, exhibiting the proportions per cent, on the 1st of January, 1844, of the numbers of Pauper Lunatics, Male and Female, in England and Wales, respectively, to the population of each sex:—

TOTAL NUMBER OF LUNATICS AND IDIOTS CHARGEABLE TO UNIONS AND PARISHES ON THE 1ST OF JANUARY, 1844.

	POPULATION of England and Wales.	LUNATICS AND IDIOTS.		
		Male.	Female.	Total.
England ..	15,535,621	7159	8442	15,601
Wales ...	944,461	542	678	1220
Totals.	16,480,082	7701	9120	16,821

PROPORTIONS PER CENT. OF PAUPER LUNATICS TO POPULATION, JANUARY 1ST, 1844.

		Population.	Pauper Lunatics.	Proportion per cent.	One Pauper Lunatic to Persons Living.
England .	Males . .	7,589,659	7159	·094	1060
	Females .	7,945,962	8442	·106	942
	Total . .	15,535,621	15,601	·100	1000
Wales . .	Males . .	463,985	542	·117	856
	Females .	480,476	678	·141	709
	Total . .	944,461	1220	·129	775
Total England & Wales		16,480,082	16,821	·102	980
Deduct Criminal Lunatics			279		
Total Pauper Lunatics not Criminals			16,542	·100	1000

It will be observed that the proportion of Pauper Lunatics to the Population is considerably larger in Wales than in England ; and that in both England and Wales the number of Females is greater than that of the Males, in proportion to the Population of the respective sexes.

It only remains to add a general abstract of the results obtained from the various sources to which we have alluded; and which contains the nearest approximation, at which we have any certain means of arriving, to the total numbers of the Insane, Private and Pauper, in England and Wales, on the 1st of January, 1844.

GENERAL STATEMENT OF THE TOTAL NUMBER OF PERSONS ASCERTAINED TO BE INSANE, IN ENGLAND AND WALES.

JANUARY 1, 1844.

Where Confined.	PRIVATE PATIENTS.			PAUPERS.			TOTAL.		
	Male.	Female.	Total.	Male.	Female.	Total.	Male.	Female.	Total.
County Asylums	130	115	245	1924	2231	4155	2054	2346	4400
Ditto, under Local Acts	—	—	—	38	51	89	38	51	89
Military and Naval Hospitals . . .	164	4	168	—	—	—	164	4	168
Bethlem and St. Luke's Hospitals .	178	264	442	86	35	121	264	299	563
Other Public Asylums.	249	287	536	177	166	343	426	453	879
Licensed Houses:— Metropolitan	520	453	973	360	494	854	880	947	1827
" Provincial	748	678	1426	947	973	1920	1695	1651	3346
* Workhouses and elsewhere . .	—	—	—	4169	5170	9339	4169	5170	9339
Single Patients under Commission .	172	110	282	—	—	—	172	110	282
Totals	2161	1911	4072	7701	9120	16,821	9862	11,031	20,893

* Including 30 Male, and 3 Female Criminal Lunatics, in Gaols, according to the Parliamentary Return for April, 1843. The numbers given under this head have been obtained by deducting from the total estimated number of Pauper Lunatics on the 1st of January, 1844, those confined in Asylums on that day, including *County* and *Vagrant* Paupers, which are not distinguished from others in the Returns made to this Board, and which (as has been stated) were not comprised in the Poor Law Returns; consequently the numbers of Pauper Lunatics "in Workhouses and elsewhere," on the 1st of January, 1844, as well as the grand totals given above, exceeded the numbers in the Table by the number of *County* and Vagrant Paupers so deducted.

IX.

CRIMINAL LUNATICS.

——◆——

It has been matter of frequent complaint, that Asylums are made receptacles for Criminal Lunatics, including all those who are confined under orders from the Secretary of State, or Royal warrants. The objections urged to their detention in Lunatic Asylums, and to the County Asylums being required to receive them, apply principally to those who have perpetrated atrocious crimes, and who are dangerous and a source of annoyance to the other inmates, whose liberty is, in some cases, abridged, in consequence of the necessity of providing for the safe custody of the Criminal Lunatics. In respect to these, the Asylum may be viewed rather in the light of a Prison than of an Hospital.

Before proceeding further with our observations upon this subject, it may be convenient to refer shortly to the leading Enactments under which Insane Persons of this description are committed to Lunatic Asylums. These are, the Acts 39 & 40 Geo. 3rd, c. 94, and 3 & 4 Vic. c. 54. The first-mentioned Act applies to persons " acquitted, on the ground of Insanity, of Treason, Murder, or Felony;" to Persons " indicted and found Insane at the time of Arraignment ;" to those " brought before any Criminal Court to be discharged for want of prosecution, appearing Insane ;" and to Persons " apprehended under circumstances denoting a derangement of mind, and a purpose to commit" an indictable crime. The Act also provides for the custody of Persons " ap-

Objections to sending Criminal Lunatics to Asylums.

Enactments respecting Criminal Lunatics.

pearing to be Insane, and endeavouring to gain admittance to Her Majesty's presence, by intrusion on any of Her Majesty's Palaces or Places of Residence." The 3rd & 4th Vic. c. 54, extends the provisions of the 39th & 40th Geo. 3rd, c. 94, to cases of Misdemeanour; and authorises the transmission to Lunatic Asylums of Persons becoming Insane, while in Prison. It applies to all persons " confined under sentence of Death, Transportation, or Imprisonment ;" " or under a charge of any offence, or for want of Sureties to keep the Peace, or to answer a criminal charge ; or in consequence of any Summary Conviction, or other than Civil process." The Act also empowers the Visiting Justices to make orders of maintenance upon Unions and Parishes, repealing certain provisions of the former Act upon that subject.—It has been assumed, in practice, that the acts above cited are compulsory upon the visitors of County Asylums, and that they cannot refuse to receive persons committed under Royal warrant.

Number of Criminal Patients in Asylums.

It will be seen by Schedule I, in Appendix G, (compiled from the Parliamentary Return lately printed) that in April, 1843, there were 224 criminal patients confined in the several Asylums in this country, and 33 in Gaols. Of the former number of criminals there were 85 in Bethlem Hospital, leaving 139 distributed in various County and Private Asylums.

Nature of crimes.

A considerable number of the Patients included in the above statement were cases of Larceny, and minor assaults, and other Misdemeanours, as to which comparatively little objection existed to their being associated with other Patients in Lunatic Asylums. There were many cases, however, of an atrocious character, calculated to render the party dangerous, and an object of dread and disgust to those around him, such as Murder, Arson, and Unnatural Offences. Of these, as will be seen by reference to Appendix G, in Schedule II.

there were 50 instances in the Public and Private Asylums, exclusive of those in Bethlem. Amongst these, is the case of a furious and dangerous Maniac in the Chester Asylum, admitted in 1835, who had committed a murder, by strangling, under the most atrocious circumstances, and whom, in order to prevent him from killing or injuring those around him, it was found necessary to keep under constant restraint, both day and night. This man was, and had for some months been, the only patient under any kind of restraint in that Asylum.

We believe that care is frequently taken to conceal, from the other Patients, the fact of their associate being a Criminal Lunatic. This, however, cannot always be effected; and even were that possible, one objection only would be removed, to the practice of detaining criminals in Lunatic Asylums, possessing no proper Wards for that purpose. The risk of escape calls for arrangements more stringent than those required in the case of other Lunatics. Some consideration, moreover, is due to the feelings of the relatives of patients, who have reasonable ground to complain of atrocious criminals being forced into their society. In reference to this part of the subject, however, regard must be had to the nature of the offence committed by each Criminal; since there are, without doubt, instances in which it would be hard to condemn a " Criminal Lunatic " to confinement in a separate Ward, or a distinct Institution. These cases, however, are exceptions, and leave the general objections untouched.

Criminality of Lunatics frequently concealed from other Patients.

Risk of escape.

In reference to the subject of Escape, we may mention the fact which came to our knowledge in the course of one of our Visits, that a criminal Lunatic had escaped from a Private Asylum at Plympton for the third time, and had not been re-taken; and also that a male patient, committed by a Magistrate, as a dangerous Lunatic, to a Private Asylum at Nunkeeling, had escaped three times, had twice attempted the lives of his Keepers, and once to set fire to the Asylum; and that the Proprietor of the Asylum had applied in vain to the Secretary of State, and to the Magistrates of the District, for the purpose of his being removed to a place of safe custody. At Gateshead Fell Asylum, also, there is a Maniac, who formerly escaped from the house, murdered his wife and daughter, and was (after his Trial) re-admitted as a Criminal Lunatic, and is now generally hand-cuffed, in order to prevent his again committing murder.

Practice at the Home Office,

The practice at the Home Office (as we learn from Mr. Capper's evidence before the Lords' Committee on Gaols, in 1835) is (upon being applied to in the case of any person acquitted on the ground of Insanity) to communicate with the Visiting Justices, with a view to ascertain whether there is any Lunatic Asylum in the County, to which they propose his removal. Mr. Capper stated that considerable difficulties existed upon the subject, to which we need not advert. We may mention, however, the fact stated by him, that, as regarded the County of Middlesex, the Visiting Justices had remonstrated against Criminal Lunatics being sent from Newgate to Hanwell, although Middlesex prisoners, on the ground that the Hanwell Asylum afforded no

Mr. Capper's evidence,

security for that class of offenders. Mr. Capper, in his evidence, adverts also to a class of Criminal Lunatics of which we have found instances, both in County and Private Asylums, viz., those who after trial and acquittal on the ground of Insanity have proved not to be Insane, or who have become perfectly sane within a short period after their committal to a Lunatic Asylum, and yet are, "in many cases, too dangerous to " turn upon the public, having committed crimes of a " serious character." Mr. Capper suggests that, for such persons, a particular class should be formed in Prisons.

We now beg to draw your Lordship's attention to some observations made by the Lord Chancellor of Ireland, contained in a letter produced and read by Opinion of
Lord Chancel-
lor of Ireland. Mr. White (Inspector-General of Prisons) to the Lords' Committee, upon the state of the Lunatic Poor of Ireland, in 1843. They are as follows :—" Solid objections exist to Criminal Lunatics being received into District Asylums, which never were intended for prisons. The advantages of bringing together all the Criminal Lunatics under the immediate eye of the Governor (*i. e.* of the Richmond Asylum, with which it was proposed to connect a detached Criminal Lunatic Establishment) is obvious. Their security could easily be provided for, and strangers could be prohibited from visiting that Department from motives of curiosity."

We entertain a strong opinion that it is highly desir- Separate care
and custody of
Criminal Luna-
tics highly desir-
able. able that arrangements should be made for the separate care and custody of Criminal Lunatics ; and we would submit to your Lordship that, as respects all Criminal Lunatics who have been charged with serious offences, and whom it is necessary to detain in custody, it is desirable that arrangements should be made with one or more Public Institutions, as Bethlem Hospital, or that a separate class should be formed in some convenient Prison, so as to prevent their association either with other Prisoners, or the Inmates, generally, of Lunatic Asylums.

X.

WALES.

WE have now brought to a conclusion all the obser- Neglected state
of the Insane at
Wales. vations which we feel it necessary to make at present with regard to the care of Lunatics in England; but it is our duty to bring under your Lordship's special consideration the very destitute and neglected state of the insane within the principality of Wales.

With the exception of the small Asylum at Haver-fordwest (so totally unfit for its purpose) before adverted to, there was no Asylum throughout the whole of the Principality until last year, when a House was licensed for Pauper and Private Patients, in Glamorganshire.*

In 1843 there were in Wales 1177 Pauper Lunatics, according to the Poor Law Returns recently printed by the House of Commons.

Of these 1177 Pauper Lunatics, it appears that thirty-six were in English County Asylums, forty-one in English Licensed Houses, ninety in Union Workhouses, and 1010 boarded with their friends and elsewhere. It has been represented to us that many of the Welsh Luna-tics, who have been in the English Asylums, have been very violent, and have been sent to them in a wretched and most neglected condition. When at Briton Ferry, we made the inquiries, directed by the Act, as to the condition of the Paupers on admission, and we were shown a letter, addressed by a Parish Officer to the Proprietor of a Licensed House, of which we give a copy.

"BLAENBWCH, 19th December, 1843.

"SIR,—We have got an Insane Female Pauper of the Union of Buillht, Breconshire; she has been so for some years. Something has took her in her limbs about two years ago, until she is quite a cripple. I suppose it is owing to being kept in a close place, having no practice to walk. Please to write me the lowest you charge per week."

In illustration of the statements we have received, as to the deplorable condition in which some of the Pauper Lunatics of North Wales have been found, and the necessity of providing an Asylum for them, we may

* We are happy to be enabled to state that an Asylum, for Private and Pauper Patients, is about to be erected near Denbigh. The county of Flint has resolved upon uniting with Denbigh for this purpose. Two other counties of North Wales have decided against a union.

mention four cases described in a letter to the Editor of
the North Wales Chronicle, dated 28th October, 1842,
of which we have the permission of the Dean of St.
Asaph to say, that he avowed himself the author. He
states, " I have seen one secured in a dark and loath-
" some shed, lying extended upon straw, (for the space
" did not admit of his standing erect,) in a state of filth
" that I dare not describe. A second was fettered and
" manacled, and basking in the public street, exposed
" to the rude gaze of the thoughtless passers by. A
" third I have seen led about the streets, and even to
" Church, in the restraint of a strait waistcoat. A
" fourth (I copy from a letter now before me of a Jus-
" tice of one of the Welsh counties), died some time
" ago in the most deplorable state, having been, for
" about fifteen years, chained like a wild beast in an
" out-house."

We have recently received a letter containing important particulars from the principal Medical Practitioner
at Denbigh, a copy of which is set forth in the note.*

DENBIGH, June 14th, 1844.

* " A few months ago a poor woman, who was under great excite-
" ment from the mischievous teasings of a crowd of boys and girls,
" appealed to me in the streets of this town for protection. When I
" got her into my house, and endeavoured, by kind and conciliatory
" language to soothe her, I found she had been chained by her hus-
" band in a cottage, in a village four miles off, for many weeks. She
" had been in an Asylum in England for some time ; but for want of
" knowledge of her native language, no good could be effected.

" I sent her to her friends under proper protection, and she was, I
" lament to say, again consigned to the tender mercies of her husband,
" who, to do him justice, had no other means of preventing the poor
" creature from inflicting injury upon herself and others. She is now
" more calm, and goes about the country unprotected occasionally.

" A few years ago, a poor girl not above a hundred yards from my
" residence became deranged. From a dislike to send her from
" home, amongst strangers unacquainted with her language and habits,
" she was consigned to the care of a neighbour, who tied her down in
" bed.—She made violent struggles to get away, and, in attempting to
" escape from her keeper, fell down stairs and fractured her head.

" I heard of a man a few months ago, whose family I am acquainted
" with in Carnarvonshire, who was confined in a small room, unshaved

Other cases of a similar description were detailed at a recent meeting of the Committee of Magistrates of the County of Carnarvon. Among these, that of Griffith Jones excited painful attention. He had for some time been confined in a place in which there was no window, and the smell arising from it was nearly such as to suffocate the Medical man who visited him. His bed was in a most filthy state, and his body covered with vermin; and he was altogether the image of starvation, despair, and wretchedness. He is since dead.

In our visits to Wales, and upon other occasions, when inspecting houses in England, in which Welsh Pauper Patients were confined, we have made various inquiries as to the state of the Insane Poor belonging to the Principality, and the information which we have received gives us every reason to believe that there is but little provision for the support, and still less for the cure, of these poor people, who are for the most part placed singly, either with their friends, (who are in the poorest station of life) or with strangers; a small pittance only being allowed in each case for their support. So

"and uncleaned for nearly twenty years. He was once a Student of the "University of Oxford.*

"There is now a man in Flint Jail, who was tried the last sessions "for cutting a poor woman dreadfully with a reaping hook, whilst in a "state of mania. He had been allowed to ramble about the country "for months in that state.

"I am acquainted with two or three cases in this town at the "present time, who are unfit to be at liberty. I had myself a very "narrow escape some time ago of being killed by an infuriated Idiot, "who had been tormented by some boys, and who threw a paving-"stone at my head as I was passing by.

"The state of the Welsh Lunatic, in general, is most pitiable and "miserable,—with no place of protection in his own country ; and the "only alternative is an English Asylum, where no real good can be "effected, and that at an enormous expense to his parish or his friends.

"It is to be hoped that the Legislature will throw its protection over "him, as I fear his own Country will not without compulsion."

(*Signed*)　　"R. LLOYD WILLIAMS, Surgeon."

---

* All the other persons alluded to, were Parish Paupers.

strongly are we impressed with the necessity of remedy-ing these evils, that we have directed some Members of our Board, who are about to visit the districts bordering on Wales, to make special inquiries, in reference to the general condition of the Insane throughout the Princi-pality, and we feel it our duty to bring distinctly under your Lordship's notice the fact that Wales, containing no less than 1177 Pauper Lunatics, has at present within its limits only one house Licensed to receive 36 Insane Pauper Patients, in addition to the Asylum at Haverfordwest, upon which it has been our duty so strongly to animadvert.

ASHLEY, (Chairman).
SEYMOUR.
R. VERNON SMITH.
J. HANCOCK HALL.
R. W. S. LUTWIDGE.
R. GORDON.
THOMAS TURNER.
FRANCIS BISSET HAWKINS.
B. W. PROCTER.
J. R. GOWEN.
H. H. SOUTHEY.
J. W. MYLNE.
JOHN BARNEBY.
W. H. SYKES.
THOMAS WATERFIELD.
J. C. PRICHARD.
J. R. HUME.

SUGGESTIONS FOR THE AMENDMENT OF THE LAW.

———

In the expectation that the Law, as it regards Lunacy, will shortly be subjected to revision. We trust that we shall not be thought to have exceeded the limit of our duties in offering the following suggestions to your Lordship.

1.

That there be provided for the Insane Poor of every County some proper and convenient Hospital or Hospitals for the reception of all recent cases.

2.

That the provisions of the Law, enabling Counties to unite for the formation of Asylums, be extended to parts of Counties, Towns, and places with separate jurisdictions; and also to the union of Counties and Districts having no Asylums with others possessing such Institutions.

3.

That the 15th section of the Act 9 Geo. IV. c. 40, be amended, by enabling a majority, being not less than two-thirds of the Justices of the Peace present at any General or Quarter Sessions, to direct or authorise tenants at rack-rent to detain out of their rent one-half of the full amount of all or any rates hereafter to be levied for building, enlarging, and repairing County Asylums, or in reference thereto.

4.

That in any County Asylum or Hospital hereafter to be erected, into which curable Lunatics (either alone, or together with incurable Patients,) shall be received, the number of Patients shall not exceed 250 in the whole. (See pp. 23, 24.)

5.

That some provision be made for the removal, from time to time, of Incurable Paupers from County Asylums, in order to make room for such as are curable.

6.

That in the more populous Counties, such as Middle-sex and Lancashire, separate receptacles be established for Chronic cases; to be conducted in a manner adapted to the wants of the Patients, but upon a less expensive scale than the present County Asylums.

7.

That if it be deemed a matter of necessity, under present circumstances, to confine some incurable Pauper Lunatics elsewhere than in receptacles expressly esta-blished for the purpose, they shall be kept, not in all Workhouses indiscriminately, but in some one specified Workhouse, or part of a Workhouse, within each dis-trict; and that every such Workhouse, or part of a Workhouse, be properly adapted and exclusively appro-priated to the reception of Lunatics, and be regularly inspected by competent Visitors, and have regular Medi-cal Officers.

8.

That all Pauper Lunatics, confined elsewhere than in Asylums, be periodically visited; and that periodical Reports be made upon their condition.

9.

That the Sites, Plans, and Estimates for every County Asylum hereafter to be erected, be referred to some Board or authority, constituted for the visitation and supervision of Lunatics, for the purpose of receiving suggestions, previously to the final adoption thereof by the Magistrates.

10.

That the Orders and Medical Certificates for the admission of Pauper Patients into any Asylum, or other place of confinement, be the same as are now required for their admission into Licensed Houses, and that no order be given unless the party signing has previously seen the Patient.*

11.

That the Orders and Medical Certificates for the

---

* At present, a Pauper is sent to an Asylum on one Certificate, and it does not appear necessary that the Magistrate, or other person signing the order for his confinement, should previously see the Patient.

admission of Private Patients into any Asylum, or other place of confinement, be the same as are now required for their admission into Licensed Houses. (See p. 163.)

12.

That no person certifying as to a Patient's Insanity, sign an order for his confinement.*

13.

That, with a view, amongst other things, to the formation of a complete Register of the Insane, notice of the admission, discharge, and death of every certified Patient, Private as well as Pauper, (excepting only those Patients of whom "Private Returns" ought to be made), be sent to the Metropolitan Board, within two days after every such admission, discharge, and death; and that in every notice of Admission, the day on which the Patient was received shall be stated, such day also to be endorsed upon the original order, and certificates.†

14.

That every County and Public Asylum or Hospital shall have a resident Medical Officer.

15.

That the Orders and Medical Certificates for the admission of Patients be a sufficient authority for re-taking them, in case of escape, at any time within eight days after such escape.

16.

That all Asylums and Hospitals for the Insane be subject to official visitation. (See page 33.)

17.

That the Official Visitors have power, at their discre-

---

* In one or two cases, we have found that the brother or father of the Patient, being a medical man, has signed the order for confinement, and also certified as to the Lunacy.

† This will also facilitate the examination of the orders and certificates upon the admission of private Patients into Asylums, and dispense with the necessity of referring to the Register of admissions in order to ascertain that the Patient was received within the period limited by law

tion, to give an order for the admission of any relation, trustee, or friend, to visit a certified Patient, wherever confined.   (See page 75.)

18.

That the Official Visitors have power to fix and alter the Dietary of Pauper Patients in all Lunatic Asylums. (See page 49.)

19.

That the Lord Chancellor be empowered, upon the representation of the Board of Metropolitan Commissioners, to suspend the Licence of any House licensed for the reception of the Insane.

20.

That it be lawful for the Proprietor or Superintendent of an Asylum, with the permission, in writing, of the Official Visitors, to take or send a Patient to any specified place, for a limited time, for the benefit of his health.

21.

That, in the event of any Proprietor quitting a Licensed House for another licensed to him, it shall be lawful for him, with the previous permission, in writing, of the Official Visitors, to transfer his Patients from the one to the other, without fresh Orders and Medical Certificates.*

22.

That Licences be granted, in all cases, to the *Proprietors* of Licensed Houses, and not, as now, in some instances, to the Resident Superintendents.

23.

That no dangerous Lunatic be removed from any Licensed House against the advice of the Medical Attendant of the House, without the previous sanction of the Official Visitors.   (See page 171.)

24.

That a full statement be published, annually, by

* The want of such a provision occasioned considerable inconvenience in a case which was brought under the notice of the Commissioners.

every County Asylum, of all receipts and disburse-
ments; also of the property of the Asylum, the sources
and amount of Income, and the application of the same.
(See page 26).

25.

That in all Asylums, Public and Private, Registers
and Medical Records be required to be kept, in a specified and uniform shape; and that annual statements
of admissions and discharges, in a form to be prescribed, be made up to the 31st of December in each
year, and transmitted to the Metropolitan Board. (See
page 179.)

———————

The following, amongst other suggestions, have been
received from the Clerk* to the Visitors of a County
Asylum, who is also Clerk to the Board of Guardians,
and are submitted for your Lordship's consideration.

That the order of Commitment to the County Asylum should be made without requiring any adjudication
of Settlement, so far as the Asylum is concerned.

That the Union to which the Pauper is chargeable,
should be liable to the weekly payments for Pauper
Lunatics, until an order of payment shall have been
made by Justices upon another District or Parish, upon
application of the Board of Guardians.

* EXTRACT FROM A LETTER RELATIVE TO THESE
SUGGESTIONS.

" The reason for these alterations arises from the difficulty too frequently experienced in obtaining the requisite evidence for the Justices
to act upon, at the time the Patient is required to be sent to the Asylum; and having recourse to the other provisions of the Statute is
attended with many difficulties, as will appear from the cases decided
by the Court of Queen's Bench, not one of which, I believe, has
stood the test of a Judicial scrutiny, the Union from which a Patient
is sent ought, in common fairness, to be chargeable with the expenses,
until the place of legal settlement is found out—and I am of opinion
that the practice should be assimilated to that under the Poor Law.
—A Pauper is admitted into the Workhouse from the parish in which
he last resided, and it is for that parish to get rid of the burthen by
finding out the place of his legal settlement."

APPENDIX A.

COUNTY ASYLUMS,

ERECTED UNDER THE ACTS 48 GEORGE III. c. 96, AND 9 GEORGE IV. c. 40.

COUNTY.	Superintendent.	Date of opening.	Weekly charge for Paupers.	Numbers, Jan. 1, 1844.		
				Private.	Pauper.	Total.
			s. d.			
BEDS.	J. Harris, Surgeon. .	1812	(a) 7 6	..	139	139
(Bedford) . .			Out County. 8 6			
CHESTER . . .	J. Leete, Surgeon. .	1829	(b) 4 1	9	155	164
(Chester) . .			Out County. 10 0			
CORNWALL . . .	D. F. Tyerman, M.D.	1820	5 6	20	133	153
(Bodmin) . .			Non-Contributory Dist. 10 6			
DORSET . . .	G. P. Button, M.D. .	1832	(a) 7 0	..	107	107
(Forston, near Dorchester) . .						
GLOUCESTER . .	S. Hitch, M.D. . . .	1823	(a) 9 0	68	189	257
(Gloucester) . .						
KENT	G. S. Poynder, Surgeon.	1833	(a) 8 6	.,	249	249
(Barming Heath, near Maidstone)						
LANCASTER . . .	S. Gaskell, Surgeon . .	1816	(a) 6 0	..	611	611
(Lancaster Moor)						
LEICESTER . . .	H. F. Prosser, Surgeon.	1837	(b) 8 6	27	104	131
(Leicester) . .			Out County. 12 0			
MIDDLESEX . . .	— Godwin, (Governor)	1831	(a) 7 7	..	*975	975
(Hanwell) . .			Out County. 14 0			
	Visiting-Physician } J. Conolly, M.D.					
	House-Surgeons { J. Begley, M.D. Davies, M.D.					
NORFOLK . . .	Ebenezer Owen . . .	1814	(a) 5 3	..	164	164
(Thorpe, near Norwich) . .			Out County. 8 0			
NOTTS	T. Powell, Surgeon. .	1812	(a) 8 0	52	125	177
(Nottingham) .						
STAFFORD . . .	Jas. Wilkes, Surgeon.	1818	(a) 7 0	62	183	245
(Stafford) . .						
SUFFOLK . . .	J. Kirkman, M.D. .	1829	(a) 5 10	7	206	213
(Melton, near Woodbridge) . .			Out County. 8 10			
SURREY	S. Hill, Surgeon. . .	1841	(a) 9 0	..	382	382
(Springfield, near Wandsworth) .						
YORK WEST RIDING	C. C. Corsellis, M.D.	1818	(a) 7 0	..	433	433
(Wakefield) . .						
			Totals . . .	245	4155	4400

(a) Including clothes.   (b) Not including clothes.   * Sept. 30, 1843

LUMS MADE, BY LOCAL ACTS, SUBJECT TO THE PROVISIONS
OF 9 GEORGE IV. c. 40.

	Superintendent.	Date of Opening.	Weekly Charge for Paupers.	Number 1st Jan., 1844, (Paupers.)
ospital, Bristol.	— Brady, Surg.	Incorporated 1696.	. . .	72
mbroke, Haverfordwest.	G. Hampson.	. .	. . .	17
Kingston-upon-Hull.*				
			Total . . .	89

HOSPITALS.

	Nature.	Principal Medical Officer.	Numbers 1st January, 1844.		
			Commissioned Officers.	Non-Commissioned Officers and Privates.	Total.
ce, Chatham	Military	Andrew Smith, M.D.	21	49	70
ital, Gosport	Naval	Sir W. Burnet, M.D.,	29	69	98
				Total . . .	168

TALS.

Where situate.	Steward.	Numbers, Jan. 1, 1844.		
		Curable.	Incurables.	Criminals.
St. George's Fields .	Mr. Nicholls .	181	84	90
Old Street, City Road	Mr. Stinton .	93	84	—
		274	168	90

Name of Asylum.	Superintendent.	Weekly charge for Paupers.	Numbers, Jan. 1, 1844.		
			Private	Pauper.	Tot.
St. Thomas's	Luke Ponsford, Surgeon.	s. d. 15.0	47	1	48
Lunatic Ward	— — —	—	25	–	25
Lunatic Asylum . . .	W. Graham . . . . House Surgeon.	(b) 10 0	30	73	103
Lunatic Asylum . . .	G. Tyrrell.	12 0	37	36	73
Lunatic Asylum . . .	— — —	—	36	–	36
General Lunatic Asylum	T. O. Prichard, M.D. .	(b) 9 0	50	181	231
Bethel Hospital . . .	— King.	—	†66	–	66
Warneford Asylum . .	F. T. Wintle, M.D. . .	—	42	–	42
Asylum	S. Alderson, Surgeon. .	(a)M. 7 6	105	52	157
		Fem. 6 6	98	–	98
Friends' Retreat . . .	J. Thurnam, M. D. . . .				
		Totals . .	536	343	879

) Including clothes.   (b) Not including clothes.
o the knowledge of the Commissioners that this Workhouse is, by a Local
nstituted an Asylum, subject to the County Asylum Acts.

METROPOLITAN LICENSED HOUSES.

RECEIVING PRIVATE PATIENTS ONLY.

PROPRIETOR.	HOUSE, AND WHERE SITUATE.	No. of Patients, Jan. 1, 1844. Private.
Ayres, William (Surgeon)	Mare Street, Hackney	5
Bell, Robert	Manor House, Chiswick	16
Birkett, Richard	Northumberland House, Stoke Newington.	46
Bradbury, Mrs. Mary	Earl's Court House, Old Brompton	26
Burrow, Miss	Grove House, Stoke Newington Green	13
Bush, John (Surgeon)	Retreat, Clapham	12
Cole, James	Dartmouth House, Lewisham	13
*Costello, W. B., M.D	Wyke House, Sion Hill, Brentford	
Diamond, W. B. (Surgeon)	Western House, St. Pancras	13
Fleming, Mrs. Mary	Warwick House, Fulham Road	5
Haines, W. F. (Surgeon)	Harefield Park, Uxbridge	2
*Horner and Co., Edward	Lawn House, Hanwell	
Jackson, John Thompson	Turnham Green Terrace	2
Kerr, Alfred George (Surgeon)	17, Pembroke Square, Kensington	2
Magnall, Mrs. Martha	Hanwell	5
Monro, E. T., M.D.	Brook House, Upper Clapton	34
Oxley, William (Surgeon)	London Retreat, Hackney	28
Parkin, John (Surgeon)	Manor Cottage, King's Road, Chelsea	15
Philp, F. R. M.D. and Finch, C. H.M.	Kensington House, Kensington	55
Pierce, Miss Mary Ann	Beaufort House, Fulham	5
Roy, D. T. (Surgeon)	Hope House, Brook Green	8
*Sloman, Harriet, Mrs.	Oak Tree Cottage, Harrow	
Smith, William	Lampton House, Hounslow	10
Steward, J. B., M.D., and Daniel, G.W. (Surgeon)	Southall Park	9
Stilwell, Arthur (Surgeon) and W.	Moor Croft House, Hillingdon	30
Sutherland, A. R., M.D.	Blacklands House, Chelsea	30
Sutherland, A. R., M.D	Otto House, Fulham	22
Symmons, Eliza, Mrs. and Co.	Cowper House, Old Brompton	39
Talfourd, Ann, Mrs.	Normand House, Fulham	18
Tow, James	Althorpe House, Battersea	12
Williams, Walter Davis, M.D.	Pembroke House, Hackney	95
Wood, Susan, Mrs.	Elm Grove House, Hanwell	7
Warburton, John, M.D.	Whitmore House, Hoxton	41

RECEIVING PAUPERS.

		Weekly Charge for Paupers.†	Private.	Pauper.
		s. *d.*		
Armstrong, Peter	Peckham House	10 0	48	203
Lee, Henry Boyle (Surgeon)	Hoxton House, Hoxton	9 0	81	315
Warburton, John, M.D.	Bethnal Green	9 8¼	226	336

* House Licensed since 1 Jan. 1844.   † For maintenance, medicine, and clothing.

	PROPRIETOR.		Numbers, Jan. 1, 1844.
BEDS.	Harris, J. (Surgeon)	Springfield House, Kempston, Bedford	25
BUCKS.	Horner and Harper, Messrs.	Denham Park, near Uxbridge	17
DEVON	Rich, James (Surgeon)	Ford House, Church Stanton	2
DORSET	Mercer, J.	Portland House, Halstock	10
	Symes, W. (Surgeon)	Cranbourne	6
ESSEX	Allen, M. (M.D.)	High Beach, near Epping	41
GLOUCESTER	Conolly, W. (M.D.)	Castleton House, Charlton Kings, Cheltenham }	8
	Eyre, T. D.	Upper Bath Road, Bristol	
	Fox, H. H. (M.D.)	Northwoods, Winterbourne	20
	Mules, C.	Ridgeway House, near Bristol	11
	Taylor, M. (Mrs.)	Whitehall House, St. George's, Bristol	9
HANTS	Burnet, C. M. (Surgeon)	Westbrook House, Alton	4
HERTS	Smith, James (Surgeon)	Hadham Palace, Much Hadham	13
KENT	Harmer, J.	Hawkhurst	2
	Newington, J. N. (Surgeon)	Goudhurst	2
LANCASTER	Edwards, E.	Blakeley House, near Manchester	25
	Haigh, E. (Mrs.)	Heath Green, Newton, do.	12
	Lomas, G.	Clifton Hall, do.	8
	Kershaw, P.	Billington Whalley, near Tew	6
	Owen, J.	Brook Villa, West Derby, Liverpool	32
	Squires, Richard (Surgeon)	Walton Lodge, near Liverpool	30
LEICESTER	Benfield, C.	Wigston House, Great Wigston	6
LINCOLN	Willis, F. (M.D.)	Shillingthorpe House, near Stamford	11
NORFOLK	Nichols and Watson (Messrs)	Heigham Hall, near Norwich	12
	Pedgrift, Robert (Surgeon)	Loddon	8
	Steele, H. (Surgeon)	Stoke Ferry	4
	Wright, W. (M.D.) & Dalrymple & Cross, Messrs. (Surg.) }	Heigham Retreat, near Norwich	16
NORTHUMBERLAND	Keenlyside, J. W.	Belle Grove House, Newcastle-on-Tyne	15
OXON	Batt, E. A. (Surgeon)	Witney	12
	Mallam, Richard (Surgeon)	Hook Norton	
SOMERSET	Fox, F. K. (M.D.) and C. J. (M.D) }	Brislington House, near Bristol	90
	Langworthy, R. A. (M.D.)	Longwood House, Ashton, do.	10
STAFFORD	Bakewell, G. S. (M.D)	Oulton House, Stone	28
	Woody, Alice (Mrs.)	Moat House, Tamworth	3
SUFFOLK	Chevallier, J. Rev. (M.D.)	Aspall Hall, near Debenham	4
	King, Jane (Mrs.)	Wherstead Road, Ipswich	
SURREY	Chapman, (Sir J.) & Co. (Surgs.)	Great Foster House, Egham	19
	Stedman, Jas. (M.D.), & others	Lea Pale House, Stoke, near Guildford	3
SUSSEX	King, W. (M.D.)	Ringmer, near Lewes	3
	Newington, C. (Surgeon)	Asylum, Ticehurst }	59
	Do. do.	Highlands, do.	
WARWICK	Brown, Henry (Surgeon)	Henley in Arden	4
	Boddington, G. (Surgeon)	Driffold House, Sutton Coldfield	8
	Burman, H. (M.D)	Henley in Arden	27
WILTS	Ogilvie, G. S. (Surgeon)	Calne	7
YORK, E. R.	Allanson, W. (Surgeon)	Retreat, Rillington, near New Malton	2
	Atkinson, J. (Surgeon)	Weaverthorpe, near Sledmere	
Do. W. R.	Durham and Haigh, (Messrs.)	Field Head House, Wakefield	2
	Hodgson, H. B. (Surgeon)	Acomb House, near York	10
	Kitching, J. (Surgeon)	Painthorpe House, near Wakefield	13
	Smith (Surgeon), Smith, P. (M.D.) }	Castleton Lodge, near Leeds	11
Do. City & Subs.	Allis, T.	Osbaldwick, near York	6
	Belcombe, H. S. (M.D.)	Clifton House, York	15
	Dawson, W.	St. Maurice House, York	6
	Tose, E. (Mrs.)	Terrace House, Osbaldwick	6

PROPRIETOR.			Weekly Charge for Paupers.	vate.
			s. d.	
DERBY	Brigstocke, (M.D.)	Green Hill House	(b) 9 0	9
DEVON	Lancaster, John	Workhouse, Stoke Damerel, Devonport	5 0	
	Langworthy, R. C. (Surgeon)	Plympton House, Plympton St. Mary	(b) 10 6	17
DURHAM	Eales, J., and Sister	West Auckland	(b) 6 to 7	8
	Glenton, F. and P. (Surgeon)	Bensham, near Gateshead	(a) 8 0	17
	Gowland, Jacob	Wreckenton, do.	(a) 7 to 8	5
	Kent, S.	Gateshead Fell	(a) 8 0	6
	Wilkinson, J. E.	Dunston Lodge, Whickham	(a) 8 0	23
ESSEX	Tomkins, J. (Surgeon)	Maldon Lane, Witham	1 0 0	17
GLOUCESTER	Bompas, G. G. (M.D.)	Fishponds, Stapleton, near Bristol	(a) 10 0	48
	Iles, A	Fairford	(a) 8 to 9	21	1
HANT	Middleton, H. (Mrs.)	Grove Place, Nursling		19
	Riches (Surgeon)	House of Industry, Carisbrooke		
	Scales, G. J. (Surgeon)	Hilsea Asylum, Portsea Island	(a) 9 to 9 6	6
	Twynam, J. (M.D.)	Lainston House, Winchester	(a) 9 0	10
HEREFORD	Gilliland, J. (Surgeon)	Hereford	(a) 10 to 12	7
	Millard, S. (Surgeon)	Whitechurch, near Ross	(a) 10 0	9
KENT	Rix, Jane (Mrs.)	West Malling Place, West Malling		34
LANCASTER	Mott	Haydock Lodge, Winwick		
NORTHUMBERLAND	Smith, N. (M. D.) and McIntosh, D. (M.D.)	Newcastle-on-Tyne, Lunatic Asylum	m. f. (a) 9/6 9	21
OXON	Mallam, Richard (Surgeon)	Hook Norton	(b)8/6 to 9	
SALOP	Gough, (Surgeon, Governor of House of Industry)	Morda, Oswestry	2 6†	2
	Jacob, James	House of Industry, Kingsland, Shrewsbury	(b) 6 to 10	11
SOMERSET	Gillett, W. E. (Surgeon)	Fairwater House, Staplegrove, near Taunton	(b) (a)	46
	Terry, Stephen (Surgeon)	Bailbrook House, Bath Easton	8 9	28
STAFFORD	Rowley, T. (M.D.)	Sandfield, Lichfield	(b) 9 (a)10	4
SUFFOLK	Shaw, James (Surgeon)	Belle Vue House, Ipswich	*	12
WARWICK	Gibbs, M. (Mrs.)	Haugh House, Packwood		3
	Lewis (Messrs.)	Duddeston Hall, near Birmingham	(a) 10 0	20
WILTS	Finch, W. (M.P.)	Laverstock House, Salisbury	(a) 7/6 to 8	91
	Finch, W. C. (M.D.)	Fisherton House, Fisherton, Auger	(a) 8 0	22
	Langworthy, C. C. (M.D.)	Kingsdown House, Box	(a) 8 to 9	36	1
	Phillips, T. (Surgeon)	Belle Vue House, Devizes	(a) 8 0	8	14
WILTS	Spencer, C. F.	Fonthill Gifford, Hindon	(a) 8 0	3
	Willett, R.	Fiddington House, Market Lavington	8 0	36	14
WORCESTER	Ricketts and Hastings, (Messrs.) Surgeons	Droitwich	(a) 9 0	26	8
YORK, N. R.	Martin, James	Gate Helmsey, near York	(b) 8 7	30	4
Do. E. R.	Beall, Jos.	Moo Cottage, Nunkeeling, near Brandsburton		9
	Casson, Richard (Surgeon)	Hull and East Riding Refuge	(b) 8 0	13	9
	Gofton, Robert	Southcoates, Hull	(b) 8 0	4
Do. W. R.	Hornby, B. (Surgeon)	Dunnington, near York	(a) 5 to 9	7	2
	Taylor, C. A. (Miss)	Hessle, near Hull	(b) 8 0	3
	Taylor, Isaac	Acomb, near York	(b) 8/6m.8f.	12	1
	Walker and Matterson, (Messrs.) Surgeons	Heworth, near York	(b) 8/6m. 7/6f.	1

WALES.

| GLAMORGAN | Leach, R. V. (Surgeon) | Britton Ferry, near Swansea | | 1 |

APPENDIX B.

COUNTY ASYLUMS.

ACCOMMODATION AND COST OF ERECTION.

BEDFORD.—*Opened August, 1812.—Pauper.*

Land . . . . . . 9 Acres.

Cost . . . . . Total Cost of Buildings, Furnishing, and Land, 20,500*l.*

Accommodation . 90 Males, 90 Females. Total, 180.

Average Cost per head, 114*l.*

CHESTER.—*Opened August, 1829.—Private and Pauper.*

Land . . . . 10¾ Acres.

Cost . . . . Total Cost of Buildings and Land, &c., originally about 28,000*l.*

Accommodation . Originally built for 96; viz.—10 Male and 10 Female Private Patients, and 38 Males and 38 Female Paupers, to each of whom was assigned a separate Sleeping Room.

The Sleeping Rooms in the Pauper Galleries are 10 ft. by 8 ft., and from 11 ft. 3 in. to 12 ft. in height; and two Beds are now, for the most part, placed in each Room, affording present accommodation for 152.

Average Cost per head to County.—Calculated on first Cost of Erection and original Accommodation . . . £292

——————— on present Accommodation . . £184

CORNWALL.—*Opened* 1820.—*Private and Pauper.*

Land.— Acres, presented by the Corporation of Bodmin.
Cost of Buildings, not including Furnishing :

Original Building £15,000
New ditto 3,780
_____
Total to present time . . . £18,780

Accommodation . . Original part . 112
,, ,, Additional Buildings 60
_____
Total, Pauper, 129; Private, 43 . . 172

Average Cost per head : On first Accommodation . . £134
,, ,, On present Accommodation . £109

_____

DORSET.—*Opened August 1st*, 1832.—*Pauper.*

Land . . . 8¾ Acres.—Land, with original House, presented by F. J. Browne, Esq., who also vested 4000*l.* in the Funds, the Dividends to be applied towards the Annual Charges of the Establishment.

Cost of Building £13,156
—— Furnishing 1,561
_____
Total £14,717

Accommodation . 51 Males, 62 Females. Total, 113.
Amount of Subscriptions £3,155
Defrayed by County 11,562
_____
£14,717

Average Cost per head . On total Outlay, £130
,, ,, Borne by County, £102

GLOUCESTER.—*Opened 24th July, 1823.*—*Private and Pauper.*

Land . . . Original Purchase .	7 Acres for £1,660		
Building, &c. First Cost of Building	£38,500 0		
Cost . . ,, Fittings	2,696 7		
	—————— 41,196 7		

Total first Cost . . . £42,856 7

	Males.	Females.	Total.
Original Accommodation . . Private .	30	30	60
,, ,, . Pauper .	30	30	60
Total .	60	60	120

First Cost per head . . . £357

How defrayed (as well First Cost, as of Additions) :—

$\frac{8}{20}$ by Subscription Fund, or Charitable Institution.

$\frac{11}{20}$,, County $\Big\}$ of Gloucester, by Rate.
$\frac{1}{20}$,, City

Additional Land . . Second Purchase .	7 Acres for £1,250	
,, . . . Third Ditto . . $\frac{3}{4}$,,	450	
	£1,700	

N.B.—Ten Acres also Rented.

Total Cost to present Time :—

Buildings, about	£44,000
Furniture, Fittings, and Apparatus . .	4,000
Land	3,360
Total . .	£51,360

	Males.	Females.	Total.
Present Accommodation . Private ,	32	39	71
,, ,, . Pauper .	95	95	190
Total .	127	134	261

Total Cost of Asylum, defrayed by—

Subscription Funds . . .	£20,544
County	28,248
City	2,568
	£51,360

217

Average Cost per head for Paupers borne by County and City, 162*l.*
The sum annually paid by the County and Subscribers for Repairs and Alterations is about 800*l.*, $\frac{9}{20}$ of which is paid by the Subscribers.

KENT.—*Opened 1st January, 1833.—Pauper.*

Land . . . 37 Acres . . 6,000*l.*
Total Cost to present Time, of Buildings, Furniture, and
   Land . . . . 64,056*l.*

		Males.	Females.	Total.
Accommodation	Wards	137	137	274
„	Infirmaries	13	13	26
	Total	150	150	300

In single rooms { Males . . . 102
                { Females . . . 102
                         204

Average Cost per Head . . . 213*l.*

Details of Cost of Asylum :—

Original Buildings, Walls, &c. (about) .	£35,000
Land (37 Acres) . . .	6,000
Furnishing, Apparatus, Baths, &c. .	9,000
Hospitals	2,056
New Wings	12,000
Total as above . . .	£64,056

LANCASTER.—*Opened 28th July, 1816.—Pauper.*

   Land . . . . 15 Acres.
Of this Land Five Acres, first purchased, are within the Boundary Wall, about one-fourth being covered by Buildings. The remaining Ten Acres are cultivated as a Farm. They are separated from the Asylum by a public road, and the ground is swampy.

   Thirty Acres from the adjoining Moor have been recently purchased under the powers of a local Act obtained in 1843.

Total Cost of Asylum to 23rd March 1843 :—

Building	. . .	£91,848 11 3
Furnishing	. . .	5,487 9 3
Repairs and Sundries	.	2,232 12 3
15 Acres of Land	. .	1,127 4 0

Total Charge to County £100,695 16 9

Accommodation . No. of Beds in Apartments { Males 295 / Females 298

Total of Beds in Apartments 593

		Males.	Females.
Of these there are in	Single Rooms . .	91	53
"	Double-bedded . .	—	56
"	Three Beds each .	66	42
"	Four " .	4	—
"	Five " .	20	10
"	Six " .	—	12
"	Twelve " .	36	—
"	Thirteen " .	26	26
"	Fourteen " .	14	—
"	Fifteen " .	—	15
"	Sixteen " .	—	32
"	Nineteen " .	38	—
"	Twenty-one " .	—	21
"	Thirty-one " .	—	31
	Total Beds . . .	295	298
	Total No. of Rooms . .	126	106

Average Cost per head, 170*l.*

N.B.—The actual number of Patients for whom accommodation is provided is about 620.

LEICESTER.—*Opened May* 10, 1837.—*Private and Pauper.*

Land . . . 8¼ Acres.

First Cost of Asylum:—Buildings, Fences, Planting, Wells, Pipes and Water-works, Ventilation
and Warming, Roads, &c. £16,893 12 0
—— Furnishing and Baths. 2,166 11 3
—— Land 2,070 10 0

Total £21,130 13 3

How defrayed:—Donations and Subscriptions,
with Proceeds of Old Institution, Buildings, and
Funded Property £7,375 3 5
Charge on County Rate . . . 13,755 9 10

Total as above . . . £21,130 13 3

	Males.	Females.	Total.
First Accommodation.—In single Sleeping rooms	28	28	56
—— Dormitories, 6 to 10 Beds each . .	24	24	48
	52	52	104

Average Cost per head, Private and Pauper . . 203*l.*
Cost of additional Buildings and Furniture, about . 6,500*l.*
Total Cost of Asylum to present time, about . . 27,630*l.*
Present accommodation . 76 Males, 76 Females. Total 152.
Average Cost per head, about . . 180*l.*—This is calculated
upon the entire outlay and total accommodation. Assuming the
accommodation for Paupers to be equivalent to their actual
number on 1st January, 1844, viz. 104, and charging the
County with the Cost of the additional Buildings, the average Cost
per head to the County for Paupers will be 194*l.*

MIDDLESEX.

HANWELL.—*Opened* 16*th May,* 1831.—*Pauper.*

Land, 53 Acres.

The original Cost appears to have been 124,456*l.* 14*s.* 5*d.*, out of
which the following Payments were made:—

For 44 Acres of Land £10,925 0
For the original Buildings 77,271 10
For Furniture, &c. 8,806 16

The additional Buildings erected in 1837 appear to have cost 20,000*l.*

We have not obtained the particulars of the costs of this Asylum, but were informed by the Accountant that it has amounted to 160,000*l.* This sum does not include 36,000*l.*, which has been also paid in different annual sums by the County since the 9th of July 1835, for Furniture, Fittings, and Labour about the Asylum, and which now annually amounts to about 4,000*l.*, and is exclusive of what is paid by the Parishes. The sums which appear to have been paid on this account in the year 1843, seem to have amounted to 6,637*l.* 12*s.*

Accommodation . . 1,000 Patients, Male and Female.
Average Cost per head . 160*l.*

NORFOLK.—*Opened* 18*th May*, 1814.—*Pauper.*

Land . . . . 4½ Acres.
Cost of Asylum to present time : Building, Furnishing, and Land, (say) 50,000*l.*
Accommodation . . . . . . Males 110 — Females 110. — Total 220.
Average Cost per head . . . 227*l.*

NOTTINGHAM.

Land . . . . 8 Acres.
Total Cost of Asylum to present time :—
Buildings and Furniture, Apparatus, &c., about £34,000
Land, Planting, &c. 2,800
                                                    ————
                    Total £36,800

towards which, about 6,800*l.* appears to have been contributed in the shape of legacies, benefactions, and parochial collections.

Present Accommodation . Males 85—Females 85.—Total 170.

Average Cost per head . . 220*l.*—This is estimated on the total outlay and amount of accommodation. Assuming the Asylum to afford accommodation, according to the existing arrangement, for 125 Paupers, the number 1st Jan. 1844, and 30,000*l.* as the total outlay borne by the county, the average cost per head for Paupers will be 240*l.*

STAFFORD.—*Opened* 1*st October*, 1818.—*Private and Pauper.*

Land . . . . 30 Acres.

Cost of Erection and original Accommodation :—The total original cost of Land, Buildings, and Furniture, appears to have been about 36,500*l.* ; whilst the Asylum was calculated to accommodate 120 Patients only.

Present Accommodation—250 Males and Females, viz. about 65 private Patients, and 185 Paupers. Much additional accommodation for Paupers has been obtained by converting the Galleries, by means of folding partitions, into Dormitories. The outlay on account of additions and improvements cannot be stated.

SUFFOLK.—*Opened* 1*st Jan.*, 1829.—*Almost exclusively Pauper.*

Land . . . . 30½ Acres.

Cost of Buildings, Land, &c.—

Purchase of House of Industry and Land . .	£8,000
Expense of conversion into an Asylum, Furnishing, &c.	22,000
Extension of Wings, &c. . . . . . . say	2,000
Total	£32,000

Accommodation . . . . 90 Males—90 Females.—Total 180.
Average Cost per head . 177*l.*
N.B.—Additions and improvements are in progress, by which
accommodation will be made for 30 more Patients. At present
the Asylum is much crowded.

SURREY.—*Opened 14th June, 1841.—Pauper.*

Land . . . . . . 97 Acres.
Cost of Buildings, Land, &c.—

Buildings	£67,467	1	10
Furnishing, &c., and preliminary expenses	7,514	19	3
Land, &c.	8,985	9	5
Total . .	£85,366	19	1

Accommodation . . . Males 180—Females 180.—Total 360.
Average Cost per head . 237*l.*

YORKSHIRE, W. RIDING.—(WAKEFIELD.)

Land.—In addition to Pleasure Garden and Grounds, 40 acres cultivated as Farm and Kitchen Garden.

Accommodation	Originally built for 150
	Additional Wings 154
	304
Actual Numbers accommodated . .	420
Total Cost of Land	£8,846
—— Buildings, Fittings, &c.	38,000
	£46,846
Average Cost per head, on present Numbers . .	£111

APPENDIX C.

COUNTY ASYLUMS.

BEDFORD . At the Asylum for the County of Bedford we were informed that the general condition of the Paupers was much improved of late, and that they were now brought to the Asylum soon after the attack of Insanity.

CHESTER . The information obtained at the Chester County Lunatic Asylum was, that "The Paupers are brought in a very bad state, in filth and in rags, and, from too long delay, in a state when there is little or no chance of cure."

CORNWALL . At the Asylum for the County of Cornwall it was stated by the Medical Superintendent, that in a large proportion of cases admitted during the year 1842, owing to long detention by friends or parishes, the prospect of recovery had been entirely precluded; and that it had been the custom in the County of Cornwall not to send a Patient to the Asylum until he had become, either from dirty habits, or dangerous propensities, unmanageable in a Workhouse, or in lodgings. The attention of the Magistrates of the County had been called to the subject in the last Annual Report of the Asylum.

DORSET . The Medical Superintendent of the Asylum for the County of Dorset has for some time past directed

the attention of the Magistrates of that County to
the condition in which Pauper Lunatics are sent to
the Asylum. Out of thirty-seven cases admitted
during the year 1842, only six were received within
three months after their being first attacked, eight
within twelve months, five had been insane between
two and five years, and the remaining Patients had
been afflicted from seven to thirty years. Those
admitted within three months after the first attack
of the disease had all recovered, and were discharged
within four months from the time of their admission, excepting one female, aged seventy-five, who
had been for some time in a state of senile imbecility. Amongst the evils complained of in relation to
this subject, is a habit on the part of the Clerks and
Officers of Unions, after they have received orders
from Magistrates to send Lunatics into the County
Asylum, of retaining them at their houses upon a
temporary mitigation or suspension of their attacks,
and of afterwards sending them to the Asylum upon
a return or an increase of their disease. In confirm-
ation of this complaint, the particulars of two Cases
were given, in which the Officers of Unions had
kept Pauper Lunatics in lodgings for several months
after Orders had been received from the Magistrates
to remove them to the County Asylum. In both cases
the Officers were subsequently obliged to send the
Paupers to the Asylum. One case occurred in April,
and the other in October, 1843. The full details of
these cases are in the Office of the Metropolitan
Commissioners, and the attention of the House of
Commons was called to one of them in the last Session of Parliament by Lord Ashley.

GLOUCESTER. All the Paupers who are now received are either sent
from the Workhouses, or are found wandering
about; and in general they are not now detained
more than a few days in the Workhouse before they

are removed to the Asylum. Their condition when first admitted is considered to be much more debilitated than it used formerly to be, a change which the Superintendent ascribes to the prevailing pressure of the times, and the increase of distress and extreme poverty among the Poor.

KENT The Paupers are generally brought to the Kent Asylum in a very advanced stage of their disease.

LANCASTER . At the Lancaster Asylum the statement made was, that nearly all the Patients admitted into the Asylum were brought from Workhouses, where they had in general been detained a considerable time, and consequently the malady had become more or less confirmed, thus diminishing the probability of recovery.

LEICESTER . The information obtained at the Leicester Asylum was that the condition of Pauper Lunatics generally, when admitted, was most unfavourable. The majority of cases are of a chronic description, from detention elsewhere, and treatment totally inadequate to their condition. The consequence was stated to be confirmed disease, a low average of recoveries, and a large amount of Incurables. "This state of things "to use the words of the Superintendent, is produc-"tive of irreparable mischief to the poor Lunatic, and "in a pecuniary point of view entails on his Parish "a very serious expense, which in most cases might be "obviated by early and efficacious treatment in the "recent stage of the malady, to say nothing of the "gratification it would afford to every rightly consti-"tuted mind, to restore a wretched Maniac to health, "to reason, and to a wife and family dependent upon "him."

MIDDLESEX . From the 1st of January to the end of March, 1844, forty cases were refused admission at this Asylum, so that there is in reality little chance of recent cases gaining admission at Hanwell.

NORFOLK . The result of our inquiries at the Norfolk Asylum was, that many Patients, Males and Females, were admitted in very feeble health, and suffering from the effect of pressure; but that, generally speaking, they were not detained long in Workhouses.

NOTTINGHAM Such has been the bad condition in which Paupers have been brought to this Asylum, that Dr. Blake, the late Physician, presented a petition to the House of Lords, calling their attention to the incurable state in which Paupers had been sent, from being kept away long after the commencement of their disease. The result of our latest inquiries at this Asylum has been that, since the new Poor Law came into operation, an increased reluctance has been exhibited on the part of the parish authorities to send their poor to an Asylum, and that the Patients frequently come in a very exhausted and debilitated state. Great advantage is said to be taken of the use of the word "dangerous" in the 45th section of the Poor Law Amendment Act; and many curable cases are detained in Union Workhouses in the rural districts.

STAFFORD . At the Stafford Asylum we were informed that the Paupers were generally sent soon after the commencement of the disease, but often very dirty, sometimes in manacles, and with scarcely any clothing.

SUFFOLK . At the Suffolk Asylum we were told that it had long been a source of complaint that Patients were sent to the Asylum wretchedly fed and wretchedly clad, and occasionally in an exhausted and almost dying state. This, however, it was said, had not been so much the case in recent times as formerly. Nevertheless, the Patients are still rarely received in an early stage of their malady. Cases have occurred in which Patients have been brought to the Asylum in improper conveyances, and not sufficiently protected from the weather, and where "death was probably accelerated by the journey and consequent exposure."

SURREY. . At the Surrey Asylum it was stated that the Paupers were frequently detained too long in Workhouses, and under the care of their friends, especially in recent cases, so as to afford little chance of cure or benefit from medical treatment. They are sent to the Asylum in some cases to die.

YORK, W. RIDING. We were informed at the Asylum at Wakefield, that the Paupers were very commonly retained so long in the Workhouse as to leave little chance of recovery. The reason assigned was said to be obvious. In the Asylum 7s. a week is paid for their maintenance; while in the Workhouse they are maintained for less than half that sum.

LUNATIC HOSPITALS RECEIVING PAUPERS.

LINCOLN. . The House Surgeon of the Lincoln Asylum stated that a great number of Paupers were sent into the Asylum in a state of mental and bodily health which rendered all chance of their recovery hopeless. He instanced three cases, in one of which the Patient died within four days; in another within twenty-five days, and in the third within eight days after admission; and in each of these Cases the Patient had been previously kept some time in the Workhouse. In one instance, Mr. Smith, the House Surgeon, refused to admit a Patient brought to the Asylum in a dying state, without the sanction of one of the Physicians. Dr. Charlesworth, one of the Visiting Physicians, entirely confirmed this statement, and called our attention to the remarks upon this subject in the Report of the Asylum for the year 1842.

NORTHAMPTON. The Medical Superintendent of the Northampton Asylum, stated that some few of the Unions which send their Paupers to the Asylum acted with liberality and sent them at the commencement of their malady; but that the greater number of the Unions either keep them in the Workhouses or farmed them out to other poor people at a small sum, in some cases not exceeding 2s. 6d. a week, until they were in a state, in which, either from becoming destructive of their clothes or dangerous to the persons about them, they could no longer be kept with economy nor safety; and that thus they arrived at the Asylum when their bodies as well as minds were beyond the reach of cure or remedy.

LICENSED HOUSES RECEIVING PAUPERS.

DURHAM . In this County the Paupers are stated to be sent to Asylums earlier than they used to be, in 1843.

DEVONSHIRE. At Plympton St. Mary, near Plymouth, the Patients are generally sent in a bad state. They are the refuse of the Workhouses, many of them are Epileptics, and upon an average eight out of ten are incurable.

GLOUCESTER. Fairford-—Some of the Paupers have been sent to this Asylum in a very bad state, and particularly during the last year. The late Medical Attendant left an entry in the Medical Register, stating that many of the Paupers had entered the Establishment who were not suffering from any acute disease, but had the functions of life so languidly performed that it constituted, in a great degree, their mental malady; the unsoundness of mind consisting more in the want of power than in any perversion of the reasoning faculty, or in any delusion. Thirteen cases were instanced in which persons died in the year 1842 very soon after their admission into the Asylum, having been brought there in a very bad state of bodily health.—1843.

HEREFORD . Hereford Asylum.—The Pauper Patients in Mr. Gilliland's opinion are kept too long in Workhouses before being sent to the Asylum to give them a fair chance of recovery.

Whitchurch.—Paupers are frequently sent in a very bad condition, much reduced, and under great exhaustion.

MIDDLESEX . At Dr. Warburton's, at Bethnal Green, not one out of ten Paupers who are admitted arrive in a curable state.

Hoxton. The information received from this Asylum is, that in the majority of instances the Pauper Patients received have undergone some previous treatment, though some cases are quite recent. The greater number of chronic cases admitted have been for some time inmates of Workhouses.

NORTHUMBERLAND. Newcastle.—Paupers are received at an earlier stage of disease than they used to be. They are frequently brought ill-clad and very dirty.

Gateshead Fell.—Paupers are received at an earlier stage of their disease than formerly.

Dunston Lodge.—Paupers are received in a better state and earlier than they used to be. A female, however, had, immediately previous to one of our visits, been received who had been Insane twenty years, and was sent because she was noisy and troublesome.

OXFORD . Hook Norton.—The majority of the Paupers sent into the Asylum are old cases which have previously been kept for some time in the Workhouse, a circumstance which is considered to operate unfavourably to their recovery.

SHROPSHIRE. Kingsland, near Shrewsbury.—The Paupers are not sent to the Asylum in so bad a condition as formerly. They are even now kept too long, so that the chance of cure is in many cases small.

SOMERSETSHIRE. Fairwater House, near Taunton.—The prospect of recovery as regards the Pauper Patients is but slender, their cases being generally of long standing before their admission.

Bailbrook House, near Bath.—The condition of the Paupers who come from the Bath district is such as in general to afford little prospect of recovery. From other districts the prospect of recovery is now more favourable, because they are usually sent on the first outbreak of the disease.

HAMPSHIRE. Hilsea Asylum, near Portsmouth.—The Paupers are frequently sent in an advanced stage of their disease, and in a bad state. They are usually sent, in the first instance, to the Parish Workhouse, and are kept there as long as they can be managed, and when they become violent or dirty, they are removed to the Asylum.

Nursling, near Southampton.—The Insane Poor are not unfrequently detained improperly in Workhouses, and many of them come in a state of great debility and exhaustion from having refused food.

SUFFOLK . Belle Vue House, near Ipswich.—Pauper Patients are generally detained as out-door Paupers by their friends until they become unmanageable. The blame is considered not to rest so much with the Relieving Officers of Unions, as with the friends under whose care the Pauper Lunatics are placed by the Parish Authorities.

WARWICK . Duddeston, near Birmingham. More than half the Patients under the care of Mr. Lewis belong to the parish of Birmingham, where the practice is to detain them in the lunatic wards of the Workhouse until they become unmanageable, when they are sent to

Duddeston. It is stated, not only that the worst cases are sent to that Asylum, but that those who are in a state of improvement are prematurely removed back to the Workhouse.

WILTSHIRE . Fisherton House, near Salisbury.—The Paupers are frequently kept, either at their own houses or in Union Workhouses, so long after the attacks of their disease that their chances of recovery are much diminished.

Laverstock House, near Salisbury. — Since the establishment of Unions, Paupers are sent in an earlier stage of their disease than they used to be.

Belle Vue, Devizes.—Some of the Paupers are brought in a very bad state, being detained as long as they are manageable, or can be kept cleanly. Many from Wales are violent, and bad cases when they arrive.

WORCESTER . Droitwich.—Paupers are very frequently sent in an extremely bad condition, having been previously detained for a considerable time in Workhouses, and then brought to the Asylum in carts, bound with cords.

YORKSHIRE . Gate Helmsley.—At our first visit the information was, that Paupers were frequently brought in an advanced stage of their disease, so as to afford little prospect of recovery. They are said to be now brought in a better state.

Dunnington.—The Paupers are often sent in a very filthy state, bound with cords, and otherwise restrained. In some cases the Patient has been kept a long time after the commencement of the disease before he is brought to the Asylum. In others he is brought soon after the commencement of his illness.

HULL . . . Refuge, Hull.—It is stated that the Paupers are admitted in the last stage of disease, and that little medical history of the cases can be obtained from

Parishes. As an instance of the condition in which they are sometimes brought to the Asylum, the case of a female pauper was mentioned, who was received in November last, from Blighton, near Gainsborough. She was in the last stage of phrenitis, was conveyed to the Asylum wrapped up in a blanket, which was thrown over her head; and she was, when received, in a profuse perspiration. She died within eight days of admission. The Parish Officers of Hull are said to have been more cautious in this respect of late years than formerly, partly, as it is believed, in consequence of a male Pauper Lunatic detained in the Workhouse having, in a paroxysm of mania, stabbed three or four of his fellow paupers, one of whom died of his wounds.

WORKHOUSES.

REDRUTH . In the Union Workhouse at Redruth, visited on the 6th October, 1843, there were 41 Insane Persons, besides 5 others of weak intellect, and unable to take care of themselves, but who had not been returned as insane in the return of Lunatics made to the Clerk of the Peace in the year 1842. Out of these 41 Insane Persons there were 6 Idiots. Several of the women were stated to be occasionally violent; one of them sometimes requiring handcuffs, a second having attempted to escape, and a third to break windows. Several had delusions: one female, who had attempted to destroy herself, fancied her body not to be her own. Amongst the men, some were at times violent; others who had been very violent were become enfeebled. It was stated that if any of the men required restraint it would be employed. One woman was extremely dirty, and addicted to disgusting habits.

BATH . . In the Union Workhouse at Bath, visited on the 20th of October, 1843, there were 21 Insane Persons ; 12 Males, and 9 Females. Of these, 3 were subject to fits, and 3 were Idiots—one woman was in bed and had on a strait waistcoat, and was constantly under such restraint. Another woman was excited and in bed ; the rest of the Lunatics appeared in tolerable health. One man had been in the House since the 22nd of June previous, and from his own statement, confirmed by the Master of the House, it appeared that he had had no medicine or medical treatment since his admission, although his case appeared to be one that was susceptible of improvement by proper remedies.

LEICESTER . In the Union Workhouse at Leicester, visited on the 6th October, 1843, there were 30 Insane Persons, namely 11 Males and 19 Females. Of the males, W. K. was a noisy Maniac, very cunning, and occasionally striking the other men in the ward. P. R. was subject to maniacal attacks, during which he was placed in a strait waistcoat. He was raving mad about two months before our Visit, and was constantly fastened to his bed at night to prevent him from injuring or annoying the other inmates. A. H. was violent and passionate, and tried to cut others with knives ; and all these persons were dangerous. Amongst the other cases, were, J. L., an Epileptic ; J. D. a case of Melancholia ; J. G., formerly in the Asylum, and still Insane, noisy, and abusive. The rest of the Males of this class appeared to be either harmless Idiots, or in a state of mental imbecility. The three most dangerous of the females were, C. B., admitted June 12th, 1839, a destructive and dangerous Idiot; M. H., admitted 23rd of February, 1839, an abusive and dangerous Lunatic. She was brought to the Workhouse in a state of violent excitement, by two policemen. M. A. R., admitted 24th of February,

1841, a quarrelsome and dangerous Idiot, once knocked out the teeth of a child. To these may be added the following, as properly coming within the description of dangerous Lunatics :—M. B., a sullen ill-tempered person, who refused to be employed, and had threatened, when at home, to kill her mother. A. W., in the Workhouse three years, an abusive Lunatic, who had occasionally struck most of the women in the ward, particularly a paralytic patient who could not defend herself. J. S., an irritable mad woman, who threw knives at those with whom she happened to have a dispute. E. H., a violent, irascible person, subject to maniacal excitement, and dangerous when irritated. She had been twenty-six weeks in the County Asylum, having become unmanageable at home after the death of her mother, sixteen years ago,—and was said to strike the inmates maliciously. A. H., a harmless Lunatic, with delusions, was most improperly sent to the Workhouse, instead of the Asylum, four years ago. Besides the above, there were in the House 6 quiet female Lunatics, all confirmed cases, and 5 Idiots. There were in the House altogether, 3 Males and 9 Females, properly to be classed as dangerous Lunatics.

PORTSEA . In the Workhouse at Portsea, near Portsmouth, visited on the 28th of August, 1843, there were 26 Lunatics ; 15 Females, and 11 Males. Of these, 7 were Epileptics, and 2 Idiots. Many of the Patients, although not strictly speaking, imbecile persons, were individuals of weak intellect. Some of them, however, were decidedly Insane, and occasionally violent and unmanageable unless restrained, and some of them were labouring under delusions.

BIRMINGHAM. In the Workhouse at Birmingham, visited on the 29th of September, 1843, there were 71 Lunatics. Amongst them was an unusual proportion of Epileptics, namely, 11 Males and 16 Females. Several

of these were Idiots : others were subject, after their
paroxysms of Epilepsy, to fits of raving madness, or
Epileptic furor, during which they were stated to be
excessively violent.   Besides these, there were several
patients who were occasionally under great excitement,
and furiously maniacal. Two of the females had strong
suicidal propensities, and one of them had attempted
suicide.   There is no class of persons more dangerous
than are those Epileptics who are subject to attacks
of Epileptic furor or delirium.   It is well known
that many fearful homicides have been perpetrated
by persons afflicted with this form of mental disease.

APPENDIX D.

List of Counties having County Lunatic Asylums exclusively for Paupers, with the numbers of Pauper Lunatics in each county, and the numbers for whom there is accommodation in each Asylum.

PAUPER LUNATICS.		Numbers in County, 1842.	Accommodation.	
			Numbers for whom there is.	Numbers for whom there is not.
BEDFORD.				
Lunatics in County	135	155	141	..
Accommodation in County Asylum	180			
CHESTER.				
Lunatics in Unions	273 ⎱	296	155	141
Not in Unions	23 ⎰			
Accommodation in County Asylum for	110			
DORSET.				
Lunatics in County	227	227	113	114
Accommodation in County Asylum for	113			
KENT.				
Lunatics in Unions	465			
Not in Unions	13			
	478			
Accommodation in County Asylum for	300	478	300	178
LANCASTER.				
Lunatics in Unions	979			
Not in Unions	123			
	1102			
Accommodation in County Asylum for	600	1102	593	509
MIDDLESEX.				
Lunatics in Unions	884			
Not in Unions	735			
	1619			
Accommodation in County Asylum for	1000	1619	1000	619
NORFOLK.				
Lunatics in Unions	401			
Not in Unions	69			
		470	220	250
	470			
Accommodation in County Asylum for	220			
SUFFOLK.				
Lunatics in County	361	361	180	181
Accommodation in County Asylum for				
SURREY.				
Lunatics in Unions	521			
Not in Unions	70			
		591	360	231
	591			
Accommodation in County Asylum for	350			
YORK, WEST RIDING.				
Lunatics in Unions	664			
Not in Unions	363			
		1027	420	607
	1027			
Accommodation in County Asylum for	420			

* According to the Poor Law Returns for 1842; since which the numbers of Pauper Lunatics, (as will be seen by reference to Appendix F), and consequently the deficiency of accommodation in Asylums have increased.

List of Counties having County Lunatic Asylums for Paupers
in union with Subscription Asylums, with the numbers of
Pauper Lunatics in each County, and the numbers for
whom there is accommodation in each Asylum. The
numbers of Pauper Lunatics belonging to Parishes not
in Unions have been calculated at one in a thousand of
the population, according to the Census of 1841.

PAUPER LUNATICS.		Numbers in County. 1842.	Accommodation.	
			Numbers for whom there is.	Numbers for whom there is not.
CORNWALL.				
Lunatics in Unions	273			
Not in Unions	24			
Total Lunatics	297			
Accommodation in County and Subscription Asylum for Bodmin	129	297	129	168
GLOUCESTER.				
Lunatics in Unions	398			
Not in Unions	100			
Total Lunatics	498			
Accommodation in County and Subscription Asylum for	190	498	190	308
LEICESTER.				
Lunatics	244			
Accommodation in County and Subscription Asylum for	104	244	104	140
NOTTINGHAM.				
Lunatics in County and County of Town	261			
Paupers in County and Subscription Asylum for County and Town in 1842	125	261	125	136
STAFFORD.				
Lunatics in Unions	384			
Not in Unions	68			
Total Lunatics	452			
Paupers in County and Subscription Asylum in 1842	177	452	185	267

List of Counties in England, with the numbers of Pauper
Lunatics, and the total accommodation for them in Public
and Private Asylums in each County. The numbers of
Pauper Lunatics as to that part of the population which
is not comprised in Unions have been calculated at one
in a thousand of the population, according to the Census of
1841.

Pauper Lunatics and total Accommodation, in Public and Private Asylums.	Numbers in County, 1842.	Accommodation.	
		Numbers for whom there is.	Numbers for whom there is not.
BEDFORD.			
Lunatics in County	135		
Accommodation in County Asylum for	180	135	180	. .
BERKSHIRE.			
Lunatics in County	241	241	. .	241
BUCKINGHAMSHIRE.			
Lunatics in County	127	127	. .	127
CAMBRIDGE.			
Lunatics in County	159	159	. .	159
CHESTER.			
Lunatics in Unions	273		
Not in Unions	23		
	296		
Accommodation in County Asylum for	110	296	155	141
CORNWALL.			
Lunatics in Unions	273		
Not in Unions	24		
	297	297	129	168
Accommodation in County and Subscription Asylum at Bodmin .	129		
CUMBERLAND.			
Lunatics in County	161	161	. .	161
DERBY.			
Lunatics in Unions	164		
Not in Unions	52		
	216		
Accommodation in Licensed House, Hill Lane, Derby, for . .	24	216	24	192
* DEVON.			
Lunatics in Unions	508		
Not in Unions	103		
	611		
Accommodation in House at Plympton, licensed for . .	70		
Workhouse at Stoke Damerel licensed for 100, but only room for .	30		
	100	611	100	511

Pauper Lunatics and Accommodation, Public and Private.		Accommodation.	
		Numbers for whom there is.	for whom there is

DORSET.

Lunatics in County	227
Accommodation in County Asylum for	113

DURHAM.

Lunatics in County	210
Accommodation in Private Asylums at	
Wreckenton, licensed for . .	45
West Auckland, do. for . .	40
Gateshead Fell, do. for : .	82
Benshams, do. for . .	52
Dunston Lodge, do. for . .	78
	297

ESSEX.

Lunatics in County	325
Accommodation in Licensed House at Witham for	2

GLOUCESTER.

Lunatics in Unions	398
Not in Unions	100
	498
Accommodation in County and Sub- scription Asylum for . . .	190
Private Asylum at Fairford, licensed for	120
„ „ Stapleton, do. for .	5
	314

HEREFORD.

Lunatics in County	147
Accommodation in Private Asylums at	
Hereford, licensed for . .	28
Whitchurch, do. for . . .	20
	48

HERTFORD.

Lunatics in County . . .	214

HUNTINGDON.

Lunatics in County	56

KENT.

Lunatics in Unions	465
Not in Unions	13
	478
Accommodation in County Asylum for	300
Private Asylum at West Malling for .	12
	312

LANCASTER.

Lunatics in Unions	979
Not in Unions	123
	1102
Accommodation in County Asylum for	593
In Liverpool Asylum in 1842 . .	36

Pauper Lunatics and Accommodation, Public and Private.	Numbers in County.	Accommodation.	
		Numbers for whom there is.	Numbers for whom there is not.
LEICESTER.			
Lunatics in County	244		
Accommodation in County and Sub- scription Asylum for . . }	130	244 130	114
LINCOLN.			
Lunatics in County	296		
Paupers in Lincoln Subscription Asy- lum, in 1842 . . . . }	73	296 73	223
MIDDLESEX.			
Lunatics in Unions . . .	884		
Not in Unions	735		
	1619		
Accommodation in County Asylum for	1000		
Private Asylums at Bethnal Green, licensed for . . . }	260		
At Hoxton, licensed for . . .	300	1619 1560	59
MONMOUTH.			
Lunatics in County	105	105 ..	105
NORFOLK.			
Lunatics in Unions	401		
Not in Unions	69		
	470		
Accommodation in County Asylum for	220		
Paupers in Bethel Hospital, in 1843 .	72		
In Bethel Infirmary or Poorhouse .	27		
	319	470 319	151
NORTHAMPTON.			
Lunatics in County	269		
Accommodation in Subscription Asy- lum at Northampton, in 1842 . }	181	269 181	88
NORTHUMBERLAND. .			
Lunatics in County	321		
Accommodation in Private Asylum at Newcastle, licensed for . . }	58	321 58	263
NOTTINGHAM.			
Lunatics in County and County of Town . . . . . }	261		
Paupers in County and Subscription Asylum for County & Town in 1842. }	117	261 125	136
OXFORD.			
Lunatics in Unions	172		
Not in Unions	20		
	192		
Private Asylum at Hook Norton, licensed for . . . }	74	192 74	118
RUTLAND.			
Lunatics in County	24	24 ..	24
SALOP.			
Lunatics in Unions	244		
Not in Unions	47		

Pauper Lunatics and Accommodation, Public and Private.	Numbers in County.	Accommodation.	
		Numbers for whom there is.	Numbers

SALOP—*continued.*

Brought forward	291		
Accommodation in Private Asylum, at Kingsland, near Shrewsbury, licensed for	} 80		
At Morda, near Oswestry, in 1842 .	14	291	

An Asylum is in progress of erection in this County.

SOMERSET.

Lunatics in County	572		
Accommodation in Private Asylums, at Bailbrook, near Bath, for .	} 65		
At Fairwater House, near Taunton, licensed for	} 8		
	73	572	

SOUTHAMPTON.

Lunatics in Unions	405		
Not in Unions	43		
	448		
Accommodation in Private Asylums, at Lainston, near Winchester, licensed for	} 80		
Nurstling, near Southampton, licensed for	62		
Hilsea, Portsmouth, licensed for . .	38		
In Carisbrook, in 1843 . . .	27		
	207		

STAFFORD.

Lunatics in Unions	384		
Not in Unions	68		
	452		
Paupers in County and Subscription Asylum in 1842	} 185		
Private Asylum, Sandfield, near Lichfield, licensed for . . .	} 30		
	215		

SUFFOLK.

Lunatics in County	361		
Accommodation in County Asylum for	180		
Private Asylum, Belle Vue, near Ipswich, licensed for . . .	} 16		

SURREY.

Lunatics in Unions	521		
Not in Unions	70		
	591		
Accommodation in County Asylum for	360		
Private Asylum at Peckham, licensed for	210		

SUSSEX.

Pauper Lunatics and Accommodation, Public and Private.		Numbers for whom there is.	Numbers for whom there is not.
WARWICK.			
Lunatics in Unions	225		
Not in Unions	181		
	406		
Accommodation in Private Asylum at Duddeston, licensed for . . .	60	60	346
WESTMORELAND.			
Lunatics in County	50	..	50
WILTS.			
Lunatics in Unions	357		
Not in Unions	25		
	382		
Accommodation in Private Asylum at Laverstock, near Salisbury, licensed for	35		
Fisherton, near Salisbury, for . .	90		
Devizes, licensed for . . .	180		
Market Lavington, licensed for . .	135		
Hindon, licensed for	2		
	442	442	.
WORCESTER.			
Lunatics in County	284		
Accommodation in Private Asylum at Droitwich, licensed for . .	60	60	224
YORK, EAST RIDING.			
Lunatics in Unions	173		
Not in Unions	14		
	187		
Accommodation in Private Asylums at			
Nunkeeling, licensed for . .	20		
Heple, near Hull, do. for . .	24		
Hull Retreat, do. for . . .	96		
Somercoats, near Hull, do. for .	3		
Hunington, near York, do. for .	30		
	173	173	14
YORK, NORTH RIDING.			
Lunatics in Unions	144		
Not in Unions	23		
	167		
Accommodation in Private Asylum at Gate Helmsley, licensed for .	40	40	127
YORK, WEST RIDING.			
Lunatics in Unions	664		
Not in Unions	363		
	1027		
Accommodation in County Asylum for	420		
,, at Private Asylum at Acomb, in 1842 . . .	15		
	435	435	592
AINSTY, AND CITY OF YORK, AND SUBURBS.			
Lunatics	38		
Private Asylum at Heworth, licensed for	13	13	25

WALES.			
Pauper Lunatics and Accommodation, Public and Private.	Numbers in County.	Accommodation.	
		Numbers for whom there is.	Numbers for whom there is not.
GLAMORGAN. Lunatics in . . . . . 155 Private Asylum at Briton Tarey, } 36 licensed for	155	36	119
PEMBROKE. Lunatics in . . . . . 105 County Asylum at Haverfordwest . 18	105	18	87

Counties in England and Wales in which there are no Asylums of any kind, either Public or Private, and the number of Pauper Lunatics chargeable to Unions in each County, August, 1843 :—

ENGLAND.

PAUPER LUNATICS.

BERKSHIRE	260
BUCKINGHAMSHIRE	147
CAMBRIDGE	143
CUMBERLAND	173
ESSEX	354
HERTFORD	225
HUNTINGDON	65
MONMOUTH	117
RUTLAND	26
SUSSEX	278
WESTMORELAND	57

WALES.

ANGLESEY	65
BRECON	66
CARDIGAN	119
CARMARTHEN	162
CARNARVON	149
DENBIGH	84
FLINT	60
MERIONETH	83
MONTGOMERY	107
RADNOR	22

APPENDIX E.

DIETARIES OF PAUPER PATIENTS.

NOTE.—The Weekly Charges for Pauper Patients will be found in the Lists of Asylums, Appendix A.

COUNTY ASYLUMS.

BEDFORDSHIRE.

BREAKFAST.

MALES.	FEMALES.
Milk Porridge, with 8 oz. of Bread.	Milk Porridge, with 7 oz. of Bread.

Tea and Bread and Butter for a portion of the Patients, instead of Milk Porridge.

DINNERS.

Sunday, Tuesday, and Thursday.	*Sunday, Tuesday, and Thursday.*
6 oz. Meat, with Vegetables.	5 oz. Meat, with Vegetables.
Monday, Wednesday, and Friday.	
8 oz. Bread, with Soup, made from Meat boiled the preceding day.	*Monday, Wednesday, and Friday.* 7 oz. Bread, with Soup.
Saturday.	*Saturday.*
1 lb. Suet Pudding.	¾ lb. Suet Pudding.

SUPPER.

Bread, 8 oz.; cheese, 2 oz.; and half-a-pint of Beer.	Bread, 7 oz.; cheese, 1½ oz.; and half-a-pint of Beer.

Tea and Bread and Butter for a portion of the Patients, the same as Breakfast, each day, instead of Bread, Cheese, and Beer.

Patients employed in the House and Garden have half-a-pint of Beer twice each day.

Sunday afternoon, all the Female Patients have Tea and Currant Cake.

Patients, who require it, have anything that is ordered by the Medical Superintendent.

CHESHIRE.

	BREAKFAST.	DINNER.	SUPPER.
MONDAY . .	Porridge, with Milk, 1 quart; for Men, 2 oz. Bread in Porridge.	Strong Meat Soup, with Vegetables and Seasoning, 1 quart; Bread, 6 oz.	As Breakfast.
TUESDAY . .	Ditto.	6 oz. Beef or Mutton, or other Meat.	Ditto.
FRIDAY . . .	Ditto.	6 oz. Bread.	Ditto.
SATURDAY . .	Ditto.	1 lb. Potatoes.	Ditto.
WEDNESDAY .	Ditto.	Pudding, with Treacle for Sauce (much approved.)	Ditto.
THURSDAY .	Ditto.	1 quart of Soup, as above; 6 oz. Bread; 1 lb. Potatoes.	Ditto.
SUNDAY . .	Cocoa or Coffee, with Sugar, Milk, Bread and Butter.	1 quart Meat Scouce or Irish Stew, seasoned with Onions and Pepper; 3 or 4 oz. Bread; Bacon sometimes added, well chopped, to the Stew.	Ditto.

One horn of Beer allowed each Man with his Dinner, daily.

CORNWALL.

MALES.

BREAKFAST . Sunday, Monday, Tuesday, Wednesday, Friday; } Broth, 1 pint; Bread, 7 oz.

Thursday, Saturday, { Milk, ½ pint; Water, ½ pint; Oatmeal, 3 oz.; Bread, 6 oz.

DINNER . . Sunday, Monday, Thursday, Friday, } Peas Soup, 1¼ pint; Bacon, 2 oz.; Bread, 4 oz.

Tuesday, { Stew, 2 lbs.; Meat, 2 oz.; Suet Dumpling, 4 oz.

Wednesday, Saturday, } Soup, 1½ pint; Vegetables; Bread, 6 oz.

SUPPER . . . . Oatmeal Porridge, 1½ pint; Bread, 4 oz.

FEMALES.

BREAKFAST . . . . Oatmeal Gruel, 1½ pint, containing Milk, ½ pint; Oatmeal, 1½ oz.; Cake, 5 oz.

DINNER . . Sunday, Thursday, } Same as Males.

Monday, . Same as Males, with 3 oz. of Bread.

Tuesday, Thursday, } Same as Males.

Wednesday, Saturday, } Same as Males; Bread, 5 oz.

SUPPER . . . . Tea, with 5 oz. of Bread and Butter.

DORSET.

DINNER . . Sunday, Monday, Wednesday, Thursday, } Meat, 5 oz. cooked, free from bone, and Vegetables.

Tuesday, . 1 pint of Soup; Bread, 6 oz.

Friday, . . Suet Pudding, 1 lb.

Saturday, { Pie Crust, ½ lb.; Potatoes; Meat, 3 oz.; Beer, ½ pint daily.

BREAKFAST.

MALES.	FEMALES.
1 pint Milk Porridge, thickened with Oatmeal; Bread, 6 oz.	1 pint Milk Porridge, thickened with Oatmeal; Bread, 5 oz.

SUPPER.

Bread, 6 oz.; Cheese, 2 oz.; Beer, ½ pint.	Bread, 5 oz.; Cheese, 2 oz.; Beer, ½ pint.

The Female Patients, who make themselves generally useful, have Tea and Butter, if preferred.

The out-door Workers and Laundry Women have an extra quantity of Beer daily.

GLOUCESTER.

BREAKFAST. . 1 lb. of Bread with Butter, and three parts of a Quart of Milk Gruel.

1 part Milk.

2 " Water.

1 " Flour and Oatmeal.

SUPPER. . . ½lb. Bread with about 1 oz. Cheese, and a Pint of Table Beer for the Men.

Tea and Bread and Butter for Women (no limit).

DINNER. . . 6 oz. of dressed meat (Beef or Mutton) on *Tuesdays*, *Thursdays*, and *Sundays*, with Potatoes and Bread, and one Pint of Table Beer. (Healthy Male Patients 8 oz.)

Saturday.—Meat Pies and Irish Stew.

Monday.—Broth with Bread, and Vegetables, 6 oz. Bread, Potatoes in addition. No Beer.

Friday.—Rice Pudding and a slice of Bread. No Beer.

KENT.

	BREAKFAST.	DINNER.	SUPPER.
SUNDAY .	Porridge of Oatmeal and Milk, with 6 ounces of Bread, every morning, for all the Patients.	For Men 6 oz. of Boiled or Roast Beef, free from bone; 4 oz. of Bread, and ½ Pint of Table Beer. —The Women have 4 oz. of Meat, &c. &c.	For Men 2 oz. Cheese, and ½ Pint Beer every evening; for Women Tea, with Bread and Butter in the proportion of 1 oz. Tea and 3½ oz. Butter a week.
MONDAY . .	Ditto.	Beef Pudding, Vegetables, and Beer, as before.	Ditto.
TUESDAY . .	Ditto.	Soup made from the bones of the preceding days, with thin Beef added, thickened with Scotch Barley, Oatmeal, and Vegetables, and 6 oz. of Bread.	Ditto.
WEDNESDAY .	Ditto.	Meat Pies or Pudding, as before.	Ditto.
THURSDAY . .	Ditto.	Rice or Suet Pudding; Men, 12 oz., Women, 10 oz.; Bread, 4 oz.	Ditto.
FRIDAY . . .	Ditto.	Meat in quantities the same as on Sunday.	Ditto.
SATURDAY . .	Ditto.	Soup as on Monday, or Suet Pudding as before.	Ditto.

A Pint of Beer and 2 oz. of Meat on Pudding Days.

LANCASTER.

MEN.

	BREAKFAST.		DINNER.			SUPPER.			
	Bread.	Oatmeal and Flour.	Mutton or Beef uncooked, with Bones.	Bread.	Flour.	Bread.	Oatmeal and Flour.	Cheese.	
SUNDAY .	5 oz.	3½ oz.	7 oz.	——	——	7¼ oz.	——	——	Coffee.
MONDAY .	5 —	3½ —	7 —	——	——	5 —	3½ oz.	——	Porridge.
TUESDAY .	5 —	3½ —	3½ —	——	4 oz.	7¼ —	——	2 oz.	Beer.
WEDNESDAY.	——	7 —	7 —	2 oz.	——	7¼ —	——	——	Tea.
THURSDAY .	5 —	3½ —	7 —	——	——	5 —	3½ —	——	Porridge.
FRIDAY .	5 —	3½ —	7 —	——	4 —	7¼ —	——	2 —	Beer.
SATURDAY .	5 —	3½ —	7 —	——	——	7¼ —	——	——	Tea.
Total	30	28	45½	2	8	46¼	7	4	

WOMEN.

	BREAKFAST.		DINNER.			SUPPER.	
	Bread.	Oatmeal and Flour.	Mutton or Beef uncooked, with Bones.	Bread.	Flour.	Bread.	
SUNDAY	5½ oz.	2¾ oz.	7 oz.	——	——	5½ oz.	with Tea.
MONDAY . . .	3½ —	2¾ —	7 —	——	——	5½ —	" Coffee.
TUESDAY	3½ —	2¾ —	7 —	——	——	5½ —	" Ditto.
WEDNESDAY . .	3½ —	2¾ —	7 —	——	3½ oz.	5½ —	" Tea.
THURSDAY . .	3½ —	2¾ —	3½ —	——	4 —	5½ —	" Coffee.
FRIDAY . . .	3½ —	2¾ —	7 —	1 oz.	——	5½ —	" Ditto.
SATURDAY . . .		4 —	7 —	——	——	5½ —	" Ditto.
Total	21	20½	45½	1	7½	38½	

LEICESTERSHIRE.

BREAKFAST . Sunday,   Porridge of Oatmeal and Milk, with 4 oz. of Bread; the Males being allowed 1½ pint; the Females 1 pint.

DINNER . . . . . Roast or Boiled Meat, 8 oz. for the Men, and 6 oz. for the Women, when cooked and free from bone; Potatoes and other Vegetables; 1 pint of Table Beer for the Men, ½ pint for the Women.

TEA . . . . Allowed the Females only. 6 oz. of Bread, and 1 oz. of Butter per day, with 1 oz. of Tea, and $\frac{1}{4}$ pound Sugar per week.

SUPPER . . . . Bread and Cheese and Table Beer; the Men being allowed 6 oz. of Bread, 1 oz. of Cheese, with 1 pint of Table Beer; the Women 4 oz. of Bread, $\frac{1}{2}$ oz. of Cheese, with $\frac{1}{2}$ pint of Table Beer.

Monday, Soup, made from the Liquor in which the Meat had been boiled the day previous, thickened with Peas and other Vegetables; $1\frac{1}{2}$ pint for the Men, 1 pint the Women; Bread and Cheese, 6 oz. of the former, and 1 oz. of the latter, for the Men; the Women being allowed 4 oz. of Bread, $\frac{1}{2}$ oz. of Cheese. Tea and Supper as before.

Wednesday, Soup, as on Monday, with the same allowance of Bread and Cheese and Table Beer. Tea and Supper as before.

Tuesday, Boiled Mutton, Men, 8 oz., Women, 6 oz., with Vegetables; Men 1 pint, Women $\frac{1}{2}$ pint of Table Beer. Tea and Supper as before.

Thursday, Boiled Beef, in the same quantity as the Mutton on Tuesday, with Vegetables and Table Beer. Tea and Supper as before.

Friday, Soup, as on Wednesday, with the same allowance of Bread and Cheese and Beer. Tea and Supper as usual.

Saturday, Meat Pies, or Suet or Rice Puddings, 1 lb. to the Men, $\frac{3}{4}$ lb. to the Women, with Bread and Cheese and Table Beer.

This Dietary is occasionally varied by the addition of Fruit Puddings in the season.

MIDDLESEX. (Hanwell.)

Males.

BREAKFAST . . . Milk, thickened with Oatmeal and Flour, 1 pint; Bread, 6 oz.

DINNER . . Sunday, ⎫ Meat, 5 oz. cooked.
Tuesday, ⎪ Yeast Dumpling, 4 oz.
Wednesday, ⎬ Beer, $\frac{1}{2}$ pint.
Friday, ⎭ Vegetables.
Monday, . 1 pint Soup; Bread, 6 oz.; Beer, $\frac{1}{2}$ pint.
Thursday, ⎰ Irish Stew, 12 oz.; Bread, 6 oz.; Beer, half-a-pint.
Saturday, ⎰ Meat Pie Crust, 12 oz.; Meat, $1\frac{1}{2}$ oz.; Beer, half-a-pint.

SUPPER . . . . Bread, 6 oz.; Cheese, 2 oz.; Beer, half-a-pint.

EXTRAS TO WORKMEN.

Out-door Workers to be allowed $\frac{1}{2}$ pint of Beer at 11 o'clock, A.M. and at 4 P.M. daily, and 1 oz. of Tea and 4 ozs. of Sugar per week.

Females.

BREAKFAST . . . Bread, 5 oz.; Butter, $\frac{1}{2}$ oz.; Sugar, 4 oz. per week; Tea, 1 pint.

DINNER . . Sunday, ⎫ Meat, 5 oz. cooked.
Tuesday, ⎪ Yeast Dumpling, 4 oz.
Wednesday, ⎬ Beer, half-a-pint.
Friday, ⎭ Vegetables.
Monday, ⎰ 1 pint Soup; Bread, 6 oz.; Beer, half-a-pint.
Thursday, ⎰ Irish Stew, 12 oz.; Bread, 5 oz.; Beer, half-a-pint.
Saturday, ⎰ Meat Pie Crust, 12 oz.; Meat, $1\frac{1}{2}$ oz.; Beer, half-a-pint.

SUPPER . . . . Milk, thickened with Oatmeal and Flour, 1 pint; Bread, 5 oz.

EXTRAS TO LAUNDRY WOMEN, &c.

Laundry Women to be allowed half-a-pint of Beer at 4 P.M., and together with Helpers, &c., 1 oz. of Tea and 4 oz. of Sugar per week, in lieu of the ordinary Supper.

NORFOLK.

MEN.

BREAKFAST (DAILY) . Bread, 6 oz.; Milk Broth, 1½ pint, or 1 oz. of Cheese and 1 pint of Beer.

DINNER . . Sunday, Beef or Mutton, 4 oz. cooked; Bread, 2 oz.; Potatoes, 1 lb.; and Beer, 1 pint.

Monday, { Suet Pudding, 10 oz.; Potatoes, 10 oz.; Beer, 1 pint.

Tuesday, { Beef or Mutton, 4 oz.; Bread, 2 oz.; Potatoes, 1 lb.; Beer, 1 pint.

Wednesday, { Suet Pudding, 10 oz.; Potatoes, 10 oz.; Beer, 1 pint.

Thursday, { Beef or Mutton, 4 oz.; Bread, 2 oz.; Potatoes, 1 lb.; Beer, 1 pint.

Friday, { Suet Pudding, 10 oz.; Potatoes, 10 oz.; Beer, 1 pint.

Saturdays, . Ditto ditto ditto.

SUPPER (DAILY) . . Bread 6 oz.; Meat Broth, 1½ pint, or Cheese, 1 oz.; Beer, 1 pint.

WOMEN.

BREAKFAST (DAILY) . Milk Broth, 1¼ pint, or Tea, half-a-pint, or Beer, half-a-pint; Bread, 5 oz., in lieu of Broth (if preferred); 1 oz. Cheese or ½ oz. Butter.

DINNER . Sunday, Beef or Mutton, 4 oz. cooked; Bread, 2 oz.; Potatoes, 1 lb.; Beer, half-a-pint.

Monday, { Suet Pudding, 10 oz.; Potatoes, 10 oz.; Butter, ½ oz.

Tuesday, { Beef or Mutton, 4 oz.; Bread, 2 oz.; Potatoes, 1 lb.; Beer, half-a-pint.

Wednesday, { Suet Pudding, 10 oz.; Potatoes, 10 oz.; Butter, ½ oz.

Thursday, { Beef or Mutton, 4 oz.; Bread, 2 oz.; Potatoes, 1 lb.; Beer, half-a-pint.

Friday, { Suet Pudding, 10 oz.; Potatoes, 10 oz.; Butter, ½ oz.

Saturday, Ditto ditto ditto

SUPPER . . Sunday, Meat Broth, 1¼ pint; and Bread, 5 oz.; or Cheese, 1 oz.; and Beer, half-a-pint, or Tea, half-a-pint; and Butter, ½ oz.

Monday, { Bread, 5 oz.; Cheese, 1 oz.; or Butter, ½ oz.; and Beer, half-a-pint.

Tuesday,	The same as on Sunday.
Wednesday,	The same as on Monday.
Thursday,	The same as on Sunday.
Friday,	The same as on Monday.
Saturday,	Ditto ditto.

NOTTINGHAM.

MALES.

	Meat.		Bread.	Potatoes.	Flour.	Suet.	Milk.	Oatmeal.	Beer.	Peas.	Salt.	Pepper.	Onions.
	Raw.	Without waste.											
	lb.oz.	lb. oz.	lb.oz.	lb.oz.	lb.oz.	lb. oz.	Pint.	lb.oz.	Pint.	lb. oz.	lb.oz.	Dms.	
Sunday . . .	0 10	0 6	0 13	0 10	0 4	0 1	1	0 3	1	..	0 1/4	0 1/4	
Monday . . .	..	..	1	1 0	1 0	1 1/2	1	0 3	1	0 3	0 1/4	1/3	
Tuesday . . .	0 10	0 6	1	1 0	1 0	..	1	0 3	1	..	0 1/4		
Wednesday . .	..	..	1	1 0	1 0	1 1/2	1	0 3	1	0 3	0 1/4	1/3	
Thursday . .	0 10	0 6	1	1 0	1 0	..	1	0 3	1	..	0 1/4		
Friday . . .	..	..	1	1 0	1 0	1 1/2	1	0 3	1	0 3	0 1/4	1/3	
Saturday . .	0 4	0 4	1	1 0	1 0	0 1	1	0 3	1	..	0 1/4		
lbs.	2 2	1 6	7 3	6 8	0 9 3/4	0 1	7	1 5	7	0 9	0 1 3/4	0 1 3/4	

FEMALES.

	Meat.		Bread.	Potatoes.	Flour.	Suet.	Milk.	Oatmeal.	Beer.	Peas.	Salt.	Pepper.	Onions.	Tea.	Sugar.	Butter.
	Raw.	Without waste.														
	lb.oz.	lb.oz.	lb.oz.	lb.oz.	lb.oz.	lb.oz.	Pint	lb.oz.	Pint.	lb.oz.	lb.oz.	Dms.		lb.oz.	lb.oz.	lb.oz.
Sunday .	0 9	0 5	0 11	0 12	0 3	0 3/4	0 7	1 0	0 3/4	..	0 1/4		..	0 1/16	0 1/2	0 1/2
Monday .	..	..	1 0	0 8	0 1	..	0 7	1 0	0 3/4	0 2	0 1/4	1/3	..	0 1/16	0 1/2	0 1/2
Tuesday .	0 9	0 5	0 15	0 12	..	..	0 7	1 0	0 3/4	..	0 1/4		..	0 1/16	0 1/2	0 1/2
Wednesday .	..	..	1 0	0 8	0 1	..	0 7	1 0	0 3/4	0 2	0 1/4	1/3	..	0 1/16	0 1/2	0 1/2
Thursday .	0 9	0 5	0 15	0 12	..	..	0 7	1 0	0 3/4	..	0 1/4		..	0 1/16	0 1/2	0 1/2
Friday .	..	..	1 0	0 8	0 1	..	0 7	1 0	0 3/4	0 2	0 1/4	1/3	..	0 1/16	0 1/2	0 1/2
Saturday .	0 4	0 4	0 15	2 0	0 1	..	0 7	1 0	0 3/4	..	0 1/4		..	0 1/16	0 1/2	0 1/2
lbs.	1 15	1 3	6 8	6 12	0 7	0 4/...	0 49	0 7	5 1/4	0 6	1 3/4	1 1/3	..	0 7/16	0 3 1/2	0 3 1/2

STAFFORD.

MALES.

BREAKFAST . . .		Milk Porridge, 1 pint; Bread, 8 oz.
DINNER .	Sunday,	Meat, 8 oz. cooked; Bread, 6 oz.; Beer, 1 pint; Vegetables.
	Monday,	Meat Pie, 1 lb.; Vegetables; Beer, 1 pint.
	Tuesday,	{ Suet Pudding, 10 oz.; Soup, 1 pint; Bread, 6 oz.; Beer, 1 pint.
	Wednesday,	The same as Sunday.

Thursday,	{ Rice Pudding, 8 oz.; Bread, 6 oz.; Beer, 1 pint; Soup, 1 pint.
Friday,	The same as Sunday.
Saturday,	The same as Thursday.

SUPPER . . . . Bread, 8 oz.; Cheese, 2 oz.; Beer, 1 pint.

FEMALES.

BREAKFAST . . . Tea, 1 pint, with Sugar and Milk; Bread, 6 oz.; Butter, ½ oz.

DINNER . Sunday, Meat, 6 oz. cooked; Bread, 6 oz.; Beer, ¾ pint; Vegetables.

Monday, Meat Pie, 12 oz.; Beer, ¾ pint.; Vegetables.

Tuesday, { Suet Pudding, 8 oz,; Soup, 1 pint; Bread, 6 oz.; Beer, ¾ pint.

Wednesday, The same as Sunday.

Thursday, { Rice Pudding, 6 oz.; Bread, 6 oz.; Beer, ¾ pint; Vegetables.

Friday, The same as Sunday.

Saturday, The same as Thursday.

SUPPER . . . . The same as Breakfast.

SUFFOLK.

DAY.	BREAKFAST.	DINNER.	SUPPER.
SUNDAY . .	Milk Gruel, and 6 oz. of Bread each, Oatmeal 12 lbs. and 6 galls. of Milk for about 200 Patients.	Males, 8 oz. Bread, 1½ oz. Cheese, and pint of Beer. Females, same, except 1 oz. less Bread.	Males, ½ lb. Bread, ¾ oz. Butter, and ½ pint Tea. Females, same, except 1 oz. less Bread.
MONDAY . .	Ditto.	Males, 6 oz. Meat, 4 oz. Bread, ¾ pint Beer; and Vegetables. Females, same, with 1 oz. less Meat.	Males, ½ lb. of Bread, 1½ oz. Cheese, and ¾ pint Beer. Females, same, with 1 oz. less Bread.
TUESDAY . .	Ditto.	Soup from Monday, with additional Meat, and 6 oz. Bread each.	Same as Sunday.
WEDNESDAY .	Ditto.	Males, Suet Dumpling of 1 lb. and Females, one of ¾ lb. with ¾ pint Beer each.	Same as Monday.
THURSDAY . .	Ditto.	Same as Monday.	Same as Wednesday.
FRIDAY . .	Ditto.	Same as Tuesday.	Same as Tuesday.
SATURDAY . .	Ditto.	Same as Wednesday.	Same as Thursday.

SURREY.

Day.	Breakfast.	Dinner.	Supper.
Monday	1 pint of Milk Porridge, with 6 oz. of Bread for Males, and 4 oz. for Females.	Soup thickened with barley, peas and Vegetables, with 6 oz. of Bread.	1 pint of Milk Porridge, with 6 oz. of Bread, for Males, and 4 oz. for Females.
Tuesday	Ditto.	Boiled Beef, 6 oz. free from bone, with 4 oz. of Bread, ¾ of a pint of Beer, and Vegetables.	Ditto.
Wednesday	Ditto.	Baked or boiled suet pudding, 16 oz. for Males, and 12 oz. for Females, with ¾ of a pint of Beer.	Ditto.
Thursday	Ditto.	Meat pie with Vegetables, and ¾ of a pint of Beer.	Ditto.
Friday	Ditto.	Baked Rice pudding with Treacle.	Ditto.
Saturday	Ditto.	Boiled Mutton, &c. as on Tuesday.	Ditto.
Sunday	Ditto.	Boiled or roast Mutton, or Beef, as on Tuesday.	Ditto.

The Male Patients who work in the garden and farm, as well as those employed as bricklayers, carpenters, painters, plumbers and glaziers, and in the engine-house, are allowed for luncheon, bread and cheese, with three quarters of a pint of beer for each; and the Females employed in the kitchen and laundry, bread and cheese, with half-a-pint of beer each; and the whole of the Female Patients in employment, whether in the kitchen, laundry, or wards, receive two ounces of tea, eight ounces of sugar, and eight ounces of butter.

The sick throughout the establishment are dieted at the discretion of the Medical-Officers.

YORKSHIRE WEST RIDING.

BREAKFAST AND SUPPER { Milk, 1 gallon; Water, 2 gallons; Oatmeal, 2¾ lbs.; Wheat Flour, ¼ lb.; of which each Patient is allowed 1½ pint.

DINNER . Yeast Dumplings, with Treacle Sauce, and Boiled Beef or Mutton, with Vegetables, on *Sundays, Tuesdays*, and *Thursdays;* 6 oz. of Meat, free from bone, allowed for each Patient. *Mondays, Wednesdays,* and *Fridays,* Soup made from the Meat boiled the day before; each Patient allowed 1½ pint. *Saturdays*, Rice Currie; 2 oz. Rice, 2 oz. Meat, with Vegetables, for each Patient; each Patient is allowed ¾ pint of Beer to Dinner.

St. PETER'S HOSPITAL, BRISTOL.

DINNER . . Meat, 4 oz. dressed, without bone, four times a-week; Peas Soup twice, and Boiled Rice once, with half-a-pint of fresh Table Beer each day.

BREAKFAST . A pint of Milk Porridge (one part Milk and two of thick Oatmeal Porridge) with Bread; some of the Patients have Tea, which is supplied by their friends.

SUPPER . . Bread and Cheese; 2 oz. of Cheese and a sufficiency of Bread: there is generally some left. The Patients are under medical treatment, &c., and have, once or twice a week, Roast Meat. The Vegetables are generally Potatoes; sometimes Green Vegetables in the Pea Soup.

PEMBROKE, HAVERFORDWEST.

BREAKFAST, DAILY — Milk and Oatmeal-Porridge, 2 pints, of which half is Milk—no Sugar. The Men have Bread in addition, and the Women Bread and Butter, about 8 oz. each.

SUPPER . . 1½ pint of Broth, in which Meat has been boiled, and 9 oz. of Bread. The Women are allowed also 1½ oz. of Butter every day, and the Men 3 oz. of Cheese three times a week each (in addition to the Broth).

DINNER . . *Sunday*, *Wednesday*, and *Friday*, Meat (generally fresh), about 5 oz., and 1½ lb. of Potatoes.

Monday, Beef's Head, stewed, 2 pints, (Meat and Soup together,) and 1½ lb. of Potatoes.

Tuesday, Two salt Herrings for each, and 1½ lb. of Potatoes.

Thursday, 2½ pints of Rice Milk; 4 lbs. of Rice allowed for 19 persons, no Bread nor Potatoes.

No Beer is allowed the Patients at any time.—The drink is Water.

PUBLIC SUBSCRIPTION ASYLUMS.
LINCOLN.
MALES.

BREAKFAST.	DINNER.	SUPPER.
Bread, 6 oz.	Bread, 3 oz.	Bread, 6 oz.
New milk, boiled, 1 pint.	Meat, cooked and boned, 4 oz.	New milk, boiled, half-pint.
	Vegetables, 10 oz.	

FEMALES.

Bread, toasted, 5 oz.	Bread, 3 oz.	Bread, toasted and buttered, 5 oz.
Tea, 1 pint.	Meat, cooked and boned, 4 oz.	Tea, 1 pint.
	Potatoes, 10 oz.	

Sunday . . Roast Beef.

Monday and Thursday . . } Boiled Mutton.

Tuesday and Friday . . } Boiled Beef.

Wednesday and Saturday . . } Boiled Beef; or cold meat warmed with Soup, 1 pint, for half the patients.

An Ox cheek is stewed with the soup weekly.

No Beer is allowed.

Carrots are used occasionally instead of potatoes.

NORTHAMPTON.

SOLIDS PER WEEK:—

	Males. oz.	Females. oz.
Bread, not less than	102	102
Solid Meat, cooked, about	18	16
Cheese, &c., not less than . . .	10	8
Meat pudding, ditto	16	14
Potatoes, about	72	72
Total . .	218	212

FLUIDS PER WEEK :—

	Males.	Females.
Milk gruel, about	168	112
Soup, "	72	72
Beer (three bushels to the hogshead), about	112	56
Tea . . . . :	—	56
Total . .	352	296

EXTRA DIET:—

	Males.	Females.
Breakfast, boiled milk	16	8—12
Dinner, meat every day . . .		5
Supper "		5
Bread, instead of vegetables . . .		6
Lunch, bread and cheese . . .	5	5
Beer (at 11 A.M. and 4 P.M.) . . .	8	8

Sick diet regulated by the necessities of the individuals.

YORK.

There is no regular Diet Table. The Pauper Patients have meat five times a week for dinner, with bread, potatoes, and other vegetables. For Breakfast the men have milk and oatmeal ; the women, tea. For Supper they have bread and cheese, with a pint of beer.

METROPOLITAN LICENSED HOUSES.

1.

PECKHAM HOUSE.

DIETARY FOR PAUPERS.

BREAKFAST.

Oatmeal Porridge .   .   Made chiefly with Milk. No limit to quantity.
Bread .   .   .   .   .   Do. do.

DINNER.

Sunday, ⎧ Meat   . 160 lbs., or once a fortnight Mutton 180 lbs. for 245 Patients.
Tuesday, ⎨ Potatoes . No limit to quantity.
Thursday, ⎪ Bread   . Do.   do.
         ⎩ Beer   . 1 Pint.

Monday, ⎫ Soup   . No limit to quantity.
Wednesday, ⎬ Bread . Do.   do.
Friday, ⎭

The Soup is made from the liquor in which the Meat for the whole Establishment (Private Patients, Paupers, and Servants) is boiled the previous day, together with all the bones, with the addition of Barley, Pease and green Vegetables.

Saturday Irish Stew . No limit to quantity.
          Bread   . Do.   do.
The Stew is made with 60 lbs. Meat, for 250 Patients, with Potatoes, Onions, &c.

SUPPER.

Bread .   . No limit to quantity.
Cheese or Molasses   Do.
Beer .   . One pint.

EXTRAS TO WORKING PATIENTS.

Breakfast .   .   . Tea and Bread and Butter

Forenoon, ⎧ Out-door Males . Bread and Cheese, and 1 pint Beer.
          ⎨ Wash-house Females, Do.   Do.   ½ pint Porter.

Afternoon, .   .   . Same as Forenoon.

Supper, Females . Tea, and Bread and Butter,

2.

HOXTON HOUSE.

BREAKFAST . . . Gruel with Bread. The Patients who are generally industrious, and those who are sick, are allowed Tea.

DINNER . . . Meat, (1 lh., including Bone,) and Vegetables, varied according to season, four days per week. Fresh Mackerel and Herrings when in season. Soup three times per week, made with Meat, Peas, and Vegetables. Suet, or Rice Puddings, or Fruit Puddings, when in season, substituted for Soup occasionally.

SUPPER . . . Broth, with Bread, four times a-week. Bread and Butter, or Bread and Cheese, three times.

Bread, 18 ounces per day allowed to each Patient.

Beer given with the Meat Dinners, and with the Bread and Cheese, or Bread and Butter Suppers.

3.

BETHNAL HOUSE, BETHNAL GREEN.

	BREAKFAST.	DINNER.	SUPPER.
SUNDAY .	1 Pint Gruel, 5 oz. Bread.	8 oz. Meat, uncooked, Vegetables and Bread, of each 5 oz.	Cheese, 2 oz. Bread, 5 oz.
MONDAY .	do.	Rice and Milk. 5 oz. Bread.	do.
TUESDAY .	do.	8 oz. Meat, uncooked, Vegetables and Bread, each 5 oz.	do .
WEDNESDAY	do.	Pudding, 15 oz.	do.
THURSDAY .	do.	8 oz. Meat, uncooked, Vegetables and Bread, each 5 oz.	do.
FRIDAY . .	do.	Pudding, 15 oz.	do.
SATURDAY .	do.	8 oz. Meat, uncooked, Vegetables and Bread, each 5 oz.	do.

Females, as above, 2 Pints of Table Beer per diem for Males, and one for Females. All Patients occupied in hard labour have Meat daily, and also an allowance of Porter, varying from half-a-pint to two pints a day.

Sick Diet comprehends Fish, Eggs, Rice, and light Puddings, with the addition of Ale, Wine, and Brandy, or anything else that the Medical Officer may deem necessary.

s 2

PAUPER DIETARIES IN THE FOLLOWING PROVINCIAL LICENSED HOUSES.

County.	Proprietor.	Asylum.	No.
Devon . . .	Langworthy, R. C . .	Plympton House, Plymouth .	1
Durham . . .	Glenton, Messrs. . .	Bensham, Gateshead . .	2
	Kent, S. .	Gateshead Fell . . .	3
	Wilkinson, J. E. . .	Dunston Lodge, Whickham .	4
Gloucester . .	Iles, A. . . .	Fairford	5
Hants . . .	Twyman, J. . . .	Lainston House, Winchester .	6
Hereford . .	Gilliland, J	Hereford	7
Northumberland .	Smith&Mackintosh,Mesrs.	Newcastle on Tyne . .	8
Oxford . . .	Mallam, Richard . .	Hook Norton . . .	9
Salop . . .	Jacob, James . .	Kingsland, Shrewsbury .	10
Somerset . .	Terry, St. . .	Bailbrook House, Bath . .	11
Warwick . .	Lewis, Messrs. . .	Duddeston Hall, near Birm..	12
Wilts . . .	Finch, W. . . .	Laverstock House, Salisbury .	13
Ditto . . .	Finch, W. C. . .	Fisherton House . . .	14
Ditto . . .	Langworthy, C. C. .	Kingdown House, Box . .	15
Ditto . . .	Phillips, T. . .	Belle-Vue House, Devizes .	16
Ditto . . .	Willett, R. . .	Fiddington House . .	17
Worcestershire .	Ricketts&Hastings,Mesrs	Droitwich	18
York, North Riding .	Martin, James .	Gate Helmsley . . .	19
„ East Riding .	Casson, Richard .	Hull	20

The weekly charges for Pauper Patients will be found in the list of Asylums in Appendix A.

1.

PLYMPTON HOUSE, NEAR PLYMOUTH.

DIETARY.

BREAKFAST . . . Bread only (without Butter), and Milk and Water.

The elderly Patients, however, and those who are not very strong, have Bread and Butter with their Milk and Water.

SUPPER . : . Same as Breakfast.

DINNER . Monday, Thursday and Saturday, } Boiled Rice, with Salt; Bread and Potatoes.

Tuesday, Pease Soup, with Vegetables and Bread.

261

Wednesday, Potatoe Pie.

Friday, { Soup made of Beef, with Vegetables, Potatoes, and Bread—the Meat is cut up, and given with the Soup.

Sunday { Boiled Beef and Vegetables, and Bread, no limit.

Milk and Water is given for drink, if asked for.

2

BENSHAM, NEAR GATESHEAD.

BREAKFAST . . . Boiled Oatmeal and Milk.
The Old and Invalid are allowed Tea.

DINNER . Sunday and Wednesday, } Boiled or Roast Beef, or Mutton, with Potatoes and Bread.
Monday and Thursday, } Cold Meat, Broth, and Vegetables.
Tuesday and Friday, } Irish Stew
Saturday, Fish, or Fruit Puddings

SUPPER . . Boiled Milk, Oatmeal, and Bread; sometimes Cheese.

The Patients are not limited to a prescribed quantity, which is regulated according to circumstances.

3.

GATESHEAD FELL.

Every Morning . Breakfast, Hasty Pudding and Milk.

Sunday . Dinner, Beef and Mutton with Potatoes and Broth,
Supper, Rice Milk and Bread.
Monday . Dinner, Barley Milk and Bread.
Supper, Boiled Milk with Oatmeal and Bread.
Tuesday . . . Same as Sunday.
Wednesday . Dinner, { Fish when it can be procured, or Flour Puddings with Treacle Sauce.
Supper, Same as Monday.

Thursday	.	.	Same as Sunday.

Thursday . . Same as Sunday.

Friday . . . Same as Monday, or Mince and Bread.

Saturday . . . Ox Head and Hough Soup, with Potatoes and Bread. Boiled Milk and Bread for supper.

All the Working Patients have Meat Dinners daily. Old people with the working Females have Coffee or Tea.

During illness the Diet is ordered by the Medical attendant.

4

DUNSTON LODGE, NEAR GATESHEAD.

MEN PAUPERS. DIET TABLE.

BREAKFAST . . Milk and Hasty Pudding.

SUPPER . . . Milk Gruel with Bread.

DINNER . Monday, Soup with Meat in it.

Tuesday, Meat Stew or Suet Dumplings.

Wednesday, Soup with Meat in it.

Thursday, Meat Pies or Meat Stew.

Friday, { Boiled Barley and Milk. Working Men, Meat.

Saturday, Soup with Meat in it.

Sunday, Fish, or Meat Pie, or Boiled Beef.

WOMEN PAUPERS.

SUPPER.

BREAKFAST . . Coffee, Tea.

DINNERS . . . Same as the Men, or nearly so. Their Diet is varied as much as possible, and not stinted in quantity.

FAIRFORD GLOUCESTERSHIRE.

Such of the Patients as labour have Ale and Table Beer mixed, and, occasionally, Meat for their Breakfast; and are, moreover, allowed small quantities of Tobacco and Snuff.

DIETARY.

BREAKFAST . . . Bread and Butter (in the Winter sometimes Toast and Lard), with Tea and Milk and Water; a large round of Bread.

SUPPER . . . (Women) Bread and Butter and Tea (Men) Bread and Cheese; a large round of Bread, with 2½ oz. of Cheese, and Table Beer; some have a pint and some half-a-pint.

DINNER . . Meat, generally, every day in the Summer, with Suet Puddings and Vegetables, (Potatoes, Cabbage, Peas, or Beans). The Meat consists of Beef, Mutton, Bacon, and Pork, and weighs, when dressed, about 6 or 7 oz. If Bacon alone, 5 oz. only.

In the Winter, there is always one day (sometimes, but rarely, two) on which the Patients have Pease Soup instead of Meat. On other days, the Dinner consists of one quart of Soup, having the stewed Meat in it, and Bread—Table Beer—some have one pint, and some half-a-pint, as they wish it, at Dinner. The Patients who work have Table-Beer and Ale mixed.

September, 1842.

6.

LAINSTON HOUSE, WINCHESTER.

DIETARY.

Sunday . Baked Meat, Pudding, and Vegetables.
Monday . Boiled Meat and Vegetables, with Bread.
Tuesday . Baked or Boiled Suet Puddings.
Wednesday Boiled Meat and Vegetables.
Thursday . Ditto Ditto Ditto.
Friday . Ditto Ditto Ditto.
Saturday . Soup with Vegetables, and Bread.

A pint of Table Beer to each Man, daily, and ¾ of a pint to each Woman, daily. For Breakfast, the Female Paupers have Coffee, with Milk, and Bread and Butter, In the Evenings, Tea and Bread and Butter. The Pauper Men, for Breakfast obtain Milk Porridge or Broth; in the Evening, Bread and Cheese, and Beer.

The Diet is the same for the two sexes, excepting at Breakfast as above specified. In regard to Epileptic cases, the attendants are directed to cut less.

7.

HEREFORD LUNATIC ASYLUM.

DIETARY.

BREAKFAST . . One quart of milk (skimmed) with bread, or sometimes in the winter, when milk is scarce, some of the Male Patients have 1 quart of broth with bread in it. A few of the women have occasionally Tea or Coffee, with bread.

SUPPER . . . Bread and Cheese, about 8 or 9 oz. of
Bread with about 3 oz. of Cheese, (it is
not weighed,) with 1 Pint of Beer. A
few of the women, if invalids or in delicate health, have Tea instead of Beer.

DINNER . . . Two days Rice Pudding—a large plateful
not weighed.

Two days Soup and Bread, 1 quart of
Soup with a large piece of Bread.

Three days Meat and Potatoes. It is made
into an Irish Stew, not weighed, no
Bread.

8.

NEWCASTLE-ON-TYNE LUNATIC ASYLUM.

DIETARY.

BREAKFAST . . Milk Gruel, *ad lib.*, with Bread for Breakfast and Supper.

DINNER . . . . 8 oz. of solid Meat with Potatoes, on Sundays, Tuesdays, and Thursdays.

Broth, with a proportion of Meat cut up in
it, *ad lib.*, with Bread, on Mondays,
Wednesdays, and Saturdays.

Rice and Milk, *ad lib.*, with Bread, on
Thursday.

The Working Patients are allowed Beer
and have solid Meat daily, with Tea
morning and evening.

Patients advanced in years have also Tea
morning and evening.

The Sick have Diet suitable to their respective Cases, and Fasting Patients, and
those labouring under peculiar delusions,
have anything they can be persuaded to
take

9.

HOOK NORTON, OXFORDSHIRE.

DIETARY.

BREAKFAST . . Bread and Milk, or Broth, or Bread and Butter and Coffee.

DINNER . Sunday, Boiled Mutton, with Bread and Vegetables.

Monday, Suet Pudding.

Tuesday, Bacon, with Bread and Vegetables.

Wednesday, { Rice Pudding, with a slice of Bread and Bacon for the Men.

Thursday, { Boiled Beef or Mutton, with Bread and Vegetables.

Friday, Soup with Bread.

Saturday, { Rice Pudding, with a slice of Bread and Bacon for the Men.

One pint of Beer is allowed to each Male, and half a pint to the Females for Dinner, excepting Soup day.

SUPPER . . . Bread and Cheese and Beer for the Men.

Bread and Butter and Tea for the Women.

Those who work are allowed Bread and Cheese and Beer extra.

10.

KINGSLAND, NEAR SHREWSBURY.

DIETARY.

Sunday, Monday, Wednesday, and Friday, } Breakfast . Half a pound of Bread and Milkmeal.

Dinner . Six ounces of Meat and Potatoes.

Supper . Half a pound of Bread and Broth (no limit).

Tuesday, Breakfast . Half a pound of Bread and Milkmeal.

Dinner . Pease Soup (no limit.)

Supper . Half a pound of Bread and Milkmeal.

Thursday and Saturday. } Breakfast . Half a pound of Bread and Broth.

Dinner . Eleven ounces of Suet Pudding and Broth.

Supper . Half a pound of Bread and Milkmeal.

The Men who work have Beer; the Women who work have Tea and Sugar.

11.

BAILBROOK HOUSE, BATH EASTON.

DIETARY.

BREAKFAST . . . . 1½ pint of Milk, Gruel, or Tea or Coffee, and 5 ounces of Bread as they like, (if Tea or Coffee, Butter also).

SUPPER . . . . . (Men) 5½ ounces of Bread, and 1 ounce of Cheese, 1 pint of Table Beer.

(Women) have Tea or Coffee, or half-a-pint of Beer, and 5½ ounces of Bread, and 1 ounce of Cheese.

DINNER . . . . On Wednesday, Friday, and Sunday, 6 ounces of dressed Meat without bone, and Vegetables at discretion; no Bread; 1 pint of Beer, Men—half-a-pint, Women.

On Thursday and Saturday, Baked Rice pudding, ½ pound before boiled, coarse Sugar or Treacle, 1½ pint of Broth with Bread in it, no Beer.

On Monday, 1¼ pint of Broth with Bread in it, and vegetables besides, no Beer.

On Tuesday, Suet Pudding, ¾ of a pound, Vegetables at discretion; and Beer (one pint for the Men, half-a-pint for the Women).

Patients employed at out of door or in door labour, have Meat every day, and an extra meal of Bread and Cheese and Beer, at eleven o'clock, A.M.

12

DUDDESTON HALL, BIRMINGHAM.
DIETARY.

BREAKFAST . . . Milk Thickened.

DINNER . . . 3 days a week, meat and abundance of vegetables.

2 days a week, broth.

1 day Pease Soup

Bread and Cheese once a week.

About half a pound of Bread is allowed at
each meal.

SUPPER . . . Bread and Cheese on Soup and Broth
days; and on Meat days Milk thickened.

Those who work have an extra meal of
Bread and Cheese, and also Tobacco once
a week.

13.

LAVERSTOCK HOUSE, NEAR SALISBURY.
DIETARY.

BREAKFAST . . . . One pint of Skimmed Milk, and about
half-a-pound of Bread.

Occasionally, a pint of Broth and Bread.

TEA . . . . One pint of Tea with Bread and Butter, or
half-a-pound of Bread, with 3 ounces of
Cheese, and 1 pint of Table Beer.

DINNER . Wednesday { From $\frac{1}{2}$ to $\frac{3}{4}$ of a pound of hot Meat with
Friday and Bread, ($\frac{1}{4}$ pound) and vegetables, 1 pint
Sunday. of Table Beer, (on Sundays, Suet Pud-
ding in addition).

Monday
Thursday } Cold Meat (or cheese), with Bread and
and Vegetables, Potatoes and Cabbage, 1 pint
Saturday. of Table Beer.

TUESDAY . . . . . $\frac{1}{2}$ pound of Bread, and 3 ounces of Cheese,
and 1 pint of Table Beer.

Sometimes (in the winter) pease soup, $1\frac{1}{2}$
pint, with as much Bread as they like.

14.

FISHERTON HOUSE, FISHERTON AUGER, WILTS

DIETARY.

BREAKFAST . . . . . (In Summer.) For the Men, 6 to 8 ounces of Bread, and 2½ ounces of Cheese, one pint of Table Beer.

(The Bread varies from 6 to 8 ounces, and depends on the Patient's appetite, and on the work he performs.)

(In Winter.) One pint of Broth, made with Bones, groats and vegetables, &c., and from 6 to 8 ounces of Bread; no Beer.

The Women have one pint of Cocoa, with 6 ounces of Bread, and 2 ounces of Cheese.

SUPPER . . . . . . Same quantity of Bread and Cheese and Beer as at Breakfast, for the Men.

One pint of Cocoa, with 6 ounces of Bread and 2 ounces of Cheese, for the Women.

DINNER . . . . . . Four ounces of Meat every day, together with as much Vegetables as they like. They generally have three sorts of Vegetables all the year round, that is to say, Potatoes, Greens, and Carrots, (or Parsnips). They are not allowed any Bread with their Dinner. Each Patient has one pint of Table Beer.

The Patients who work are allowed an extra meal, every day, of Bread and Cheese, and small quantities of Snuff or Tobacco are occasionally given to them.

15.

KINGSDOWN HOUSE, BOX.

DIETARY.

BREAKFAST . . . One quart of Gruel, (Milk and Oatmeal), one-third Milk, and a round of Bread.

SUPPER . . Cocoa and Milk and a quart of Broth, with a round of Bread for the Men.

The Men who work have for supper Bread and Cheese and Beer.

DINNER . . . Meat and Vegetables, five times a week, consisting of Beef, or Bacon, or Mutton, with Potatoes or Cabbage.—Each Patient has about 6 oz. of Meat; half-a-pint of Beer is allowed for Dinner on the meat days.

On Friday there is boiled Rice with Treacle, and some Milk in addition.

On Tuesday, a quart of Soup with Bread or Potatoes; water only allowed for Dinner on the Soup and Rice days.

The Men who are at work have Meat, Vegetables, and Beer, always for dinner.

16.

BELLE VUE HOUSE, DEVIZES.

DIETARY.

BREAKFAST . . . A quart of Milk Porridge (more than one-third Milk), with Bread cut into slices.

SUPPER . . . Bread and Butter, or Bread and Cheese (as much as they like), with Table Beer—more than half-a-pint—or Tea.

DINNER . . . Four days in the week, Meat; about 4 or 5 oz. of Mutton, Beef, or Bacon, with Potatoes, Cabbage, or other Vegetables, with half-a-pint of Table Beer—no Bread.

The Beef is sometimes salt and sometimes fresh. Two days Suet Pudding (no limit), with half-a-pint of Table Beer. The other day Bread and Cheese for Dinner (no limit), and rather more than half-a-pint of Table Beer.

In the winter the Patients have Pease Soup once a week, instead of the Pudding; about a quart, with Bread in it.

17.

FIDDINGTON HOUSE, WILTS.

DIETARY.

BREAKFAST . _ . 1 quart of Broth with Bread in it, or 1 quart of Milk with Bread in it.

Nearly 90 of the Parish Patients are allowed Tea.

DINNER . . . Meat, five days a week, consisting of about 6 oz. of Beef, Mutton, or Bacon, with Potatoes, Greens, or other Vegetables; no Bread; one pint of Table Beer.

On Monday, { 1 quart of Pease Soup with Bread in it, or the same quantity of Broth thickened with Rice; 1 pint of Beer.

On Saturday, { Bread and Cheese, 8 oz. Bread and 3 oz. Cheese; 1 pint of Table Beer.

Such of the Patients as work have Ale and Bread and Cheese at eleven and four o'clock, making five meals a day; and for supper, a pint of Ale extra.

18.

DROITWICH.

DIETARY.

BREAKFAST - - - Bread and Milk; Men a quart, Women a pint (containing 8 oz. of Bread for the Men, and 6 oz. for the Women).

DINNER Sunday, 8 oz. of boiled Mutton, 1 pound of Potatoes, and Beer.

Monday, Thursday, and Saturday, } Soup, a quart, with 8 oz. of Bread.

Tuesday, 1 lb. of Suet Pudding for the Men, and three-quarters of a pound for the Women, with Beer.

Wednesday and Friday, } Eight ounces of boiled Beef, and 1 lb. of Potatoes, with Beer.

SUPPER - - - Bread and Cheese and Beer, 8 oz. of Bread and 1 oz. of Cheese.

If ill, the Patient's Diet is regulated by the Medical Officer.

19.

GATE HELMSLEY, NEAR YORK.

BREAKFAST - - Milk and Oatmeal, 1½ pint, with Bread without limit.—Patients who are old, or in delicate health, are allowed Tea.

SUPPER - - - The same.

DINNER - - - Five days Meat (twice boiled, and three times roasted), the roasted Meat is not weighed, but something short of ½lb. is given to each Patient.—No Bread is allowed with the Meat (except to old or Invalid Patients), but Suet Pudding is

given, and a variety of Vegetables, with
the Boiled Meat, (which is less in quantity
than the Roasted Meat.)—Soup is served,
and Pudding, filling altogether a pint-
and-a-half vessel.

Two days (Monday and Thursday) there
are Meat Pies, with Potatoes in them : a
large plateful is given, but not weighed.
—No Beer is allowed, except to Invalids
and to Patients who work.

20.

HULL AND EAST RIDING REFUGE, HULL.

BREAKFAST Men   1 pint of Oatmeal and Milk, and 8 oz. of Bread.

Women   1 pint of Tea and 8 oz. of Bread.

DINNER Men and Women :—

Sunday,   8 oz. Meat, 14 oz. Potatoes, 1 pint Small Beer.

Monday,   1 pint of Soup, 8 oz. Bread.

Tuesday,   Ox-head Broth, with Greens, and Barley and Peas ; or,

1 pint of Meat Hash, with Potatoes and Herbs, and 8 oz. Bread.

Wednesday, Fish, and 14 oz. Potatoes ; or, Pease-Soup with Bread, and 1 pint of Beer.

Thursday, 8 oz. of Meat, with 14 oz. of Potatoes, and 1 pint of Beer.

Friday,   1 pint of good Meat and Vegetable Broth, with 8 oz. of Bread.

Saturday, 1 pint of Rice Frumety, and half-a-pint of Beer.

APPENDIX G.

SCHEDULE 1.

STATEMENT OF CRIMINAL LUNATICS, APRIL, 1843.

	In County Asylums.			In Licensed Houses.			In other Public Asylums.			Total.		
	M.	F.	Tot.	M.	F.	Tot.	M.	F.	Tot.	M.	F.	Tot.
†Beds.	2	.	2	1	.	1	.	.	.	3	.	3
Chester	10	1	11	.	.	.	.	.	.	10	1	11
Cornwall	6	2	8	.	.	.	.	.	.	6	2	8
Devon	.	.	..	6	.	6	.	.	.	6	.	6
Dorset	2	.	2	.	.	.	.	.	.	2	.	2
†Durham	.	.	.	5	1	6	.	.	..	5	1	6
Gloucester	6	3	9	1	.	1	.	.	.	6	4	10
†Hants	.	.	.	2	.	2	.	.	.	2	.	2
Kent	5	2	7	.	.	.	.	.	.	5	2	7
Lancaster	15	2	17	.	.	..	.	.	.	15	2	17
Leicester	4	.	4	.	.	.	.	.	.	4	.	4
Norfolk	1	.	1	.	.	.	.	.	.	1	.	1
*Norwich	.	.	.	.	.	.	2	.	2	2	.	2
Notts	3	1	4	.	.	.	.	.	.	3	1	4
†Oxon	1	.	1	1	.	1	.	.	.	2	.	2
†Salop	.	.	.	3	.	3	.	.	.	3	.	3
†Somerset	.	.	.	1	2	3	.	.	.	1	2	3
Stafford	2	.	2	.	.	.	.	.	.	2	.	2
Suffolk	4	1	5	1	.	1	.	.	.	5	1	6
†Sussex	.	.	.	1	.	1	.	.	.	1	.	1
†Warwick	.	.	.	1	1	2	.	.	.	1	1	2
†Wilts	.	.	.	5	3	8	.	.	.	5	3	8
†Worcester	.	.	.	3	.	3	.	.	.	3	.	3
York, West Riding	2	1	3	.	.	.	.	.	.	2	1	3
†Do. East Riding	.	.	.	1	.	1	.	.	.	1	.	1
Bethlem Hospital	.	.	.	.	.	.	64	21	85	64	21	85
Metropolitan District	.	.	.	15	7	22	.	.	.	15	7	22
Gaols	.	.	.	.	.	.	.	.	.	.	.	.
Totals	63	13	76	47	14	61	66	21	87	205	52	257

* Infirmary Bethel, a detached Lunatic Ward of the Union Workhouse.

In the Counties distinguished by a † there are no County Asylums.

APPENDIX F.

NUMBER OF PAUPER LUNATICS AND IDIOTS CHARGEABLE IN EACH UNION IN ENGLAND AND WALES IN THE MONTH OF AUGUST 1843.

ABSTRACT of RETURNS, showing the Number of PAUPER LUNATICS and IDIOTS chargeable to Parishes comprised in each UNION in *England* and *Wales*, in the Month of August 1843; distinguishing the Number of each Sex, whether Dangerous to themselves or others, where maintained, and the Average Weekly Cost per Head for Maintenance, Clothing, &c.

COUNTIES.	Population in 1841.	LUNATICS.			IDIOTS.			Grand Total Lunatics and Idiots.	Proportion per Cent. to Population.	WHERE MAINTAINED.									WHERE MAINTAINED.						AGES.								Dangerous to themselves or others.	Of dirty Habits.	Average Weekly Cost per Head for Maintenance and Clothing.			
										In County Lunatic Asylum.			In Licensed Houses.			In Union Workhouses.			With their Friends, or elsewhere.																	In County Lunatic Asylum.	Licensed House.	Elsewhere.	Average.
		M.	F.	Total.	M.	F.	Total.			M.	F.	Total.	M.	F.	Total.	M.	F.	Total.	M.	F.	Total.	0 to 5	5 to 10	10 to 20	20 to 30	30 to 40	40 to 50	50 to 60	60 to 70	70 and upwards.						

ENGLAND:

Bedford
Berks
Buckingham
Cambridge
Chester
Cornwall
Cumberland
Derby
Devon
Dorset
Durham
Essex
Gloucester
Hereford
Hertford
Huntingdon
Kent
Lancaster
Leicester
Lincoln
Middlesex
Monmouth
Norfolk
Northampton
Northumberland
Nottingham
Oxford
Rutland
Salop
Somerset
Southampton
Stafford
Suffolk
Surrey
Sussex
Warwick
Westmorland
Wilts
Worcester
York { East Riding
York { North Riding
York { West Riding

WALES:

Anglesey
Brecon
Cardigan
Carmarthen
Carnarvon
Denbigh
Flint
Glamorgan
Merioneth
Montgomery

Totals of ENGLAND

Totals of WALES

SCHEDULE 2.

CASES OF ATROCIOUS OFFENCES IN COUNTY ASYLUMS AND LICENSED
HOUSES, APRIL, 1843.

	CRIME.	In County Asylums.		CRIME.	In Licensed Houses.	
		M.	F.		M.	F.
Beds...	Murder	2	..	Cutting with intent to do bodily harm	1	..
Chester .	Murder	1	..	. . .	..	..
	Arson	2	..	. . .	..	..
Cornwall	Smothering two Children . .	..	1	. . .	..	..
Devon .	. . .	..	..	Murder	1	1
Durham .	. . .	..	..	Murder	..	..
	. . .	..	..	Maliciously stabbing	1	..
Gloucester	Murder	..	1	. . .	..	..
	Maliciously cutting	..	1	. . .	..	..
Hants ..	. . .	..	..	Murder	1	..
Kent . .	Murder	1	..	. . .	..	..
	Infanticide	..	1	. . .	..	..
	Attempting to stab her husband	..	1	. . .	..	..
Lancaster	Killing his wife .	3	..	. . .	..	..
	Killing his child .	1	..	. . .	..	..
	Other Homicides .	3	..	. . .	..	..
	Arson	1	..	. . .	..	..
Leicester	Murder of his wife	1	..	. . .	..	..
	Arson	1	..	. . .	..	..
Notts. .	Burning stacks . .	1	1	. . .	..	..
Salop ..	. . .	..	..	Arson	1	..
	. . .	..	..	Detestable crime .	1	..
Suffolk .	Murder	1	1	. . .	..	..
	Manslaughter . .	1	..	. . .	..	..
Sussex .	. . .	..	..	Maliciously cutting	1	..
Warwick	. . .	..	..	Murder	..	1
Wilts ..	. . .	..	..	Murder	..	2
	. . .	..	..	Maliciously shooting	1	..
York W. Riding	Infanticide	..	1	. . .	..	..
York E. Riding	. . .	..	..	Murder	1	..
Metrop. District	. . .	..	..	Murder	1	2
	. . .	..	..	Infanticide	..	2
	. . .	..	..	Shooting his wife .	1	..
	. . .	..	..	Killing his grandfather	1	..
	. . .	..	..	Shooting with intent to kill .	1	..
	. . .	..	..	Attempt to drown	1	..
	. . .	..	..	Cutting & maiming	1	..

INDEX.

U

283

Medical Attendants, to be appointed at General Quarter Sessions to
visit Licensed Asylums in provinces three times a year, 2;
general high character of, 8; at Hanwell, their onerous duties,
24; at Licensed Asylums, 28, 113; in County Asylums, *ib.*;
at St. Peter's Hospital, Bristol, 53; generally visit pauper patients
regularly, 74; opinions of, as to treatment of Insanity, 115—
117; as to restraint, 153, 156—159; as to tranquillising effect
of religious services, 160.

Medical Journal, neglect in keeping, 40.

Medical treatment of Patients in Lunatic Asylums, 113; difference
prevailing as to, in different classes of Asylums, *ib.*; opinions of
Medical Attendants in Asylums respecting, 116, 117; regulations
of, in some Asylums at variance with general opinion, 118; not
substituted for coercion, 121.

Melancholia, defined, 106.

Metropolitan Commissioners in Lunacy, authorised to inspect public
and private Asylums throughout England and Wales, 1; to visit
Licensed Asylums in Metropolitan district four times a year, 2;
to visit and report on Licensed Asylums in the Provinces twice a
year, *ib.*; and County and other Asylums under 9 Geo. IV.
c. 40, once a year, *ib.*; directed by Lord Chancellor to visit Royal
Naval and Military Hospitals, and all other public Asylums except
Bethlem, *ib.*; divide England and Wales into four districts, 4;
each again subdivided into two parts, *ib.*; inquiries instituted by
them *ib. et seq.*; especially as regards Lunatic poor, 6;
recommendation of, as to Medical Officers, 28; exposure
of main evils chief object in present Report of, 34; formerly
prosecuted a person for improperly receiving Insane persons as
boarders, 38; their reasons for continuing licenses to the Asylums
at Peckham and Hoxton, 44; proceedings of, with respect to
Asylum at Haverfordwest, 50 *et seq.*; endeavours used by them
to correct abuses, 65 *et seq.*; visits of, to Workhouses, 98; extract
from Report of, on Norfolk Asylum, 114; not empowered to
grant partial liberty to Patients, 169; inquiries of, as to Statistics
of Insanity extended to Scotland and Ireland, 178.

Middlesex Asylum.—See *Hanwell.*

Middlesex, County of, burdened with unusual number of paupers whose
settlements are not ascertained, 91.

Middleton, Lady, fund instituted by, for relief of Pauper Patients discharged from Nottingham Asylum, 27.

Military and Naval Hospitals, Commissioners authorised to visit, 2;
number of, 3; supported by and under control of Government,
10; at Fort Clarence, 31; at Haslar, *ib.*

Monomania, defined, 106.

Moral Insanity, defined, 106.

Morda, near Oswestry, House of Industry at, included in class of
Licensed Asylums, 10; ill-suited for reception of Patients, 143.

Morecroft House, case of beneficial restraint at, 149.

THE END.

LONDON :

BRADBURY AND EVANS, PRINTERS, WHITEFRIARS.